Ever[...]
Free to [...]

Everest:
Free to Decide

The story of the first
South Africans to reach
the highest point on earth

Cathy O'Dowd & Ian Woodall

ZEBRA

ZEBRA

Published by Zebra Press
a division of Struik Publishers (Pty) Ltd
(a member of the Struik Publishing Group (Pty) Ltd)
32 Thora Crescent, Wynberg, Sandton

Reg. No.: 54/00965/07

First published in October 1997

Editor Tamsin Shelton
DTP and cover design Neels Bezuidenhout

Reproduction by Disc Express cc, Johannesburg
Printed and bound by National Book Printers, Drukkery Street, Goodwood, Western Cape

ISBN 1 86872 101 9

To Bruce Herrod
1958 – Everest Summit 25 May 1996
South Africa will always remember

To Malcolm Duff
Without whom there would have been no beginning

And to all those who have been lost on Everest

Acknowledgements

Our sincere thanks go to all those who helped us in many different ways in making both the 1st South African Everest Expedition and this book a reality:

President Mandela, who, with his patronage and his encouragement, was a constant source of inspiration.

The government and people of Nepal, who provided us with unlimited assistance and friendship.

Our sponsors (listed in Appendix B), without whom there would not have been an expedition. To all our readers who enjoyed following the expedition and reading this book, and who feel that this type of South African adventure is important, please support the expedition sponsors by buying their products or sending them a note of appreciation.

Our families, who stuck by us through thick and thin, never letting their personal concerns undermine our determination.

Our team-mates – Ang Dorje, Pemba, Jangmu, Nawang, Deshun, Ang Sirke; our base camp support – Philip, Patrick, Shankar; our Kathmandu support – Padam Shrestha and all the staff of Sherpa Co-operative Trekking. Without them none of this would have been possible.

The South Africans who joined the expedition support treks and gave us valuable encouragement at base camp.

All the women who applied for the Woman on Everest selection and inspired us with their enthusiasm for the project. Because of your response we will be operating similar projects in future.

Jan Horn and Ivan Oberholzer for friendship beyond the call of duty.

Tamsin Shelton and Nick Pryke, who helped us turn a pile of paper into a book.

And all the others who lent a helping hand along the way.

Thank you.

Cathy O'Dowd and Ian Woodall
September 1997

Contents

Prologue

9 May 1996
17:00 – Geneva Spur, Everest

Iᴀɴ:

With a final heave I pull myself over the crest of the Geneva Spur and lie panting in the soft wet snow. I close my eyes for a moment's rest, attempting to relieve the pain in my throat and lungs burnt raw from the effort of climbing with so little oxygen.

Hell, it's cold. Just sitting and resting for a few moments has left me shaking. I can't feel my hands and my damp clothing is freezing against my body. I try in vain to breathe a little warm air into my frozen gloves. Vast armies of storm clouds chase each other among the surrounding peaks and it starts to snow heavily. The wind begins to drive harder and harder in an attempt to blow me off my precarious perch. The visibility is deteriorating by the moment.

Bloody hell, I mutter to myself, where did this lot come from? We could be in real trouble here. I hope Cathy's safe.

I shift uncomfortably to the edge of the spur to see if Bruce is visible on the fixed ropes below. As I look down, the gale-force wind channels and forces the newly falling snow up the side of the spur and blasts it out over the top like a cork from a champagne bottle, straight into my face.

'Bloody Danish weather forecasts,' I curse as I cough up the last of the powder snow and try to clear the freezing mess from my eyes without losing my contact lenses in the process.

The weather is fast developing into a full-blown Himalayan storm and with me perched on a small rock and snow outcrop at 8 000 metres, Bruce battling up the fixed ropes below me, and heaven knows where Cathy is, we are in a very serious mountaineering situation. Think now, Ian, think. Up or back down, because if you stay here you'll die. Should I wait for Bruce or press on without him?

My shaking from the cold has reached alarming proportions and I'm sure that I'm going to shake myself off the edge of the spur and back down the huge Lhotse Face. Where the hell is Bruce? Doesn't he know I'm freezing my whatnots off up here? Come on, youth, hurry up!

Suddenly the fixed ropes give a violent shudder heralding Bruce's imminent arrival.

'Bloody Danish,' Bruce swears as he hauls himself gasping and blowing on to the narrow shelf and collapses in a heap beside me.

'Beautifully put,' I smile in return as I watch my close friend lie on his back at 8 000 metres and shake his arms and legs in the air, like a shaggy dog after a cold bath, in an attempt to clear himself of the wet snow. With a last shake and thrust of his arms Bruce sits up and looks out into the raging storm.

'Where's Cathy?' he asks.

'I don't know,' I have to admit. 'Last time I saw her she was a long way in front.'

'Christ, mate, do you think she's made it safely to camp 4?'

'I hope so,' I reply.

Even through the driving snow I can see the worried look on Bruce's face at the thought of Cathy being out in this storm.

'Where does the route go from here?' he asks pointedly as there are no fixed ropes to be seen anywhere.

'That way, I think,' I reply, indicating an area of storm, wind and horizontal snow that looks exactly the same as all the other areas of storm, wind and horizontal snow.

'We'd best try to keep as close together as possible, old man,' shouts Bruce against the force of the wind.

I nod in agreement, not bothering to try to compete with the storm. Bruce shows a thumbs-up sign over his shoulder and leads off slowly into the teeth of the storm and into real trouble. The route to camp 4 and safety is a very narrow one. A slight mistake in any direction could plunge us down the icy south pillar of Everest, but we must keep moving no matter how poor the visibility, because to stop is to die.

CHAPTER I

Step Into History

12 April 1996
05:30 – Base Camp, Everest

'So whose idea was this bloody expedition, anyway?' grumbled Ian into the metal mug of tea he held cupped in his blue-gloved hands, his eyes half-open and his mind fogged by lack of sleep.

'Yours,' Bruce and Cathy replied together.

'Well, why didn't somebody stop me?' he asked in disgust.

'There's no stopping you when you've an idea on the boil,' said Bruce in his soft English accent, a broad grin emerging from the depths of his bushy beard. 'Anyway, you're the expedition leader, so by definition it's your fault.'

'Absolutely,' agreed Cathy.

The three friends sat huddled in giant blue jackets and green woolly hats, laboriously storing away cup after cup of tea as energy for later in the day, their first day's climbing on Everest.

'Are you feeling nervous?' Cathy asked, looking at Bruce.

'Me, nervous? Never!' he retorted, while acknowledging the truth with a wry smile. 'Why would I be nervous about my first day of climbing on the highest mountain in the world? It's only a big hill.'

'A very big hill,' rejoined Cathy.

'The biggest,' Ian added bluntly.

'And what about you, Cathy?' asked Bruce in reply. 'Are *you* nervous?'

'Give me strength. I'm just worried you won't keep up with me.'

> CATHY:
> To be honest, at five o'clock in the morning my only coherent thought is how nice it would be to curl back up in my warm down sleeping bag. But

twinges of excitement cut through the fog of sleepiness. A tight knot of anticipation and nervousness competes with the sickly sweet milky tea for place in my stomach. At last I will be setting foot on the mountain. And this is *the* mountain, Everest, the biggest on earth. It will be the first time I have climbed with Ian and Bruce. I glance surreptitiously across at them. God, they look so disgustingly big, strong – male. I hope I can keep up. I'm sure I can keep up.

Ian is nodding over his cup of tea, like a little old gnome swamped in the huge jacket. He looks worse than I feel. I've already realised that early morning starts are not his strong point. I don't know how someone so slight in build can be so tough. Behind the logic, the discipline, the reserve, I still don't know who he really is. But I know he'll get this job done if at all possible.

Bruce is talking. How can anyone be so cheery when it's this early and this cold? But that's Bruce. I remember when I first met him, a huge, chubby man filling up the living room of Ian's parents' home in Rivonia. Right from the beginning he came across as what he was, a cheerful, sensible, intelligent man, fully committed to working as hard as he could on whatever project he dedicated himself to. He has a clear head and an even temper, which is good for the rest of us. He balances out both my and Ian's mood swings.

And we are all about to go climbing on Everest. I don't know how it ever got to this. It all happened so fast. Six months ago the thought of climbing Everest seemed as remote as the stars. And now I am about to set foot on it.

IAN:

If you listen carefully you can hear it. Those with a sense of history can stand quietly at the site of an old battlefield and hear the shouts of excitement and feel the tingle of fear cascading down through the pages of history. If I sit quietly on the ice- and rock-strewn glacier at the foot of Mount Everest, I can hear the nervous chatter of all the climbers who have gone before us, and I can sense the wonder of the early explorers as they sat, like me, waiting for their first day's climbing on the mountain. That's what coming to climb Everest is about, to meet and experience history.

Bruce, Cathy and I have come to Everest with a simple purpose. To place the South African flag on its summit for the first time. Even as I sit here in the cold morning air, it gives me a thrill just to imagine achieving such an aim. Bruce, my closest friend and confidant, is an ideal expedition teammate. Strong of mind as well as body, he could easily be mistaken for being South African rather than English, in his drive and determination to work together for the common goal. Cathy, whom I have only known for a short while, has yet to show us whether she is physically strong enough to climb Everest, but of her strength of mind there is no doubt.

06:00 – Base Camp

Ian pulled across the blue Chinese thermos flask. The bright red roses that decorated its sides seemed incongruous in the shabby green mess tent, perched unevenly on a floor of ice and rock. He opened the flask and filled up everyone's cups of tea before re-focusing the climbers' minds on the job in hand.

'We'd best get moving in a minute, guys. We'll need to get most of the way up the icefall before the sun reaches it. The icefall is the most dangerous place on Everest and the later we leave it, the warmer and more lethal it becomes.'

Finishing off the last of his tea, Ian stood up with a groan, stretching out his cold and stiff back before moving to the door of the mess tent. The silence that lay over the camp in the form of the dark blue shadow of early morning was broken by a brief crack like that of a gunshot. Everyone jumped. It was followed by a heavy groan, and then silence again.

'Damn,' muttered Bruce. 'I hate it when that happens.'

They had learnt to recognise the strange noises that came from the glacier beneath their feet as the great weight of ice shifted and settled in its imperceptible movement down the valley. But in the week they had already spent at base camp, they had not yet got used to it. They knew that if the glacier was moving this much at base camp, the icefall would be considerably more volatile and considerably more dangerous.

Each climber pulled off their warm down jacket and replaced it with a windproof Goretex one, pulled on over a full suit of thermal underwear, fleece salopettes and a fleece jacket. Then on went gloves, hats and scarves to complete the soft furnishings. On their feet were huge plastic 'double boots', and over them nylon gaiters up to the knee to stop snow getting in.

CATHY:
Finally my rucksack is loaded on over all this paraphernalia. It sits on my back like the weight of sin. The thought of walking like this, let alone climbing, seems rather ridiculous.

Slowly we move away across the uneven, rocky terrain. The weight of the boots makes it feel like walking with cement blocks on each foot. But there is no other way up. No roads, no helicopters, nothing except two legs and a lot of will power. And a stomach full of nerves.

Because, as we walk towards the icefall, this is risk made real. It is one thing to sit in South Africa pontificating about how 'of course I know the risks of high-altitude mountaineering'. It is another to be approaching the notorious Khumbu Icefall, about to put the theory to the test. The dusky blue jumble of giant blocks that makes up the icefall has dominated both the view from base camp and the conversation of all the climbers here for the past week. It has a nefarious reputation as the most dangerous part of Everest. All those blocks are unstable and there is so little to be done to minimise the risk. We can avoid avalanches by choosing when to climb, crevasses by choosing where to climb, but with the icefall there is no choice but to go through it. The only safety lies in doing it as early in the morning, and as fast, as possible. For the colder it is, the more stable it is likely to be.

And it's only the beginning. There is an enormous amount of mountain between us and the summit, to get both up and down, and all of it is potentially treacherous. But that's part of the challenge.

IAN:

I do not court danger for its own sake, nor do I let it stand in my way. Life manifests itself in how it is lived. Sometimes that means calculated risks have to be acknowledged, faced and overcome. Climbing on Everest is dangerous, of that there is little doubt, but we feel that the experience and possible success of the expedition is worth that gamble. Where would exploration, science and medicine be if man failed to take risks? I believe it's in our make-up, in who we are as a species. Some risks may be life-threatening, some may not, but someone has to face them. So we have acknowledged the chances we are taking on Everest, and soon we will face them in the icefall. Only the powers that be know if we will overcome them.

06:15 – Base Camp

The climbers left base camp as the first rays of the morning sun were catching the peaks far down in the valley. The summit of Everest is hidden from base camp by its huge west ridge. The team hoped to reach the summit eventually by skirting round the south side of the mountain and up the Western Cwm. The cwm is a hidden valley lying bounded by the mountains of Everest to the north, Lhotse to the east and Nuptse to the south. From the top of the cwm, they would attempt to climb the South-West Face of Lhotse, the fourth highest mountain in the world. From the pass, or col, between Lhotse and Everest, which lies at 8 000 metres, they would finally turn on to the South-East Ridge of Everest and follow that to the summit.

From base camp only the rocky tip of Lhotse is visible, as it too is hidden between the West Ridge of Everest and the West Face of Nuptse. Nuptse, at just under 8 000 metres, is a long icy mountain, with a ridge resembling a silver serrated knife. Somewhere, out of sight between these colossal peaks, lies the hidden valley.

It was the pathway into the valley that concerned them now, the treacherous Khumbu Icefall. The source of the Khumbu Glacier, on which their base camp was placed, lay in the valley, which resembled a frozen lake. The icefall was the rapid at the mouth of that lake, where the ice tumbled over the lip, squeezed between the bottom of the West Ridge and the tail end of Nuptse. In a horizontal distance of about 3 kilometres, it fell nearly 1 000 metres, a gigantic confusion of frozen blocks. As the blocks were creeping slowly downwards, they were highly unstable.

06:45 – Khumbu Icefall

'Enough,' declared Bruce, stopping suddenly and looking up. 'I can see the start of the safety line that runs through the icefall just ahead of us. I'm stopping and putting on crampons.'

'Fair enough,' replied Ian, collapsing down next to Bruce, 'I just about broke my neck in those last few metres.'

As the ice gradually became steeper and steeper, sweeping up into the icefall, the climbers found their footing becoming ever more unsure, the soles of their boots battling to grip on the slick ice. They rummaged round in their rucksacks for their ice-climbing equipment. Out came harnesses, which were tied round thighs and waists, and crampons, metal plates with protruding metal spikes, which they clipped to the soles of their boots. The metal spikes could be kicked into the hard, steep ice to stop them slipping.

As the three climbers adjusted their footwear, they could see small figures from the 13 other expeditions on the mountain also moving towards the slopes. Like the South Africans, they had followed the rocky moraine that ran along the glacier's edge, and then threaded a way between the pinnacles and over the hummocks of ice of the glacier to the foot of the icefall.

'Damn, it's cold,' Cathy said to herself as her stiff, unco-operative fingers struggled to do up the tension clasps of the crampons. The chill of the shadowy icefall seemed to cut right through all the layers she was wearing. The sweat she had worked up crossing the glacier was now beginning to freeze against her skin. She needed to keep moving to stay warm.

The first to complete the preparations, Cathy picked up her rucksack and moved across to the line of safety rope, which lay slack on the snow, fixed off at intermittent intervals to anchors made of snow stakes or ice screws. She took a safety sling, one end of which was tied to her harness, and clipped the other end to the rope. If she fell on the steeper sections, she would only stop when her safety sling caught against the next anchor point below her, but she would stop. She moved off cautiously, following the rope as it ran up steep icy slopes, finding complex paths between tottering sculptures of snow and house-sized blocks of ice.

CATHY:
Dear God, what happened? Where did the ground go? Instead of smooth white snow in front of my feet, there is an ice-lipped chasm, disappearing down into uncharted depths in the bowels of the glacier. I realise that the trail does a sharp bend and follows along the edge of the crevasse, which is about 4 metres wide. But how are we going to cross it? As I move painstakingly along its edge, I stare, fascinated, into the icy slot. The white ice changes in colour with depth, passing gradually from pastel blue into indigo, before disappearing into darkness.

I see ahead a thin metal ladder spanning the crevasse, as delicate as a bracelet. So that's how we get across. I've read about such things, but it is a little different to contemplate the narrow metal spars lying nonchalantly across the drop. Not one ladder but two, tied end to end, with a little bit of bright blue rope. At either end the ladders are tied off to ice screws or snow stakes. On either side, lying slack on the snow, are further ropes. I don't feel so cheerful about this.

Still, it has to be done, but there is no way I'm trying to walk over this. The cold and my sleepiness combined with the unaccustomed weight of my rucksack and huge boots make me feel unstable enough just on flat ground. I kneel and gingerly start to crawl across the ladder, staring down in wonder at the inky depths visible between the rungs. Ice is so weirdly beautiful.

'Give us a smile then, girl. Everest style at its best yet.' Bruce's voice booms out cheerfully. I glance cautiously up to see him standing by the edge of the crevasse, photographing me. Damn. Why do I get the feeling that there is another way of doing this that I haven't caught on to? Just when I'm trying to look as if I know what I'm doing.

With sore knees and much relief, I reach the other side and stand up awkwardly in the soft snow. Ian, who has been watching in silence, casually picks up the two ropes that lie slack on each side of the ladder. He twists them round his wrists until they come taut, and then begins to walk across the ladder, carefully placing his boots so that the crampon points do not catch on the rungs, using the rope tension to keep his balance. So that's how you're supposed to do it.

I don't like the look of this at all. Crawling makes a lot more sense to me. But I'm damned if I'm going to crawl while the men walk.

The next ladder turns out to be just round the corner. No one says anything as I tentatively pick up the handrail ropes and wind them so tightly round my wrists that I virtually cut off the circulation. I step out slowly on to the ladder, one step and then another. The metal plate of my crampons grates against the rungs, but it works. I can do it.

IAN:
R2,50, that's how much the old scruffy book cost, but it took me two whole nerve-racking, desperate months to save up enough pocket money to finally buy the story of the first ascent of Mount Everest in 1953. The story was good, the writing eloquent, but what I really wanted was the pictures. Those glorious pictures allowing me to experience the dangers of the icefall with the Sherpas, the hot stifling slog up the Western Cwm with the climbers, and then strike out on my own for the summit. They never left my side for months and months. They have never left my memory. Now as we begin to make our own way across the ladders and crevasses of the icefall, I can not only recall the pictures of 1953 but I can jump inside them and experience history for myself, and I'm loving every moment of it.

07:30 – Khumbu Icefall

As ladder followed ladder the technique became second nature to the climbers, and the depths to be seen between their feet, between the ladder rungs, were barely noticed. Between the ladder sections were snowy slopes that had to be plodded up, before encountering the next chasm to be crossed.

The ladders and safety ropes that traced a safe route through the icefall were the responsibility of an Anglo-Danish Everest expedition. Other teams who used the route contributed financially towards its establishment and upkeep, because the icefall was, ever so slowly, flowing downhill, so the anchor points of the ropes and ladders had to be checked almost every day. As the weeks passed crevasses would widen or close up, blocks would tilt and fall over. The icefall route had to be constantly altered to compensate for these changes.

As Bruce, Ian and Cathy continued their slow upward climb, a climber moved down towards them with the enviable speed of those going downhill rather than up.

'Where're you off to then?' he asked in a plummy British accent.

'We're just doing a day trip to camp 1 and back,' replied Bruce. 'It's our first day on the hill.'

'Good decision,' the Englishman replied with feeling. 'I've just spent the most bloody awful night at camp 1 battling with the lack of oxygen. I'm damn glad to be on my way down. This is the second time I've tried Everest and I forget each time how unpleasant acclimatising to the altitude can be.'

'How high did you get last time?' asked Ian curiously.

'Up to 8 000 metres, climbing on the north side last year,' he replied.

'Hell, forget 8 000 metres,' muttered Ian, 'I'm having enough trouble getting up to 6 000 metres right now.'

'Enjoy it,' the Englishman shouted happily as he started back down the ropes. 'I'm off down for a cup of tea. I've earned it!'

The air pressure at base camp, and consequently the oxygen availability, was only half that of sea level. And by the time the climbers approached the summit of Everest it would be down to a third. But their bodies were still demanding the usual amount for the quantity of exercise.

Long before reaching base camp they had encountered the first symptoms caused by inadequate amounts of oxygen: shortness of breath, slow movement, mild headaches, nausea. If they pushed too high, too fast, they risked Acute Mountain Sickness, which could kill in 24 hours. The only cure was immediate descent. But if they were patient their bodies would slowly adapt, a process called acclimatisation. By going a little bit higher on each day's climb and then returning to sleep low, they were giving their bodies the push, and the time, to adapt.

CATHY:
After the welcome rest that the conversation has brought I move on slowly, reluctantly. I don't know where all the air has gone. It all looks just the same, if air can be said to 'look' like anything, but it just isn't there in the way it is at sea level. Each breath just produces a burning sensation, rather than the sweet relief of oxygen intake.

I know everyone is supposed to be able to adapt to the altitude eventually. But you've always got to wonder if you won't be the exception that proves the rule. Or if on this trip it just won't happen for you, because you do react differently each time you go high. What if I acclimatise much more slowly than the others? How long will they be prepared to wait before they strike out on their own? And what will I do then? I guess I'll deal with it when the time comes.

IAN:
I've been to high altitude many times. That doesn't mean that I'll acclimatise faster on Everest than either of my team-mates, it just means that I know my symptoms, I know my body. Our best defence against the altitude is early and quick self-diagnosis, so I have an advantage there. But acclimatisation takes patience, and of that I'm notoriously in short supply. So

as we venture into the world's thinnest air, I lecture myself, less is more, less is more!

08:30 – Khumbu Icefall

The first section of the icefall had been a winding route of ladders and inclines. Now the climbers had to tackle a series of steep snow walls. The first loomed at the head of a small valley. The line traversed below it to a point where the ropes took off upwards.

'Hell,' mumbled Bruce, wiping the sweat off his round face, 'this thing doesn't let up, does it?'

He brushed his hand over his beard, which tinkled at his touch. Cathy began to laugh.

'All that sweat is running into your beard and freezing. You've got a fringe of tiny icicles all round your mouth,' she said.

'Hmm, I had that pretty often during my three seasons in Antarctica, but the beard makes a great face warmer, and stops the sunburn.'

Cathy could see Bruce's point. Her nose was already reduced to an icy lump, and her cheeks and chin tingled from the dry, cold air. She turned to tackle the snow wall before she lost all her accumulated heat, and attached a jumar to the rope to provide a handhold. The jumar, which acted like a clamp, would move if pushed upwards but lock if weighted downwards. With one hand on the jumar, feet kicking alternately into the steep snow, and the other hand flailing around generally, she made slow progress upwards.

While the South Africans tackled the vertical ice wall one by one, several Sherpas assembled at the top, waiting for their turn to descend. The Sherpas were professional Nepalese climbers employed by expeditions to assist in carrying loads and setting camps. All were lean and strong and at home in the harsh environment of the Himalaya. Born on the edges of the mountains, they had less difficulty acclimatising to the lower altitudes on the mountain and were less affected by the cold. This, together with living in a society of manual labour, made them physically stronger in general than the western climbers.

'Bara Sahib?' called down a cheerful voice. The weather-beaten face of Ang Dorje, the team's sirdar, or chief of staff, beamed down at the climbers.

'Ang Dorje, you good-for-nothing shirt-lifter,' Ian called back in recognition of his Nepalese title as expedition leader.

'What's the matter, do you need some help in getting down?' he teased.

'Bara Sahib looks very tired,' Ang Dorje replied, shaking his head in mock concern. 'Maybe you should let Didi carry your rucksack,' he continued, gesturing at Cathy and using her Nepalese nickname.

With a wicked gleam in his eye, a ready fund of humour, and a head of thick, black, wavy hair, Ang Dorje appeared more like an urban playboy than a high-altitude mountaineer. He looked resplendent in his orange climbing salopettes, and seemed unmoved by the fact he had already been to the top of the icefall that morning and was on his way back down. Over his shoulder peered Jangmu, his face, as always, impassive and his eyes hidden behind rainbow-coloured reflective sunglasses. Behind them, grinning shyly, were the brothers Pemba and Nawang, and the anxious face of Ang Sirke. These five Nepalese climbers made up the balance of the South African expedition's climbing team, and although the expedition was still at its formative stage, the eight climbers had already become good friends. The Sherpas had left base camp even earlier than the South Africans and had already dumped their loads at the site of the first camp on the mountain.

'It's not far,' Ang Dorje assured the climbers as he slid past them, but with a mischievous grin. 'Not far at Nepali speed, but maybe a bit further for you.'

'The toe-rags are laughing at us,' Ian grumbled as the Sherpas moved on down. 'They like nothing better than to see the sahibs taking a bit of strain.'

CATHY:
I watch them go with envy, as they move so swiftly, so easily, back down the slopes I have just toiled up. They are a curious people, with their stoic acceptance of life's hardships and their easy delight in its pleasures. In the days I have spent with them at base camp, I have been gradually trading snippets of information as we gain the confidence to express our mutual curiosity about each other's lives. I visit mountains for change, for challenge, for fun, but they live here. This is home. And they must therefore see it so differently. They know these mountains in a way I never will, and there is so much I would like to learn from them. But it is not always easy to break through their reserve, or overcome the language difficulties.

IAN:
I have climbed with them and I have fought side by side with them. The Nepalese people, and particularly those from the mountain regions, have a special honour and a special pride. Had I not been so fortunate as to have been brought up a South African, I would want to be Nepalese.

09:15 – Khumbu Icefall

The trail ran through more snowy bowls, up more icy walls and then switchbacked over complex hummocks. By now the sun had emerged from behind the ridge of Nuptse and the frigid morning air was rapidly warming up as the white snow of the icefall acted as a giant reflector. The sun beat down brutally through the thin atmosphere. The climbers stopped to put on sunglasses to protect their eyes from the relentless glare of the sun-lit snow. Without these, they risked sunburn of the retina, which would rapidly lead to temporary or permanent blindness.

'Hey guys, look at this,' Ian shouted, holding up an opaque plastic tube, 'my suntan lotion's frozen.'

'That's because it's a water-based lotion,' said Bruce, ever the scientist.

'I don't care whether it's a gin-and-tonic-based solution,' Ian said in disgust. 'It's no use to me frozen.'

'You could lick it like a lollipop.'

'I'd be as sick as a dog.'

'Yes, but your tongue wouldn't get burnt.'

'You know what? We could invent a self-heating suntan lotion.'

'That's right, a solar-powered, self-heating suntan lotion.'

'It'll be worth millions,' said Ian, turning the bottle around in his fingers.

CATHY:
After the intense cold of this morning, this baking heat and dazzling glare seem so out of place. Even with sunglasses on, my eyes ache. And I can feel the sweat trickling down my spine into the small of my back. I concentrate only on moving from anchor to anchor on the safety line, trying not to look beyond that, not to search for signs of progress. With the many twists and dips in the trail, landmarks approach with agonising slowness.

I slump down in the snow and pull out my thermos flask, trying to look as if drinking is the purpose of the rest, rather than just the excuse. The cold juice brings relief to my throat, dried out by the continual mouth-breathing.

I have been leading the group up to now and am pleased with my progress. I know I am a slow but steady climber and am glad not to be in the company of 'boy racers' but of team-mates who share my style. Nevertheless, I'm glad when Bruce moves on ahead. Now all I need do is focus on the green gaiters that cover the back of his boots, and keep moving.

09:45 – Khumbu Icefall

Another convoluted crossing of another snowy bowl brought them in sight of a huge, overhanging roof of ice. Cathy caught up with Bruce, who was standing, looking at the ice roof.

'That must be the wave Mal Duff described to us,' said Cathy. 'Remember, the one bit he said is "definitely going to fall over in the next week"? I hope that today isn't its day for self-destruction.'

The big, bluff Scotsman had come over to their camp the week before to welcome them, to tell them about the icefall, and to collect their money for the use of it. Ian had climbed with Mal before, indeed had learnt most of his mountaineering from Mal. They had tried to climb the North Face of Anna-purna together, failing only a few hundred metres below the summit. This was to be Mal's third attempt to summit Everest. In between swapping reminis-cences, Mal had told the South Africans that the icefall was surprisingly stable that year and the route relatively straightforward. The only really scary bits were near the top, with the 'wave' marking the start of the tricky section. His only advice was to do it quickly, as early as possible and with fingers crossed.

'What's everybody waiting for?' asked Ian as he stopped to see what Cathy and Bruce were looking at.

'Mal's wave,' said Bruce, pointing up at the roof of ice.

'Nasty,' Ian said with a frown.

'Guys, I would much prefer it if we were standing at the top of this section rather than at the bottom,' ventured Cathy sensibly.

'I haven't been in front yet, so I'll give it a go,' Ian volunteered as he slipped his ice axe off the back of his rucksack in preparation for the steep climb.

'You guys go on,' said Bruce, 'I'll stay here and take some shots of you both climbing.'

Ian and Cathy looked at one another and shrugged. If Bruce wanted to sac-rifice himself for the sake of his art, who were they to interfere?

'Remember to keep the motor-drive going as the millions of tons of snow and ice fall on your head,' Ian joked as he led off towards the outrageous overhang.

'Are you going to climb this thing, or carry on playing with yourself?' called Bruce in reply.

Christ, thought Cathy to herself, we're standing in the most dangerous area of the Khumbu Icefall, itself the most dangerous area on Everest, and my two experienced expedition team-mates have resorted to trading toilet humour.

The Sherpas had their own way of ensuring safety on the mountain. They took the mountain extremely seriously and would not venture on to its slopes before a *puja*, or ceremony, was performed to propitiate the mountain god. The *puja* involved building a *chorten*, or stone altar, on top of a small rise near the centre of base camp. They then lit a fire of juniper at the base of the altar and laid out plates filled with sweets, rice and *tsampa* (ground grain), and bowls of water and whisky. Jangmu who, when not climbing mountains, was a lama in a monastery, led them through a long series of chants. The ceremony ended with a party involving the consumption of a lot of *chang*, the rice liquor favoured by the Sherpas. To illustrate the seriousness and effectiveness of the *puja*, they explained why one of the Sherpas with New Zealander Rob Hall's international team had fallen through a snow bridge covering a crevasse at the start of the Western Cwm: Hall's team had not performed the ceremony before their Sherpas had ventured on to the mountain for the first time. The South Africans' introduction to the icefall had been watching the Sherpa, whose leg was broken, being delicately lowered through the icefall maze strapped to a ladder. All day ant-like figures had weaved through the snowy blocks back down to base camp, their progress seeming desperately slow.

10:15 – Khumbu Icefall

To reach the wave the climbers descended into a deep depression, using a ladder to reach the bottom, and then pulled up the other side to the left-hand end of the snowy ledge that ran directly below the wave. They worked their way cautiously across the ledge, moving slower than they would have liked because of the knee-deep snow on the traverse. Above them a ceiling of rippled blue ice loomed out into space.

CATHY:
Yes, we're through! A short vertical wall leads up just beyond the wave, allowing me to escape gratefully to a large snowy plain beyond. I can feel the blood pumping through my veins, my pulse rate quickened by the adrenaline of traversing under the ice roof.

So today wasn't its day to collapse. May I never be here to see that. Although it would be spectacular … There is a curious fascination about the icefall. It is full of such bizarrely beautiful formations: ice as gnarled as ancient trees, as fragile as giant chandeliers, as intricate as lacework. And the colours are as intense as stained glass. The deep blue ripples of the ice roof are almost mesmerising in their complexity. But the temptation to stand and gawp, like a tourist in a cathedral, is soon repelled by the ever-present awareness of danger.

There is an incredible exhilaration is doing this, in being here, and especially when 'here' is on the slopes of Everest.

IAN:
This is terrific. A hard day's physical challenge in a totally unbelievable setting, with a tinge of danger, bags of excitement, and two great team-mates to share it with!

11:00 – Khumbu Icefall

The trail followed a wide loop across the plain above the wave, dodging blocks and crevasses, before swinging back again to a vertical wall seen in the distance. A long corner and slight drop revealed a crevasse to be crossed by four ladders tied end to end. The ladder bowed alarmingly beneath the climbers' weight, bouncing with each step. Then soft snow took them across to a huge vertical wall.

Progress was slow, requiring flailing of arms, legs and jumars. Now nearly 600 metres higher than their base camp, they were feeling the effects of the thinner air, gasping for breath. The wall eased off near the top, leading to a slope forever promising to transform itself into flat ground but taking an age to do so.

The three friends finally slumped down in the snow to see, just a little way ahead, a smattering of tiny tents, the various mountain homes of the different expeditions and the site of camp 1.

Although no higher than they were, it was separated from them by one final wide crevasse that had to be climbed down and across and up. They looked at each other in a unanimous moment of decision.

'That will do for one day,' declared Bruce. 'We'd best get back down the icefall before it gets caught in the afternoon heat.'

'Absolutely,' Ian agreed. 'This has, of course, everything to do with safety and nothing to do with general exhaustion.'

> CATHY:
> The relief of stopping is so sweet. Breathing comes more easily, although the air is still so thin. Six thousand metres up. On the mountains I've climbed in the Andes, this would be the top, a tiny summit with the pyramid of the mountain spreading away below me. This would be the culmination, the goal, the hard half done with only the descent left. But this time it's only a fraction of the way up, only a small spot low, low down on the slopes of the pyramid, slopes that extend upwards for nearly another 3 kilometres.
>
> A tired elation fills me. I have no idea if I'll make it all the way up this one, but I'm not out of the running yet.
>
> Ian stirs restlessly. Please no, I'm not ready to start the long wade downhill, not yet. If I can just keep the others talking for a bit, I can inconspicuously grab some rest.
>
> 'We can hardly see the base camp tents from here,' I say. 'Where have ours got to?'
>
> A bit inane, but it serves the purpose.

IAN:
We've reached the top of the Khumbu Icefall on our first day's climbing on Everest, and we've reached it together. No histrionics, no complaints, just a good solid team performance. I couldn't have wanted more, and it certainly bodes well for the rest of the expedition, because team-work is everything.

12:00 – Khumbu Icefall

The three climbers looked down on to the Khumbu Glacier, an enormous conveyor belt of ice moving in very slow motion, imperceptibly creeping its way from the mess of the icefall into the long valley below. It was hemmed in on three sides by huge mountains – Nuptse, Everest, Khumbutse, Lingren, Pumori. The base camp tents pitched precariously on its surface were so dwarfed by their surroundings that from the top of the icefall they seemed no more than tiny pimples. Everest base camp was simply a mark on a map, a site on the outside curve of the glacier, consisting of little more than a stretch of rock-covered ice hummocks, with occasional trickles of meltwater in the hollows. It was as high as yaks and porters could walk up the valley, and close to the foot of the icefall where the actual climbing began.

Yet on this barren wasteland a colourful and cosmopolitan community had sprung up, a mini United Nations of mountaineering. The South Africans had a team of Serbians as their down-glacier neighbours, although everyone referred to them as the Yugoslavs. On the other side were the Swedish, the Taiwanese and nine other expeditions. Each team erected several large tents, usually as mess and kitchen tents, with a sea of little multi-coloured living tents scattered around them. Prayer flags in bright red, green, yellow and blue ran out from the *chortens* to the various tents.

Cathy, Bruce and Ian surveyed the dots of colour, looking for the two green tents that served as the South Africans' dining and storage facilities. The black two-man tents in which they each slept were too small to see. Just to pitch these had taken half a day with a pickaxe to level a site and build a rock platform on which to place them. The environment around was inherently hostile. No natural colour existed beyond brown-grey rock, white ice and blue sky. Nothing grew and nothing lived there except birds, which followed the climbers up the valley to scavenge off kitchen scraps.

The only sound at base camp was the whistle of the wind, the cracking and groaning of the ground as the glacier readjusted to the enormous pressure it was under, and the rumble of rockfall from the nearby mountain slopes. Thankfully, the roar of avalanche remained sufficiently rare to bring everyone out of the tents, grabbing for their cameras.

Bruce at last managed to identify the South African tents.

'Somewhere inside there, too small to see, is a steaming mug of tea. If only it wasn't so far away.'

'Well, talking about it won't get us back down there,' said Ian, anxiously stamping his feet in the snow. 'I've had enough of this altitude for a bit. Let's go home.'

CATHY:
Ah, well. I guess it had to happen some time. It seems such a shame to lose all this painfully, preciously gained height. Especially knowing that we'll have to climb all the way up here again. But we're on our way towards the top. And I'm on my way! My greatest fear up until today has been not being able to keep up with my companions. And now I've proved I can do it, proved it both to them (although they never asked for that) and most importantly to myself. I feel that somehow in their eyes I have shifted from being a 'woman' to being simply a 'climber'. Despite my exhaustion, I can't wait for the next day of climbing. I'm on my way.

15:00 – Khumbu Icefall

The icefall, long enough on the ascent, seemed to have stretched even further as they descended in the baking sun. The thermal and fleece clothing layers, which had felt so insubstantial in the early morning, now clung to their skins in the sweaty heat. Vast reaches of snow materialised that they had no memory of having crossed that morning. But at last, in the distance they could see the South African flag flying above the tents, the mix of red, green, blue and yellow standing out brilliantly against the sombre mountainside.

'Now we just have to see if we can get it to fly on the summit,' Ian said thoughtfully.

CHAPTER 2

Bed and Breakfast

12 April
15:30 – Base Camp

Bruce, Ian and Cathy reached base camp, tired, but well satisfied. Ang Mu, the camp cook, was waiting for them just outside the kitchen, a structure of stone walls with a blue tarpaulin roof. He had a thermos flask in one hand and a cluster of mugs in the other. As each climber approached they received a mug of hot orange juice. They dumped their rucksacks and slumped down inside the mess tent.

Shankar pushed his head inside the tent door and started to refill the climbers' cups. Their base camp manager was a young Nepalese, slight and fragile, almost Chinese in appearance, seemingly out of place in the harsh environment of the Khumbu Glacier, but in fact exceedingly capable.

'You had a good climb?' he asked Ian.

'Yes, thank you, Shankar, not too bad, all things considered.'

'Not too tired?'

Ian stared hard at the small Nepalese man. Shankar had a roguish sense of humour hidden behind his smooth brown face.

'You want to come with us next time?' challenged Ian.

'No, no, Bara Sahib,' Shankar replied quickly. 'I'm happy here at base camp. It's warm, lots to eat. I will just look after you when you come back.'

A rattle of Nepali from Shankar sent Ang Mu scurrying back to the kitchen for more tea and biscuits. Although Ang Mu did not climb on the mountain, his job as cook was not an easy one. Water was collected from a meltpool several hundred metres from the camp and carried back in plastic drums. All food was cooked on giant kerosene cookers and, with the help of Shankar, he had to ensure that enough fuel and fresh food came up to base camp each week from the local villages. With the nearest market town four days' walk away, it took some organisation.

Deshun burst through the door of the mess tent. 'So how did it go? Tell me everything,' she demanded.

'Give us a chance, woman,' laughed Bruce. 'I'm so tired I can hardly drink, let alone speak.'

He took a long draught of the hot orange juice, and then another.

'How did you get on, Cathy?' said Deshun. 'Did you keep up with them?'

Cathy, smiling, raised her eyebrows at Ian.

'So, Ian, Cathy did all right then?' Deshun asked, rising to the bait.

'Suppose so,' Ian mumbled.

'Sorry, Ian, I didn't hear that. What did you say?' she pressed.

'Okay, all right,' said Ian, putting down his tea on the metal table with a bang. 'Cathy did very well, she kept up with us the whole way, and in actual fact led most of it. Satisfied?'

Cathy and Deshun looked at one another and nodded their agreement.

'Not bad for a woman,' chipped in Bruce.

'Just what I was going to say,' agreed Ian quickly, and the two men ducked to avoid flying biscuits.

'Don't listen to them, Deshun,' Cathy said. 'Hopefully you'll be climbing with us soon and then we'll show them what the women can do.'

'Promises, promises,' Bruce whispered to Ian.

Ian had always wanted to include a South African woman as part of the expedition climbing team, but not knowing any women climbers himself, he advertised the vacant place in the South African media. Having received an immediate response of over two hundred applications, he decided to take six of those who applied to Mount Kilimanjaro in Tanzania, so that they could all get to know one another, compatibility being so important on an expedition such as Everest. After two weeks in the African mountains Ian asked both Cathy and Deshun to join the expedition as far as Everest base camp, after which one of them would be invited to fill the vacant climbing place. The other one could choose either to stay with the team and assist at base camp or to return home. In the event Cathy was chosen to fill the climbing role, and when Deshun asked if she could remain at base camp, everyone was thrilled that she would be staying on as part of the support team. Subsequent to the team starting to climb, however, the Nepalese government changed the permit restrictions for the number of climbers allowed on Everest, and Ian was now trying to get her on to the permit to climb as well. So, although not initially part of the climbing team but still desperate to join them, for the moment Deshun could only sit and wait, as the decision would be made at the Ministry of Tourism in Kathmandu and not at base camp.

Deshun watched wistfully as the climbers pulled off their big mountaineering boots. Cathy smiled at her. The two women had been through a lot together and although Cathy had finally got the place on the team that they had both been vying for, the friendship remained strong. She understood something of Deshun's frustration.

Her boots off, Cathy removed her hat and undid the band securing her plait. She shook her head to release her waist-length brown hair but nothing happened. Inspection revealed her hair to be a mass of tangles. She sighed heavily and, taking her rucksack, headed to her tent in search of a brush.

> CATHY:
> I spread out on the soft support of my down sleeping bag, luxuriating in the weariness of my body and the knowledge that I don't have to go anywhere soon. I really can't be bothered to try to deal with my hair. I'll worry about that tomorrow.
>
> A great day. The icefall is so spectacular and the mountain beyond so inviting. And my companions aren't too bad. I might even decide that I like them. I'm bitterly tired, but that should just be the lack of acclimatisation. It can only get better.

Ian and Bruce picked their way wearily towards their own tents to change into warm, dry clothes and to put their feet up for a few hours before dinner. Although the camp was warm in the soft afternoon sun, as soon as the sun sank behind the mountain of Pumori it would be cast in deep blue shadow and the temperature would drop rapidly. Anyone who hadn't put on warmer clothes in anticipation of this would quickly become chilled.

The two men stopped at the door of Bruce's tent and Ian looked across at the smiling face of the Englishman, half hidden behind his thick brown beard. Bruce was the biggest of them all, a tall, broad-shouldered man. His chubby chipmunk cheeks and happy disposition hid a fiercely bright mind, which had earned him a doctorate in Geophysics. He had since given up that profession to take up travel photography, specialising in mountains. Bruce had become someone Ian could bounce ideas off, someone who would tell him when he was being stupid, and someone who would encourage him when he became demoralised by the sheer load of leadership.

'A job well jobbed, I think,' said Ian as they stared up at the icefall together. 'I'm glad to be able to get back to being a climber. Ever since I thought up the idea of a South African Everest expedition I've been swallowed up in a nightmare of logistics, an endless sea of administration.'

'Yes, it was good to stretch the old legs,' said Bruce. 'And Cathy did pretty well. I must say, old man, I was rather dubious about your idea of including a novice woman on the team when you first came up with it. But your choice isn't bad. I think she is capable of climbing this mountain.'

'Yes, I think she is as well,' replied Ian.

> IAN:
>
> I ease what's left of my body gently back against my blue plastic equipment barrel and with an audible sigh relax and look around my little base camp tent. Well, not exactly home yet, but I've lived in worse! I smile to myself at this afternoon's horseplay. We're very much at the formation stage of our development as a team, but the signs so far are good. Deshun is keen and excited, but with a quiet appreciation of how steep a learning curve she's really on, and as for Cathy and Bruce ... Well, it already feels like we've been climbing together for years. Now if I can just concentrate Herrod's mind on the climbing and not on other things, we may get up this thing. Devil that he is!

19:00 – Base Camp

'Soup ready, soup ready.' Rajan Khatri, the kitchen assistant, was doing the rounds calling everyone to dinner. The camp rustled to the sound of climbers emerging past frozen flysheets. They shuffled over the uneven ice and rock to crowd on to the canvas chairs set around the metal table in the mess tent. Dinner dress was down jackets, woolly hats, gloves and thick socks, as the wind came whistling under the canvas tent flaps. The meal was lit by a kerosene lamp, and started with a huge pot of soup, spiced with peppery poppadoms, enough to give everyone at least two helpings. Next came curried vegetables, meat with beans, meat pies, potato pie and gravy. As always, there was far too much, but the kitchen staff would finish off the rest. Dessert was warm, tinned, mixed fruit, followed, as ever, by tea, coffee or hot chocolate.

As the climbers sat with their gloved hands cupped round their hot mugs reflecting on a satisfactory first day's climbing on Everest, Ang Dorje poked his head through the tent door.

'Bara Sahib, the loads you have left us to take to camp 1 tomorrow, they are fine for two Sherpas, but what are the others going to carry?'

Ian stared at him in amazement. That afternoon he'd put out loads of food, tents, stoves and gas that needed to be moved up the mountain. In doing so he had estimated what he thought five climbers could reasonably carry in one day, but now Ang Dorje, his co-leader, was querying the lightness of their rucksacks, so Ian had to go out into the cold and find more equipment to fill up their loads.

'Incredible, aren't they?' said Deshun when he returned. 'They are just so fit and strong.'

'Bloody lunatics more like it,' Ian replied, throwing away his hot chocolate, which had chilled in his absence. 'When I was in Kathmandu last November, I put word out that I was looking for Sherpas for Everest and then interviewed the various applicants, but I didn't think I'd employed a team of Rambos.'

'You said you wanted them hungry for the summit,' Cathy commented.

'"So hungry they can taste it" is what I recall you saying,' chipped in Bruce.

'"Sufficiently experienced to climb on their own, but not having reached the summit before,"' Deshun quoted.

'All right, all right,' Ian submitted. 'At least they're keen.'

'Except Ang Sirke,' Cathy said knowingly.

Bruce burst out laughing.

'He swore to me in Kathmandu he was a camp 2 cook,' said Ian defensively.

'Look, mate,' said Bruce, trying to compose himself, 'Every time we talk to the Sherpas about what food to take to camp 2 for Ang Sirke, the other four collapse in fits of laughter. I saw them teasing him this afternoon by trying to explain to him what a kettle was for. Face it, mate, Ang Sirke is a very ambitious climber who took whatever job he could get to be on this expedition. But he definitely isn't a cook.'

'Well, as long as he does his job and carries loads to camp 2, then I'll be satisfied. We can always eat hill food if we have to,' Ian replied with a shrug.

13 April
07:30 – Base Camp

'Tea ready, Didi. Tea ready, Sahib.'

Rajan was moving from tent to tent with a thermos flask of black tea and a bowl of sugar. For the climbers burrowed into their down cocoons, it acted as a wake-up call. Ian pulled his sleeping bag firmly over his head, Cathy curled up in a ball and Bruce tried desperately to pretend he hadn't heard. But Rajan's call was as insistent as an alarm clock. Eventually heads came peering out of tent doors like rabbits peering out of burrows and gloved hands were extended to accept the cups of tea.

Everyone disappeared back into their bags with the tea, to wait for the sun to reach their tents and rapidly raise the temperature. Within half an hour the tent ceilings changed from dark grey-blue to light blue and then to white; the tents themselves changed from iceboxes to hothouses and the sleeping bags rapidly became too warm to stay in. The frosting of ice from a night's breathing quickly melted and evaporated.

'Breakfast ready,' Rajan called. Climbers gradually crawled out of their shelters. They all assembled in the mess tent to receive the usual breakfast offering of porridge with omelette or toast, and many, many cups of tea.

The team gathered in the storage tent after breakfast.

'Okay, everyone, listen in,' Ian began. 'We had a good day's climbing yesterday, but we don't want to get ahead of ourselves logistics wise. We have a mound of equipment that needs to be sorted and re-packed, and Bruce has all his sponsors' photographs to shoot. So I suggest that we spend the next four days here at base camp as work days, and then move straight up to camp 2 on the seventeenth, for about three nights' acclimatisation. A short rest at base camp after that and we should be fit to move back up to camp 2 permanently.'

'Ian, what's the plan for fixing ropes on the mountain?' Cathy asked.

'Well, Bruce and I have a meeting with all the other expedition leaders later today,' he replied, 'so we should be able to get an agreement to share the route-fixing work with some of the other teams.'

'Do you know exactly how many teams there are here?' asked Deshun. 'There seem to be a lot of climbers about.'

'I worked it out at 13,' replied Ian, 'from 16 countries and 5 continents.'

'But they're not all on our route?' Cathy wondered.

'No, I think three teams are on the south pillar route,' he said.

'And one on the South-West Face,' confirmed Bruce.

'All in all there's an impressive wealth of experience here,' Ian added. 'The climbers at base camp at the moment have notched up 50 to 60 successful ascents of Everest between them, with Sherpa Ang Rita of the Swedish expedition holding the world record with 9 ascents.'

The team sat quietly for a few moments reflecting on how experienced everyone else seemed to be in comparison with their small team.

'Well,' said Deshun, rubbing her hands together, 'I guess this equipment won't sort itself out.'

The equipment had originally been packed into loads for carrying up the trail to base camp by porters and yaks. Now it needed to be sorted between what would remain at base camp and what needed to be moved on up the mountain. Then the equipment that was to be moved up had to be re-packed so that it could be carried on the backs of the climbers, and to ensure that the right items were carried to the right camps. The climbers began to open the piles of barrels and boxes, which were all leaning at crazy angles on the uneven floor, threatening to collapse. The floor of the storage tent became a chaos of stoves, gas canisters, food packs, tents, clothing, and dozens of sundry items. Cathy made up food packs of cheese, biscuits, powdered drinks, chocolate and various sealed, pre-cooked meals. Ian sorted out the tents, checking that each one had all the necessary extras, like poles, guy-ropes and pegs. Deshun ploughed through the sponsors' promotional material, sorting out T-shirts and flags, in preparation for Bruce's photographic shoots, while Bruce himself started checking the medical equipment.

11:30 – Base Camp

Rajan stuck his head through the tent door.

'Tea ready,' he called.

'Thank God for that!' said Bruce. 'How we're ever going to move all this equipment up the mountain I just don't know.'

Everyone collected cups of tea and handfuls of biscuits and moved outside to sit in the warmth of the morning sun. The icefall glistened in the sunlight, and they could just make out the tiny black dots of other climbers up on the mountain.

Ang Dorje came walking towards them as they sipped their tea.

'We are back, Bara Sahib. We all took loads to camp 1. Jangmu and Pemba have gone on to set up a tent at camp 2.'

'That's terrific, Ang Dorje, well done,' replied Ian, offering his chief of staff a stool and pouring him some tea. 'I want the Sherpas to rest now for the next two days before moving anything else up the mountain. It could turn out to be a long season and we don't want you guys burning yourselves out too soon.'

'Okay, Bara Sahib,' replied Ang Dorje. 'Route is not fixed higher up anyway.'

'That's right, so you can rest while the logistics are sorted out with the other teams.'

'*Ramro*, Bara Sahib, very good,' Ang Dorje agreed as he took his leave of the climbers and headed back to the other Sherpas to tell them the good news.

'Well, that puts us up to speed with the other teams,' said Ian well satisfied. 'Three other teams have also got tents up at camp 2, but no one has slept up there yet.'

Cathy found Ang Dorje sitting outside the kitchen tent, legs stretched wide, enjoying the rest in the sun.

'Did you have a good day, Ang Dorje?' she asked.

'Oh yes, Didi. The icefall is good this year. Not as dangerous as before.'

'Do you actually like climbing,' she asked curiously, 'or is it just a job?'

'It is a job, a good job. My wife is always happy with the money I bring home. But also I enjoy doing it.' He stared up towards the mountain. 'I have been to 8 400 metres before, almost to the South Summit. But this year I hope to make the summit,' he replied, breaking out into a broad smile.

'But Ang Dorje, aren't you a bit old for that?' teased Cathy. 'You should be settling down and having grandchildren.'

'No, I am a young man. I am only…' Ang Dorje paused for thought, '36!'

'Last time I asked you, you were 39,' Cathy protested. 'And even then you looked shifty saying it.'

'Well,' Ang Dorje turned his most charming smile on her and banged his chest, 'my heart is young.'

15:00 – Base Camp

'I've never seen so many egos packed into so little space,' Ian announced as he and Bruce sat down in the mess tent after returning from the expedition leaders' meeting.

'The leaders stood up one by one, and announced who they were and what climbing they'd done,' said Bruce, looking around for any sign of some tea.

'They all seem to have been on Everest before,' Ian continued, 'and New Zealand leader Rob Hall stood up and announced that he had reached the summit of Everest four times already, a record for a western climber.'

'I thought Ian was going to burst into tears when he had to humbly confess to never actually having climbed Everest before,' laughed Bruce.

'I certainly felt like it,' Ian agreed, shaking his head. 'I think we're viewed with a kind of amused condescension. They wish us well but nobody thinks we have a hope in hell of actually making the summit. Anyway, once they'd finished handing out Oscars to each other we managed to agree some basic logistics.'

'The Yugoslavs are fed up with all the mucking about,' Bruce explained, 'and have seized the initiative. They said that they would fix the ropes up the Lhotse Face from camp 2 to camp 3, or at least their Sherpas would.'

'We've agreed to help the New Zealand and French teams fix from camp 3 to camp 4 on the South Col,' Ian said.

'Will we be acclimatised enough by then?' Cathy asked.

'No, none of the climbers will be,' he replied. 'We'll have to leave it to the Sherpas from our three expeditions.'

20:00 – Base Camp

The climbers sat round the mess tent table with mugs of coffee or hot chocolate. Deshun came bursting back in, head-torch in hand. She quickly sat down shivering, and grabbed for the thermos flask of hot water.

'I don't think I'll ever get used to going to the toilet in this cold,' she declared, 'especially in the middle of the night.'

During the cold nights, a trip to the toilet, which was situated well away from the main camp and built round a plastic barrel so that the human waste could later be removed back down the trail, became an exercise in suffering.

'Why are you going in the middle of the night?' asked Bruce. 'It's definitely cold enough to be using a pee bottle in the tent. Then you just have to empty it in the morning. Once it unfreezes, of course.'

Deshun gaped at him and began to giggle.

'I'm quite serious,' he said. 'Once we get on the mountain, and especially if we get caught in storms, no one is going outside, however strong the call of nature.'

'Bruce, that reminds me,' said Ian, 'did I ever tell you the trouble I had in finding pee bottles for this expedition?'

'No, go on,' said Bruce slowly, already beginning to smell a rat.

'The problem was that I was buying all our equipment in the UK,' Ian continued.

'Yes, well, so what?' asked Bruce, still unsure where this was leading.

'Well, I could only find English pee bottles, the ones with the very small openings. And being a South African expedition we need the huge …'

Ian was cut short by howls of derision from Cathy and Deshun, while Bruce just sat there shaking his head, admonishing himself for being led on so easily.

'The real shame of the nights being so cold is that we never appreciate the stars,' commented Cathy once some order had been restored. 'I only look at them in the two minutes it takes me to get from the mess tent back to my tent, and even then I can't look too long or I'll trip over something.'

'I'd love to photograph the mountains at night,' said Bruce, 'but it takes too long. I don't know what would freeze first, me or my camera.'

Shankar came into the mess tent to collect the water bottles to be filled with hot water. They would act first as hot water bottles to warm up cold sleeping bags, and later as a source of liquid for thirsty throats during the night. Once all the bottles were back they were quickly tucked down the front of jackets and the climbers made their way to their little tent bedrooms and 12 hours of glorious sleep.

The mountains stood out as giant, jagged black masses on all sides. The spectacular sky was filled with thousands of bright stars never seen in urban environments. As silence overtook the camp, the mountains took on a mysterious life of their own. The glacier creaked and groaned, while rock and icefall rumbled in the distance. But each person was safe in their tiny world of warmth within their sleeping bags.

14 April
07:00 – Base Camp

CATHY:
I jerk awake, my throat raw and my chest heaving. Rolling over I begin to cough, long, jerking spasms. This is not good. On the walk-in I went down with bronchitis and I don't need that again. I shouldn't climb with this. It will only get worse and that could end any chance I have. If I can just persuade the others to wait a day or two, I should get over it.

08:30 – Base Camp

'So what do you think?' asked Cathy apprehensively.

Bruce peered intently at her over the mess table.

'Sounds like a weak excuse to me, young woman. I think you just want a few more days of lounging around in the sun.' He smiled to take the sting out of the words. 'But of course we'll wait. My legs are still pretty stiff from the day before yesterday and, to be quite honest, my stomach is playing up. I'd be glad of the extra rest as well. That's not a problem, hey, Ian?'

Ian took a few moments to consider the request before answering.

'No problem,' he replied finally. 'Each of us will get sick at some time or other, and we're at a very early stage in the expedition, so there's no need to risk Cath's health. We'll wait here at base camp for an extra couple of days, and then move up to camp 2 on the twentieth instead.'

'Thanks, Ian, I'm sure I'll be better by then,' said Cathy.

'There's no need to thank me, it's just sensible logistics,' Ian replied with a smile.

IAN:
I'm not unduly concerned by Cathy's loss of health. We are all likely to get sick at some point on the expedition, and the dry air, the rock-dust and the mouth-breathing of the climbers combine to make throat infections the most common ailment at base camp. At any one time about a third of base camp seems to have coughs or chest infections. Everyone is sucking on throat lozenges, and there is a brisk trade going in cough medicine. Stomach complaints are the next most common problem. The glacial grit in the water, the different food, the poor washing facilities, all make stomach problems easy to pick up.

I haven't known Cathy for very long, but I'm already impressed with her mountaineering maturity. Most climbers on their first major expedition will go to the ends of the earth to try to hide any ailments that they may have, fearing that if they own up to them, it will place them in a less favourable light for going high on the mountain, and may even affect their chance of a summit bid. The reverse is true, however, although it's almost impossible to get the youngsters to understand that. Cathy obviously has, and that's a very good sign for the future.

It also means that she trusts my experience and my logistics. I remember when we first assembled together as a team and I explained that there would come a time during the expedition when we would be leaving for the summit. I made it quite clear then that there would be no restrictions on who made the final bid and who did not, and anyone who felt that they were fit and ready could join in. I said that that may turn out to be all of us or none of us. I wondered to myself then whether any of them really believed me when I said everyone would have an equal chance. At least I know now that Cathy does.

09:00 – Base Camp

Cathy and Bruce walked back towards their tents, in agreement that they would take the morning off and do nothing more than recover. As they approached the tents, Cathy noticed a long line of thermal underwear laid out to dry on the rock in front of Bruce's tent.

'You've been most industrious,' she said, 'doing all that washing. Whatever got into you?'

'Yes, I thought I was a very good lad,' replied Bruce. 'I was up before breakfast, got a basin of hot water from the kitchen and washed all my underwear and socks, and they certainly could do with it. They were about to start a breeding colony in the bottom corner of my tent. It took several basins of water, actually. And then I laid them all out to dry before breakfast.'

He picked up a pair of thermal long johns to see if they were dry.

'Oh no, look at this!' he exclaimed.

He held up the long johns by one ankle: rather than hanging from his hand, they stretched out in front of him, as rigid as a board.

'They haven't dried. They've frozen solid! Now what do I do?'

Cathy picked up one of his tops and shook it vigorously. The ice flew off in little plates. She handed the top to him.

'There you go. It's only a little bit damp. It's the glacial quick-dry method.'

'I'd settle for the conventional way, thank you,' he replied. 'That's what I get for being too organised. Next time I'll do the washing in the middle of the day.'

15:00 – Base Camp

'Okay, you lot,' said Ian suddenly. 'I've got a game we can all play.'

Bruce, Cathy and Deshun looked up from their reading and letter writing in curious amusement. Ian was by far the least gregarious member of the team and community games seemed a far cry from his normal logistics and planning.

'What did you have in mind?' Cathy asked.

'All in good time, but first let me show you the grand prize for the winner.'

With a flourish Ian produced two large bars of Nestlé Crunch chocolate from his jacket and placed them proudly in the centre of the mess tent table. Although the expedition had only been at base camp for nine days, a bar of Crunch hadn't been seen in quite a while and two whole large slabs certainly caught everyone's attention.

'Ah,' said Ian gleefully, 'I thought that would wake you all up. Right, the game is called "Why I want to climb Everest". We each get a turn to come up with the most banal, sickly, stomach-turningly awful reason why you want to climb the mountain. The most dreadful reason wins the chocolate. Everyone understand?'

There were smiles of acknowledgement all round.

'Oh, and by the way, "Because it's there" doesn't count, as someone has already won a similar competition with it.'

'Okay,' said Bruce rising to the occasion, 'I'll start.' He frowned for a few moments before continuing. 'It all started when my single-parent, abused grandmother was lying on her death bed, suffering from three, no wait, four terminal diseases, and she made me promise before she slipped away that I wouldn't rest until I'd climbed Everest.'

Cathy, Ian and Deshun immediately broke into spontaneous applause.

'Bravo, bravo,' cheered Ian. 'Herrod, you're a natural. You could lie for England.'

'Thank you, thank you,' he replied, while taking a bow. 'Cathy, it's your turn. And remember, you've got a hard act to follow.'

'Very hard, very hard,' agreed Ian, moving the chocolate bars more towards Bruce's side of the table.

'Okay, let's see,' pondered Cathy. 'I want to climb Everest as a statement highlighting how the destruction of the world's rainforests and the loss of the whales is being caused by the world's overpopulation of refrigerators.'

'Oh deep, very deep,' Ian commented. 'A different genre, but still very deep. She's definitely in the lead.'

'Damn,' said Bruce, pushing the chocolate back into the centre of the table.

'Okay, now yours, Ian,' Cathy demanded.

'Right,' said Ian in his most theatrical voice. 'My quest for the Holy Grail of the summit of Everest started when I was climbing in South America many years ago. I was in a life and death situation on the mountain and an old Aztec god came to my rescue and saved my life. Well, as you can imagine, I was pretty grateful to him, so I asked the Aztec god what I could do to repay his kindness, and he said to me in his deep booming voice, "Bury the afterbirth of your first male child on the summit of Everest." So I've got it in a little jar ...'

'Woodall, you're a lying toe-rag,' interrupted Cathy.

'Cheat,' Deshun added. 'You know that story comes from the leader of the French expedition.'

Ian and Bruce looked at one another, trying to keep straight faces, before the strain became too much and they broke down into hoots of laughter. They were remembering how the leader of the French expedition had told them a few days ago, in all seriousness, how he carried the afterbirth of his son around in a jar and was going to bury it on the summit of Everest.

'You're disqualified,' said Cathy decidedly.

Ian sat up and wiped the tears from his eyes.

'Okay, it looks like Cathy is firm favourite for the chocolate, but maybe Deshun can snatch it away from her at the last minute.'

'Even Everest penetrated down to the bottom of deepest, darkest Africa,' said Deshun at last. 'When I was young I watched a lot of TV, documentaries on things like Eskimos, Alaska and wolves. Once there was a programme on Sir Edmund Hillary's ascent of Everest. I was fascinated by all that snow and towering ice, by the idea of trying to live in such a weird place. I wanted to tell my grandchildren that I'd done something like that. I decided one day I would climb that mountain too. I didn't even know where on earth it was.'

'My God, that is so awful,' Bruce declared, 'it should have a government health warning.'

'Vicious, vicious,' agreed Ian, officially handing Deshun the chocolate bars. 'I've heard some nasty ones in my time, but that was in a class of its own.'

'Good, I'm glad you liked it, because it was the truth,' Deshun said with delight, and skipped out of the tent before any of her prized chocolate could be repossessed.

15 April
09:00 – Base Camp

The team members were sitting in the sun outside the mess tent, their canvas stools balanced precariously on the uneven ground, enjoying a breakfast omelette and a cup of tea.

'I've acquired a dog,' said Cathy. 'Last night I found a small black dog asleep in the bell of my tent. It seemed a bizarre thing to find so far from any village, but I ignored it and went to bed. It was still there this morning and turned out to be a large black puppy. It's now lying happily asleep in the middle of all our washing.'

'Are you sure it wasn't one of your male admirers from another team trying to sneak into your tent in disguise?' teased Bruce.

'The men here *are* a bit desperate,' Deshun agreed. 'Cathy and I went over to the Yugoslavian team again yesterday evening. Their radio operator still can't make contact with Belgrade on his ham radio set because it seems that Pumori is in the way, but he's being besieged by South Africans interested in us. So as we were talking to some guys in Cape Town suddenly all these climbers just appeared out of nowhere to give us the eye.'

'It was quite eerie,' Cathy added. 'When we left their radio tent we found them waiting outside for us. Two walls of Slavic manhood, all apparently identical, all six-foot-three, with massive shoulders and swarthy bearded faces. They stood in complete silence except for the occasional unintelligible remark in their native tongue.'

Cathy began to cough again, her throat irritated by the effort of talking. Bruce watched her closely but made no comment. Ian raised an eyebrow in her direction, but he could see that Bruce was keeping a close watch, so he went back to his equipment sheets.

17 April
13:00 – Base Camp

Pale sunshine spread over the camp. The climbers pulled the canvas chairs out from the mess tent and sat in the sun eating their lunch. The braver ones were wearing T-shirts. Bruce even removed his to expose his chest.

'No!' protested Cathy and Deshun in unison as the light reflected dazzlingly off the milky white expanses of his stomach.

'What's wrong with my chest?' he asked, patting it thoughtfully. 'A fine figure of a man.'

'A plentiful figure of a man,' Cathy retorted, eyeing the ample stomach.

'Nonsense, this is just inbuilt supplies for use on the mountain. You'll see. When you lot are reduced to pale wraiths, I'll be trim, slim and fighting fit. Now *there's* a sight to turn stomachs,' Bruce exclaimed, noticing the figure walking towards them. 'Our illustrious leader has at last emerged. And just look at those legs!'

Ian was walking towards them in a white T-shirt and baggy khaki shorts.

'The shorts in which Britain conquered the empire,' Cathy commented. 'And no wonder. The poor natives were probably too busy laughing to fight.'

'Ian, mate,' said Bruce, 'I'm not sure it's fair to inflict those legs on us this early in the day.'

'What! These are go-anywhere legs, these are,' Ian protested. 'They may not look like much but they've been all over the world.'

He walked into the mess tent to find some food.

By the time Ian came out, Cathy had returned to her tent. All the coughing was making her feel dizzy, and she was getting a sore-muscled feeling, as if she was getting flu. She hoped that she might be able to sleep it off.

'She's getting worse,' Bruce said to Ian. 'Her tent is right next to mine and she coughs through the night, seemingly in her sleep. She's not going to recover at this altitude. She should go down.'

'I had a look at her this morning and I don't think it's that serious, Bruce. It's just a bad case of base camp cough. Let's give her a couple more days and see what happens,' replied Ian.

CATHY:
I lie in the tent, head aching, muscles sore, trying to stay still and not start another spasm. But the little, irritating itch builds up, more and more intense, until I can't bear it. The coughing tears at my throat and doesn't reach the itch, but I can't stop myself. I reach for the bottle of cough mixture I found in the medical supplies. Anything to make this stop.

I can see the look in the guys' eyes. The 'at what point do we stop the sympathy and just shoot her' look. Such stupid small things that stop us from achieving what we want. But I *will* get there. I just need patience, not to wreck everything by going up before I'm ready.

18 April
09:00 – Base Camp

Shankar stuck his head into the mess tent.

'Bara Sahib, a message has come up with the porters who've brought us some more fresh food. The liaison officer should arrive this afternoon.'

'Thanks, Shankar. Could you please see that a tent is put up for him? Caths, can you help me find all his clothing and bedding?'

'Who is this guy?' asked Cathy.

'Mr Murari Khatiwada, our LO.'

The Nepalese government posts a government official with each expedition to ensure that they follow all the rules and regulations of climbing in Nepal, particularly those with regard to environmental protection. These cover everything, from making sure that all equipment is removed from the mountain at the end of the expedition, to ensuring that no human waste is disposed of in base camp, but is sealed in barrels and taken down the trail to where it can be safely disposed of. He was also there to ensure the fair treatment of the Nepalese staff by the westerners.

'We're going to have to look after this guy,' Ian explained. 'We've been assigned the senior officer. He's not only in charge of the South African expedition but also in overall charge of all the liaison officers at Everest base camp this season. He's very experienced. He told me when we met in Kathmandu that he's been working in the Ministry of Tourism as a planning and promotion officer for 17 years, and this is his tenth duty as a liaison officer on an expedition.'

15:00 – Base Camp

Bruce walked over to Ian's tent and hammered against the door.

'What's up?' came the muffled reply.

'We need to have a quiet chat, youth,' said Bruce.

Ian switched off his Walkman and unzipped the tent door. Bruce crawled in to join him among the muddle of barrels, packets, clothes, tapes and sleeping bag. He settled himself comfortably with his back against a barrel and took a deep breath.

'Ian, we have to get moving on this mountain. The days are passing us by. We're now really well acclimatised to base camp altitude, but we have a lot higher and further to go.'

'You don't have to tell me,' replied Ian. 'Another 3,5 kilometres straight up.'

'We need to move up to camp 2 and spend some time acclimatising there now,' Bruce continued. 'Most other teams are already established at camp 2, and we can't afford to fall behind. The end of the season will creep up on us and we won't be ready to go for the summit.'

Although the official end-of-season date on the climbing permit issued to the team by the Nepalese government was 31 May, that meant little. The season, which ran through April and May, really ended when Everest became engulfed by the summer monsoon storms, sometime during the last week of May. If the South Africans hadn't climbed the mountain by then, they would have no chance.

'I've been hoping Cathy would shake off that cough. She can't risk going up another 1 000 metres with that,' said Ian.

'Certainly she can't,' Bruce agreed. 'But we can't risk waiting either.'

'I appreciate that, but if you and I go up on our own and leave her behind at base camp, then she'll be out of sync with us on acclimatisation. She may never catch up, which jeopardises her summit chances.'

'I know. But waiting for her jeopardises everybody's chances. In the end the success of the project has to be more important than that of any of the individuals involved in it.'

Ian sat quietly, thinking through all the various options and possibilities, but whichever way he looked at it, he knew what Bruce said was true.

'You're right,' he said finally. 'We have to acclimatise higher than base camp as soon as possible, so we'll move up to camp 2 first thing tomorrow. Cathy'll just have to catch up as best she can.'

'You know what these expeditions are like,' said Bruce. 'It's still a hell of a long way to go. By the time the expedition plays itself out, it could be you and me flat on our backs and Cathy making a solo bid for the summit.'

'Yes, I know,' Ian replied. 'I just hope *she* sees it that way as well.'

'Do you want me to have a word with her?

'No, it's okay, mate, I'll do it.'

CHAPTER 3

Two, Going on Three

19 April
06:30 – Base Camp

'We shouldn't leave it too late,' said Bruce as he and Ian sat crouched in the mess tent.

'Yes, I know, we'll go in a minute, but I'm already frozen before we start,' Ian replied, stamping his feet into the ground.

'The climbing will warm you up,' pressed Bruce.

'Okay, no rest for the wicked,' Ian said as he finished the last of his tea and picked up his rucksack just as Mr Khatiwada entered the tent.

'Good morning, Mr Woodall, I have come to wish you good speed on your climb.'

The liaison officer, a small, rotund man, was huddled inside a giant green down jacket. Although clearly happier in the lowlands of Nepal, he took his duties seriously. A formal man who never moved on to the familiarity of first names, he was to spend most of his time nestled in his huge jacket, drinking tea and talking to his fellow liaison officers.

Ian rose and shook his outstretched hand.

'Thank you, Mr Khatiwada. We will see you again in a few days' time. If you need anything in the meantime, please just ask Shankar to help you.'

CATHY:
I sit by the door of my tent and watch the two figures slowly dwindling in the distance.

So I stay and they go. Poor Ian. He was very nice explaining the logic of it all, and how easily I will be able to catch up with them, but we both know it's a problem.

I hate this cough with a passion, yet it won't go away. The environment doesn't help. The air is so dry and filled with rock-dust from all the stone fall. But I can't push it. I can remember vividly what the bronchitis felt like, and I don't need that again. That got so bad that I had to leave the team and walk back down the valley to recover. So I have caught up before.

I'll do it again. I've not put this much into getting here to be stopped now by some stupid hacking cough. I just need patience and determination. The game's not over yet.

13:00 – Camp 1

Bruce and Ian slumped down next to the single small tent that marked the South African camp 1 at 6 100 metres. No one from the team was intending to sleep at the camp, they were just going to use it as a transit depot. Bruce began to rummage around in the tent to find some food while Ian pulled out a thermos flask of juice from his rucksack.

'Incredible how much easier it becomes the second time around,' commented Bruce through a mouth stuffed full of cream cheese and biscuits.

'Hmm,' agreed Ian through a packet of country sausage. 'We are beginning to acclimatise. But now we're moving into new territory, above 6 000 metres.'

He grinned suddenly at the thought.

'We've just passed the summit of the highest mountain in Africa!' he declared.

'I'll drink to that,' Bruce replied, holding up the thermos flask and saluting the little tent and the surrounding mountains.

Ahead of them lay the Western Cwm, the valley that lay hidden between Everest and Nuptse, with the massive form of Lhotse at its head. The climbers took off their crampons to begin the long walk towards the foot of Lhotse. The trail curved towards the West Ridge of Everest, before cutting back across the valley to hug the bottom of the slopes of Nuptse. Its path was dictated by the huge crevasses that ran across the valley, only partly visible as most were bridged in places by snow. The seamless white surface gave little indication as to whether it rested on hundreds of metres of solid compacted snow or on thin air.

The trail wound gently but relentlessly up, the ant-like figures that toiled up it completely dwarfed by the giant slopes that rose to either side. The Nuptse ridge rose up in a gargantuan sweep of fluted snow, ice and rock, the sun reflecting off the icy slopes as off burnished silver. The West Ridge of Everest was a more sedate affair, bulging snow slopes rising in waves towards the ridge. And slowly coming into view in the distance, the South-West Face of

Lhotse, appearing from the valley as a flat wall of ice. With each gain in height, a little bit more of the face would be revealed, the face which they would eventually have to surmount, just to reach their top camp.

The two climbers followed the marker wands, strips of red cloth tied to thin poles, that indicated the trail. The passing of climbers had marked a path in the snow, but it would disappear in the first snowfall. Once the crevasses were passed, the floor of the cwm undulated gently upwards. With no features it was difficult to judge distance and the men were not sure how far up the valley camp 2 was situated.

> IAN:
>
> Our situation is magnificent. I would put up with any discomfort to be here, and although the climbing is physically draining and requires continuous concentration to avoid the crevasses, it only highlights how outrageous a place the Western Cwm really is. I've read many descriptions of it over the years, maybe all of them, but standing here for myself, I realise none of them do it justice. It's the history of the place. No, it's the sheer magnitude of the surrounding mountains. No, no, it's the solitude, a place reserved for just the few souls who have ventured through the icefall. Hell, I don't know, it's just bloody marvellous.

15:00 – Western Cwm

'Damn it!' gasped Bruce, bent double over his knees. 'This isn't fun. Where on earth has camp 2 disappeared to?'

'It must be somewhere up there at the head of the valley,' Ian panted, 'but I can't see anything.'

'*Namaste*,' called Bruce to a passing Sherpa. 'Are you coming down from camp 2?'

'Yes, sahib.'

'Where is it from here? And is it far?' Bruce asked.

The Sherpa smiled broadly at the plaintive question.

'You see the thin line of brown on the left side of the valley?'

He explained to Bruce and Ian that the camp was situated on the moraine slopes coming down from the South-West Face of Everest, about three quarters of the way up the cwm and apparently a long way from where they now stood. The Sherpa moved away swiftly down the valley, while Bruce and Ian resumed their slow plod upwards.

They fixed their eyes on the moraine spit, but it seemed to hover in the distance, a mirage never getting any closer. Although the terrain was gentle and the going easy, each felt as if he was moving through treacle. Their bodies seemed only to work in slow motion. It was the insidious effect of the altitude, of attempting to make their bodies function at heights where there was too little oxygen. Whereas the obstacles of crevasses, of avalanches, of soft snow were all apparent, that of altitude was not. It was the invisible enemy, tangible only in the failure of their bodies to work properly.

The moraine spit gradually became bigger until they were at last standing at the bottom of what seemed only a short stretch up an icy gully to reach the level ground on top of the moraine where the tents presumably stood. But a walk that would have taken ten minutes at sea level now mysteriously extended itself until it came to resemble a marathon.

17:00 – Camp 2

'So where's the tea then?' Bruce puffed as he lay like a beached whale across his rucksack.

'Waiting for you to make it,' Ian replied.

'Well, yes. It's down to you and me, mate. No cook staff, no women. Just us two rugged mountaineers.'

'Rugged and thirsty mountaineers.'

'Do you want to toss for it?'

'We can't brew until we've got ice to melt. Tell you what. I'll go out and chop blocks of ice if you'll do the melting and boiling.'

Ian picked up his ice axe and walked across the rocky rubble of the moraine to the nearest ridge of ice protruding from the glacier. The need to stay hydrated was the most important of all the chores facing the climbers. They needed to be drinking 6 to 7 litres of liquid a day. Unlike at base camp, there was no running water to use for cooking, so water was obtained by melting blocks of ice or snow on a gas-powered stove. Ice was preferable because it was less likely to be polluted by human waste, and snow had the frustrating characteristic of taking enormous quantities to produce very small amounts of water.

The slow process of feeding chips of ice into the pan of lukewarm water filled up the rest of the afternoon. Once water was available cooking was fortunately a simple process. Their meals were pre-cooked and vacuum-sealed in packets that could just be put in boiling water to heat them up.

Bruce fished two aluminium packets out of the boiling water.

'Do you want the chilli con carne or the sausage and beans in tomato sauce?' he asked Ian. 'That's the one advantage of leaving Cathy behind. Now we get to pig out on all the kinds of food she hates.'

The casual remark sobered the mood.

'I wonder how she's getting on,' said Ian, in between mouthfuls of chilli eaten straight from the packet. 'Still, nothing to be done about it.' He chased the last traces round the packet with his spoon. 'So what's next on the menu?'

'A tough choice, youth. Do you want butterscotch and dumplings or chocolate pudding?'

IAN:

I lie back listening to Bruce's hoarse breathing. Well, here we are, Ian, 6 500 metres on Everest. So far so good. I feel fine now, tired but okay, but I know the dubious pleasures of an altitude headache await me in the morning. The bottom line, though, is that the expedition is going well. We're working and bonding really well together as a team, we're on a par with the other teams with our logistics, and ahead of most, and I have faith in both Cathy and Bruce as mountaineers. Not bad considering everyone, other than ourselves, has written us off as pure novelty value. History should have told them to be wary of underestimating South Africans so soon.

20 April
11:00 – Camp 2

'What the hell are you doing?' Ian snapped. He had been woken from a troubled doze by most of Bruce's camera equipment tumbling on to his head.

'Sorry about that. I knocked the pile over while trying to find some more film. These tents seem quite big when you're in one on your own, but with two of us and all our junk, it's a tight fit.'

The previous night the tent space had been neatly divided between the two of them, sleeping bags down the middle, personal equipment stacked tidily on each side. But in the course of an unpleasant morning spent nursing altitude migraines it had all dissolved into a male chaos.

'Hell, my head hurts,' Ian muttered, rolling on to his side in the hope that it might ease the gong that was reverberating inside his mind.

'And mine,' Bruce replied. 'Let's go for a walk. We've spent too long lounging around.'

They pulled on boots and jackets and crawled out of the tent. The camp 2 area consisted of two rocky ridges separated by an icy road. The various expeditions were camped on one or other of the ridges, so it was almost like a suburban street with houses on each side. The South African camp looked rather meagre compared to the other teams. At the moment there was only one tent in place, the black one they were sleeping in. Their down-glacier neighbour was an American team, housed in a cluster of orange and yellow tents. On the up-glacier side, almost hidden behind a thicket of ice pinnacles, was another American team, this one attempting to climb Lhotse, rather than Everest. Directly across the street was a third American team, with a virtual village of yellow tents.

'By God!' Bruce grumbled once he and Ian had worked out who was who. 'I knew the Yanks were taking over the planet, but this is a bit much.'

'They're a bloody menace,' agreed Ian. 'We should put something in their drinking water to stop them breeding.'

'It wouldn't help,' Bruce said, shaking his head, 'they don't breed normally. They're like amoeba, continually dividing. One minute there are two of them, then the next time you look, there are four of the perishers staring out at you.'

They walked slowly up the icy pathway between the expeditions to find the various British teams housed a bit further up the street. The Yugoslavs and the New Zealand team were perched higher up on the moraine belt.

Beyond them the moraine petered out, to return to the hard ice of the glacier. The climbers' eyes were drawn inexorably up to the head of the valley, where the glacier stopped abruptly at the foot of the huge South-West Face of Lhotse. It hung like a giant white veil, sweeping down from the rocky tiara that crowned the face.

IAN:
Standing at the foot of the fourth highest mountain in the world, I'm drawn back into the pages and pictures of my childhood book. The dramatic battle the British team had with this great face, and how the whole fate of that expedition hung in the balance, as George Lowe and his team of Sherpas fought heroically for a way up and through these breathtaking slopes of near-vertical snow and ice.

Soon it will be our turn. Firstly to place our camp 3 at 7 400 metres, about halfway up the giant face, and then to force our way across the top section of the mountain to the South Col and our camp 4 at 8 000 metres.

Some challenges are subtle or devious. Some are imaginary or far-fetched. Lhotse is none of these. It is a good old-fashioned, 'in your face', 'here I am, come and get me' sort of challenge. Just the type we like!

14:00 – Base Camp

CATHY:
I sit on the rock by my tent, watching the Sherpas coming into camp. They have been to camp 2 and back in a day, carrying loads. I find it hard to

believe. How I wish I was there, up at camp 2, with the others, directly below the summit slopes of Everest, rather than languishing here. Base camp seemed such an exciting place to be when I first arrived. Now it has become mundane, boring even. I want to move on, to move up. But I must be patient, play the long-term game.

The Sherpas, having dumped their empty rucksacks, disappear into the cook tent. I follow them, eager for news of Ian and Bruce, of happenings on the mountain.

Cathy found the five Sherpas crowded along the stone benches built into the inside of the cooking shelter. Under the blue tarpaulin the temperature was soaring, but they did not seem to mind. Deshun was already sitting with them, hands round yet another cup of tea.

'A good trip?' Deshun was asking.

'Yes, Didi,' Ang Dorje said. 'But it was very hot in the valley up to camp 2.'

Cathy watched the others as Ang Dorje talked. He always did the talking, whether in Nepalese or English. Jangmu sat to one side, still wearing his reflective glasses, as inscrutable as ever. The lama really did seem to have eyes that looked inward towards his soul rather than outward on to the world. Pemba and Nawang sat together quietly talking in Nepalese. Nawang particularly battled with poor English, but Pemba was gradually coming out of his shell. The two brothers were obviously talking about the women.

At last Pemba shyly asked Cathy, 'Do you have children, Didi?'

'No, I don't,' she replied.

'And the black didi?' he asked, meaning Deshun.

'She hasn't either.'

'Are you married?'

'No, neither of us are married.'

Pemba and Nawang lapsed into a fast babble of Nepalese. By now the other Sherpas were listening with interest.

'How old are you?' Ang Dorje asked Cathy.

'I'm 27,' she replied, 'and Deshun is 26.'

The Sherpas looked incredulous and chattered in Nepalese. All except Jangmu, who as a lama was single, had married in their early twenties. They were puzzled by this group of westerners, none of whom had offspring. That the two women could have reached such advanced ages and be unmarried fascinated them.

'I am 28 and I have two children, daughters,' volunteered Pemba. 'And Nawang, he is 26 with three daughters.' He looked worriedly at the women. 'You must marry soon.'

Cathy and Deshun burst out laughing.

'It's all right, Pemba,' Cathy said. 'It's different where we come from.' She looked across at Deshun. 'On the whole I think we are happier unmarried.'

Pemba shook his head in bewilderment.

21 April
15:00 – Base Camp

The women had gone to visit the Yugoslavs' base camp again, to talk to South Africans over their ham radio. Cathy and then Deshun spoke to a disembodied voice in Durban. It seemed strange to hear that it was 28 degrees at home, as they stood around in fleece salopettes and massive down jackets. As they emerged from the radio tent, they saw a familiar grey-headed figure staggering up the glacier.

'It's Philip,' Cathy said happily, and the two women hurried down to meet Ian's brother, who was to serve as the base camp technician. They were delighted to see him, for his friendly manner and relaxed attitude to life made him a great camp companion. He was so different from his younger brother in some ways, far more approachable and open, yet with the same underlying determination.

Philip lent over his ski sticks, trying to ignore his throbbing head, and watched the pair approaching him. Thank God, he thought. He must be almost there. He had stayed behind in Kathmandu to get all the satellite communications equipment working. Long, frustrating days had passed at the Harati Hotel, trying to establish voice, fax and data links with South Africa. Once the system was up and running, it was all carefully packed, first into a helicopter and then on to yaks, to be carried up to base camp.

'Hello, Phil, good to see you. How're you feeling?' asked Cathy.

Each woman got a big hug.

'I've come all the way from Lobuche, so I'm knackered. I can feel a bit of a headache coming on,' he replied wearily.

'Clearly a cup of tea is in order,' Cathy said, and the three began to walk back to the South African camp.

They entered the large, green mess tent to find the dining table strewn with leather masks, rubber tubes, and orange bottles piled all over the floor. British expedition leader and oxygen salesman Henry Todd had finally delivered the oxygen bottles that the South Africans had ordered from him. With his affable character and vast experience, Henry engendered a lot of respect in base camp. Although capable of fussing like a mother hen on occasion, what he had to say was always worth listening to. He was now waiting to demonstrate to the South Africans how to use the oxygen systems.

'The large leather mask is placed over the nose and mouth. A tube runs from it to the bottle. You can tell how full the bottle is by monitoring the little nipple at the mouth of the bottle. The rate of flow from bottle to mask is controlled by this regulator on the tube, which can deliver anything from 1 to 7 litres a minute.'

Henry paused for breath and another swig of tea.

'You'll probably use oxygen to sleep on at camp 4,' he continued. 'Then you should set the regulator for 1 litre a minute and a bottle should last all night. While climbing you'll use anything from 2 to 4 litres a minute, depending on how you're feeling, and then a bottle lasts about 6 hours.'

Cathy picked up one of the bottles, which was about the length of her arm. It was not as heavy as she had expected.

'A bottle weighs 2,6 kilogrammes,' said Henry, anticipating her question. 'You'll have to register all your bottles with your liaison officer, giving him the serial numbers. Nepalese environmental regulations require that you bring all bottles back off the mountain.'

Henry looked over at Philip, who had slumped down in a corner with a cup of tea to nurse his headache.

'What's wrong with him?' he asked.

'He's just arrived at base camp from Lobuche, so he's feeling the altitude,' Cathy replied.

'A perfect candidate. I'll show you what a difference oxygen can make.'

Philip suddenly found his face smothered beneath a large leather mask, and strange tangy air being pumped into him.

'Do you feel any better?' Henry demanded after a few minutes.

'No,' said Philip. 'I can't feel any difference. All I can think about is how desperately I want a cigarette.'

15:00 – Camp 2

'Hey, youth,' said Bruce suddenly, emerging from his sleeping bag and propping himself up on one elbow. 'What's it really like being a South African?'

'What sort of question is that?' Ian asked in surprise.

'No, really,' pressed Bruce. 'I've always wondered why you lot are so strange.'

Ian knew that he was being enticed into a reply, but he had to change the cassette in his Walkman anyway, so he sat up and pushed his rucksack behind him for support.

'I suppose it's a bit of a rollercoaster ride,' he began. 'We're stubborn, very critical of ourselves and very impatient. It takes us forever to be convinced that change is necessary, but once we are, then we make the change in a flash and wonder what all the fuss was about.'

'But you do have some weird right-wing characters running around the country.'

'Maybe so, no one's saying that there haven't been a few genetic slip-ups along the way, but hey, you've got John Major, so every country has their share.'

'That's true. Point taken.'

'We're not saying we're perfect, maybe not even close to perfect, but every country has its problems,' Ian continued. 'Look at America, the richest country in the world, and it can't supply health care to its population. The problem we have in South Africa is that we expect to be perfect, and to be perfect now, what's more. Tomorrow is too late.'

'But your new country, like many older ones, needs time to find solutions to its problems,' said Bruce.

'That's exactly right, but we are so impatient and self-critical, that's why it's like a rollercoaster ride.'

The two friends sat quietly for a few moments to catch their breath – holding a conversation after only a couple of days at 6 500 metres can be hard work.

'I guess if I have to sum it up, though, I would say that if trouble hits, and you have to choose a companion to stand by your side, you don't need to look past your nearest South African,' Ian concluded as he slipped back down inside his warm sleeping bag with a fresh Cranberries tape.

18:00 – Base Camp

CATHY:
I haven't coughed all day. I've been keeping a careful watch and I really seem to have shaken it this time. And I have so much unused energy rocketing round my system that I am desperate to do something. So what to do?

Do I wait for the boys to come back down and then go up with them next time? That will take days still and leave me well behind them on acclimatisation. No. I'll go up on my own. I've done the icefall before, so that's no problem, and the Western Cwm should be straightforward.

The concept of regaining the initiative, of moving rather than sitting waiting, is exciting. I don't want to be at base camp. I want to be making my way up this mountain. I'll go tomorrow.

I take a radio and walk up to the top of a rock pile behind the mess tent and look up at the silvery gleam of the icefall. Tomorrow. Definitely. My down jacket wrapped tightly round me, the radio clasped in my red-gloved hands, I press the button and call through to camp 2 to tell them.

CATHY: 'Base camp calling camp 2. Do you read?'
IAN: 'Hi, Caths. How're you feeling?'
CATHY: 'Much better, thanks. That's why I radioed you. I'm going to move up to camp 2 tomorrow.'
IAN: 'Are you sure about that? Don't do anything until that cough of yours has cleared up completely.'
CATHY: 'It's gone. I feel great. And I'm so frustrated sitting around base camp with nothing constructive to do. How have you and Bruce been coping up there?'
IAN: 'Pretty grim, quite frankly. We've decided to come down tomorrow. We've had enough for the moment of sleeping this high. Caths, be careful. If you're battling with the altitude, sleep at camp 1 tomorrow and move on to camp 2 the next day. We found base to camp 2 a real long haul.'
CATHY: 'Sure.'

She was immediately determined to do nothing of the sort.

CATHY: 'See you on the trail. This is base camp out.'

18:15 – Camp 2

'I guess she's on her way up,' Bruce said.

'Seems that way,' Ian agreed.

'It's the right thing for her to do if she wants to catch us up.'

'Yes, I know. It just means that she'll have to climb all the way from base to camp 2 on her own.'

'And almost certainly back again.'

'Well, I guess if we didn't think she was capable enough to be on the mountain on her own, we shouldn't have invited her,' Ian reflected.

'She'll be fine,' said Bruce. 'Let's give her full marks for taking the initiative to move up by herself.'

'No, you're right. She's a mountaineer and must be allowed to make her own mountaineering decisions.'

'It does mean that we may get a little peace and quiet at base camp, though,' Bruce suggested.

'That's true.'

IAN:
Bruce and I have spent two nights at 6 500 metres, and are about to sleep a third. Cathy seems well recovered and full of beans. If she can make it up here on her own and spend a few nights by herself at this altitude, then she'll have caught us up really quickly and the three of us will be back on the same acclimatisation programme. That would be terrific. But if she can't, it'll certainly mean that the expedition will split forever into two groups, with Bruce and myself in the front, and Cathy, and perhaps Deshun, making up a second slower group. I really hope it doesn't come to that, but it all depends on Cathy. Will she have the determination to see it through on her own? Only the next few days will tell.

CHAPTER 4

Beyond 7 000

22 April
06:00 – Base Camp

CATHY:

I sit in the warmth of the kitchen tent, staring at yet another cup of sweet black tea. I really don't feel like what must be my fourth or fifth cup, but I am determined to stay hydrated. Liquid provides one of the few defences we have against altitude, and by tonight I will be higher than I have ever been before.

I am excited and nervous, invigorated at the prospect of getting on the mountain again, intimidated by the thought of the long haul through the icefall and the unknown distance of the Western Cwm.

I leave before the sun rises, seeing other small figures coming out of their respective burrows and moving slowly ahead of me to a common point at the foot of the icefall.

My stomach begins to churn in discomfort and at the edge of the glacier I stop, lean heavily against a rock, and throw up most of the tea I so diligently consumed before leaving. Unsure if this is a good or a bad sign but feeling better for it, I move on. With the distance ahead of me too long to contemplate comfortably, I keep my mind in neutral, concentrating on the next step and the one after that. Anything more than that can be dealt with at another time.

As I approach one of the steep walls to be climbed, a wave of Sherpas comes pouring down over me. About 11, I count, running down the wall with the safety rope just looped around their wrists. The rush of sound and colour disappears as quickly as it materialised, leaving me once again alone in the expanse of white snow and blue ice.

It is with considerable surprise that I lift my head at the top of the escape route from the wave to see the final wall looming in the distance. At first I think my memory must be mistaken, but the closer I get the more I am convinced that the toil of the icefall is almost over.

09:00 – Camp 2

'Are you ready yet?' Bruce asked as he poked his head back into the tiny black tent.

'Won't be a moment,' Ian replied, stuffing the last of his personal equipment into his already bulging rucksack. Crawling out on his hands and knees and dragging his pack behind him, he struggled out of the tent and stood up next to Bruce.

'Why does my rucksack always look heavier than yours?' he asked, frowning at the apparent slimness of Bruce's pack.

'It's all a matter of good physics,' Bruce stated in his best doctor-of-science manner.

'It's all a matter of you being a workshy layabout,' grumbled Ian in reply.

The two friends made a brief check around their camp to ensure that nothing had been left behind before setting off down the glacier towards the broad expanse of the Western Cwm.

IAN:
Sometimes we go up, and sometimes we go down. That's the nature of big-mountain climbing. Someone once worked out that by the time a climber has reached the summit of a big mountain like Everest, they would have effectively climbed it three times with all the ups and downs. This is going to be one of the down times, and for the time being at least I am looking forward to getting back to base camp for a while. But as that great American actor once said, 'I'll be back!'

10:00 – Western Cwm

CATHY:
After some cheese, biscuits and water consumed at our camp 1 tent, I enter the Western Cwm. Clouds form and disperse in the valley, as if torn by relentless indecision whether to fill the valley or abandon it. Each time they lift briefly to reveal the head of the valley, it seems to have got no closer. Once the crevasses are passed, the white expanse gives no markers of

distance. The cwm seems elastic, ever stretching to ensure I get no closer to my goal, no matter how many steps I take.

I see two small figures moving towards me, one substantial, one slight. I recognise them eventually as my team-mates. I have been both anticipating and dreading meeting them, fearing they will pass me while I am still hopelessly far from camp 2. But I know I have covered a lot of ground and am grateful for the chance to exchange a few words.

12:00 – Western Cwm

'Good heavens, they'll let anyone on this mountain,' Ian said to Bruce as the third member of their team arrived. Cathy and the two men sat down on their packs in the snow and passed around a water bottle.

'I blame the French,' Bruce stated, shaking his head in mock resignation.

'Absolutely,' Ian agreed.

'I guess it's quite some way still?' Cathy ventured, too tired to join in the midday banter.

'Afraid so,' Bruce replied. 'You see there in the distance, the moraine ridge running on to the glacier, below the South-West Face of Everest? All the camps are on that moraine. The last half-hour slog up to the camp is a real killer, but at least ours is one of the first camps you'll find.'

'How's your time up there been?' Cathy asked, not really encouraged by Bruce's description.

'Okay, I guess, although we're glad to be on the way down. We both got some monster headaches. You need to be very careful with the altitude.'

IAN:
I'm really pleased to see Cathy, particularly as she's obviously climbing quickly to have made such great progress by midday. But most of all it's her attitude. She's totally confident about being on her own on the highest mountain in the world. There's no sign of disappointment that Bruce and I are going down but she still has to continue up. These are all very good signs for the future. I know that the other expeditions have their own opinions of Cathy being on Everest with her relative lack of experience, but I'm beginning to become really proud of her.

CATHY:
Once they have left, the featureless snow plain seems to stretch on to infinity. I begin to feel that rather than taking one step after another, I am merely taking the same step over and over again. The clouds have dissipated and

the sun is hammering down on the valley. With no shade anywhere, there is no way to escape the relentless glare. It is reflected back from all sides off the dazzling white snow. With no wind the heat builds up in the valley like an oven.

I push up the sleeves of my thermal top and curse the sweaty warmth of the black fleece salopettes I am wearing. My feet, encased in double boots designed to keep them warm in extreme cold, are now swimming in burning sweat. I drape a scarf across my face and neck for protection from the relentless blaze and plod on.

Each time I sit down for a rest, leaning back against my pack rather than bothering to take it off, my backside rapidly becomes numb with cold, while the rest of me steams gently. I pull out more sunblock from my rucksack and smear it on to my sweaty, dirty skin. God knows when my next bath is going to be.

I have got to be crazy. It is either too hot or too cold. We are either lying around bored and frustrated from doing nothing or gasping our lungs out doing too much. There has to be a better way to live your life than this.

But I could be standing up at quarter to eight in the morning to lecture to 200 bored first-year journalism students at Rhodes University about the history of the South African press. Maybe there are worse things in life than climbing Everest. With the encouraging thought that however bad it gets, I am unlikely to be asked to explain, yet again, the structure of the English press, I haul myself to my feet and plod on.

Cathy stumbled slowly up the final moraine slopes below the South African tents and flopped into her tent like a stranded fish. Lakpa, the cook for the French climber who was camped next door, brought across a cup and a thermos flask of tea. She drank the hot liquid gratefully, still lying in her semi-recumbent position.

16:00 – Base Camp

'Honey, I'm home,' Bruce called out as he and Ian approached the mess tent.

'Another hard day at the office,' Ian said, dumping his rucksack in the corner of the tent and collapsing on to one of the stools.

As they were removing their climbing harnesses, a face peered around the corner of the door.

'My God, look what the cat brought in,' Philip said with a broad smile.

'Hey, the wanderer returns,' Bruce said as he got up to shake Philip's hand. 'This calls for a celebration tonight.'

'Absolutely. And to help things along, look what I've carried all the way from Shangboche.'

With a flourish Philip produced a shining bottle of Nederberg Château Libertas from behind his back.

'Ah,' exclaimed Bruce, 'will you marry me?'

'Wait, there's more.' Philip then produced a bottle of Klipdrift brandy.

'I love a man who's bilingual,' declared Bruce.

'When you two are finished …' said Ian as he got up to shake his brother's hand.

'Hi, *boet*,' said Philip. 'How was the climb down?'

'Not too bad, but it's nice to be back here,' Ian replied. 'Any headaches?'

'Just bits and pieces really, nothing too serious.'

'I'd keep away from Herrod and that brandy for a while if I were you,' Ian advised with a laugh.

'No, it's fine. They're purely for medicinal purposes.'

'That's absolutely right,' agreed Bruce, 'purely medicinal purposes.'

18:00 – Camp 2

CATHY:

I switch off the radio, the sound of Ian's voice still ringing in my ears.

'Be careful, be careful, watch for any signs of altitude sickness.'

He can be such a worrier sometimes. But he's right. Climbing up to 6 500 metres and then descending again is one thing, sleeping at this height is quite another.

I feel the sudden heaving of my stomach again and grab for the tent door, thrusting my face out into the chilly night air to throw up. I detest this nausea, but at least I'm not getting headaches. I rinse my mouth and quickly zip up the door, trying to save what little warmth is left.

I carefully assemble the various items that need to join me inside the sleeping bag to prevent them freezing – toothpaste, Walkman, and a water bottle filled with boiling water. I wriggle into my down sleeping bag, prevented by the tight fit of the bag from pulling my knees up to my chest for warmth. Instead I cuddle the metal water bottle against my chest. Within minutes my chest is unbearably hot and my feet freezing. I know the sleeping bag will be warm once I have generated enough body heat, but right now it is frigid.

Unable to sleep, I lie awake in the darkness listening to music. Once Tchaikovsky has been rescued from sounding like a slow-motion death wail by warming up the Walkman batteries against the skin of my stomach, the music provides an escape into another world. But eventually even that begins to pall.

I lie awake contemplating the peculiar unpleasantness of not being able to sleep. As I'm usually capable of a solid ten hours, insomnia is foreign to me and deeply disagreeable. I toss and turn restlessly in the sleeping bag, each move requiring a re-ordering of the myriad of things I seem to have in bed with me. The tiny green glow of my digital watch is the only thing that proves that time is actually passing, rather than having been forever suspended.

Looking at it yet again I realise several hours have passed. It dawns on me, to my considerable disgust, that I have been sleeping while dreaming about lying awake being unable to sleep. What a waste!

23 April
07:00 – Camp 2

CATHY:

'Bed tea,' announces Lakpa cheerfully, seemingly six inches from my ear but merely at the door of the tent. I fumble sleepily with the zip to receive the usual sickly sweet Sherpa tea.

I lie for long minutes in the warmth of my sleeping bag, savouring the total comfort of the down cocoon. Only one gloved hand protrudes to allow me slowly to consume the hot liquid.

At last I reluctantly squirm out of the warmth, driven out by the rising heat as the sun comes on to the tent. It seems like time for a rubdown to remove some of the sweat of the previous day. I pull out a holder of wet wipes, only to find them frozen solid. I should have slept with them as well. Given that there's not much that can be done in the way of cleaning with a frozen wet wipe, I give that up as a bad idea and put them out in the sun to thaw.

At last I emerge, mole-like, to survey the camp scene: rock, ice, sky, cloud, and a scattering of tiny, many-coloured tents huddled together beneath the great rock wall that makes up the South-West Face of Everest.

The head of the valley is dominated by the huge ice wall sweeping up to the rocky summit ridge of Lhotse. A trail of black dots crawls up an invisible line in the middle of the face, like a train of ants, following its own mysterious path up the white tiles of a kitchen wall. Climbers, toiling up the 60-degree ice slopes of Lhotse. And I thought just walking up the valley floor of the Western Cwm was hard!

Will I ever make it up that far?

11:50 – Camp 2

Cathy woke from a light doze and summoned up the energy to dig out the radio and call down to base camp. To her delight, she got perfect reception while still lying in her sleeping bag.

IAN: 'How're you doing up there? Any problems with the altitude?'

CATHY: 'Not so good, Ian. I seem to be free of headaches, beyond a certain cotton-wool feeling behind the eyes, but instead I'm throwing up every six hours.'

IAN: 'Too much partying with the French, obviously.'

CATHY: 'I wish. No, just too little air.'

IAN: 'You're in good company down here, although it doesn't have much to do with the altitude. Herrod decided to celebrate our successful return from camp 2 last night by polishing off a bottle of red wine, in which he was nobly assisted by Philip. He added one or two things after that, and then needed help to stand long enough to throw it up again.'

CATHY: 'So how does he feel this morning? I bet he's wishing for something as easy as an altitude headache right now.'

IAN: 'I guess so. He hasn't been seen yet, and it's nearly noon.'

13:00 – Base Camp

Philip was hard at work unpacking and connecting all the communications equipment when Bruce finally staggered out of bed. He sat at the door of the storage tent, now officially upgraded to the communications or 'comms' tent, and watched Philip struggling to fit together the radio antennae.

'I love work,' he announced eventually. 'I could sit and watch it for hours.'

'Sod off,' said Philip, abandoning the antennae and joining Bruce for a cup of tea. 'You're as much help as the yak herders have been. They've been watching, fascinated, for hours, muttering to themselves about how it should be a little more this way, or a little more that. It's funny, really. The latest in twentieth-century technology, provided courtesy of transport that's been used in the Himalaya for thousands of years.'

He pointed to the various other gadgets that lay strewn across the rock and ice of the glacier. 'Satellite dish to connect us via the Indian Ocean satellite relay station to the satcom land-earth station in Malaysia, phone and fax system, Apple powerbooks and computer, printer, battery re-chargers, and so on. State of the art equipment, all brought in by yak!'

'And all equally useless when it comes to getting us even one metre higher up the mountain,' Bruce added.

'Not that I'm saying it's all useless, not at all,' he continued hurriedly, seeing the look of consternation on Philip's face. 'I'm particularly keen on seeing if we can download some of the Kodak digital photographs I've taken on to the computers. I'd love to have a look at how they've come out.'

'Well then, get off your rear end and give me a hand setting it all up,' said Philip.

Together they built a small stone-walled shelter for what was to be the heart and soul of the whole technological operation, the small, red Honda generator which would be the source of all their power.

The generator was to be Philip's special problem child. Each morning he would have to take the spark plug out and clean it, and if it looked worn, replace it. He would then fill the generator with kerosene, which first had to be filtered through a cloth to extract all the impurities, change the oil, and then start it. Or not, as the case might be, depending on the mood of the generator that particular day.

15:00 – Base Camp

'Okay, Ian, the power's on, everything's plugged in and ready to roll,' said Philip confidently.

'Is this really going to work?' Ian asked excitedly.

'I bloody well hope so,' Philip replied as he made a final adjustment to the satellite telephone.

'So, who shall we call?' Ian said, rubbing his hands together with anticipation.

Before Philip could suggest a suitable candidate, however, the telephone itself burst into action with a shrill ring. Ian and Philip both jumped back in surprise.

'This is a set-up, right?' said Ian with a smile.

'No, it must be a genuine call, or a wrong number,' replied Philip.

The telephone continued to ring out across the wastes of base camp. Fearing that the mysterious caller would hang up, Philip himself picked up the telephone.

'South African Everest base camp here,' he said in his best butler's voice.

A few moments passed before Philip gave the handset to Ian.

'It's for you,' he said.

Still convinced he was being set up, Ian took the telephone tentatively from his smiling brother.

Ian: 'Hello, this is Ian speaking.'

Cecil: 'Hi, Ian, it's Cecil. How's everything going?' [Cecil Lyons, mar-
           keting director of Radio 702, Johannesburg]

Ian: 'Hi, Cecil, it's great to hear your voice. Everything here is fine,
           we've established our camp 2 on the mountain at 6 500 metres, so
           we're ahead of schedule.'

Cecil: 'That's great news, Ian. How are Bruce and Cathy?'

Ian: 'They're both well. Bruce is here with me at base camp suffering
           from a well-deserved hangover, and Cathy is up at camp 2 at the
           moment.'

Cecil: 'On her own?'

Ian: 'Yes, but don't worry, she's very capable.'

Cecil: 'Okay, Ian, as you know, we're going to cover the whole expedi-
           tion on radio over the next month or so. Our reporter, Patrick
           Conroy, is sitting at Johannesburg International Airport at the
           moment, waiting to fly out and join you at base camp. Is there
           anything you guys need before he leaves?'

Ian: 'Thanks, Cecil, but no, we seem to be well organised here. Just tell
           Patrick to take it really slowly on the walk-in to base camp. He's
           no use to you if he's sick.'

Cecil: 'Okay, I'll tell him. I just hope that he's there before you reach the
           summit.'

Ian: 'We'll certainly be up the mountain when he arrives, but the date
           of a possible summit attempt is so difficult to predict. There are so
           many things that can go wrong that I can't really tell you one way
           or the other at the moment.'

Cecil: 'I understand. Well, good luck, send my best wishes to everyone,
           and I'll speak to you again once Patrick arrives.'

Ian:

I'm thrilled that our satellite communications system is working so well.
Philip's done a terrific job setting it up. Definitely plug and play, I couldn't
believe it!

Very few people are fortunate enough to be able to take the time out of
their busy lives to undertake a project such as climbing Everest, two and a
half years for me, three and a half months for the others. So being able to
share our experiences on Everest with the rest of our fellow South Africans
is a very important part of being a national expedition. President Mandela,
our patron, has asked us to place our South African flag as high on Everest
as possible, and as we drive to do just that, it's so important for us to be able
to draw on the support and encouragement we receive from back home.

24 April
20:00 – Base Camp

CATHY:

God, I'm tired. It has been a long day getting back down to base camp. In some ways going down is worse than going up. It is just so hard on the knees and the feet. But after two uncomfortable nights at 6 500 metres I am only too keen to wallow in the comforts of base camp. Compared to camp 2, it has all the luxuries of Club Med.

And right now, I want nothing more than a solid 14 hours fast asleep with a whole lot more air than I had at camp 2.

As I unzip my tent door to go inside, Bruce approaches, waving something at me.

'Look what Philip brought me,' he says. 'I got so sick of all the rest of you plugging into your Walkmen that I asked him to buy me one, with speakers.'

'That's nice, Bruce,' I reply, not really paying any attention. I just want my warm sleeping bag and oblivion.

I have just slid nicely into sleep when Pink Floyd's 'The Wall' comes surging through my mind at a million decibels. What the hell? I jerk awake, bewildered.

Bruce and his bloody speakers. I try to shut it out but it hammers insistently through my head. It is not the kind of bedtime music I fancy after a long day.

Eventually I yell at him to turn down the volume, but to no effect.

'He can't hear you over the noise,' shouts Deshun unhelpfully. She is camped on the other side of my tent and is not as badly affected by the terrible noise. Her relaxed amusement does nothing to improve my frame of mind.

I wait. Maybe he will get tired of it.

No, looks like I am going to get the entire album.

My anger rises. I scramble out of my sleeping bag, pull on my down jacket, push my feet into cold boots and stumble out into the icy night. The brilliant blaze of stars above is totally wasted on me. I peremptorily unzip Bruce's door and stick my head in.

'This,' I announce icily, 'is a total sense of humour failure on my part. Turn that damn thing down. Don't you own earphones?'

'No,' apologises Bruce humbly, looking startled. 'I'm sorry. I didn't realise.'

'Don't do it again,' I order loftily and withdraw.

My anger has dissipated, replaced by amusement at Bruce's surprise.

25 April
09:00 – Base Camp

Ian took advantage of a late breakfast to explain to the team the movement plan for the next few days.

'Okay, everyone,' he began. 'We're very pleased to welcome Cathy back to base camp, and are thrilled that she's caught up with Bruce and myself in acclimatisation.'

Bruce and Ian raised their mugs of tea in a morning toast while Cathy smiled back her appreciation.

'Now that we're back together as a team, the plan is for us to rest here for the next four days, after which we'll all move up *en masse* for camp 2 on the twenty-ninth and make that our base for the rest of the expedition. A day of rest, or possibly two, at camp 2 and we should be ready to make the big jump to camp 3 at 7 400 metres.'

Bruce and Cathy nodded their approval of the basic plan, although everything would depend on favourable weather. Ian noticed that Deshun had been very quiet all morning and was looking into the depths of her coffee mug while he was speaking. She obviously realised that as the team continued to make good progress up the mountain, so she fell further and further behind. There was nothing more that Ian could do about speeding up her permission to climb on the mountain, but he made a mental note to have a quiet word with her later in the day.

29 April
06:00 – Base Camp

'By God, man, where are you putting it all?' asked Ian in fascination as Bruce downed yet another cup of tea in the warmth of the kitchen. 'I kept count up until five, but then they began to blur into one another.'

'It's very important,' replied Bruce pompously, 'that the mountaineer be properly hydrated. Liquid intake is our greatest source of prevention against altitude sickness. I intend to be fully prepared for living up at 6 500 metres.'

'I reckon it's the British influence,' offered Cathy as she filled up her water bottle with juice. 'You and I run on food, Ian, but the British run on tea.'

'Enough is enough,' said Ian. 'The Sherpas have already left. You surely can't want any more, Bruce?'

'Just you wait and see,' he replied. 'I'll beat you all to camp 2.'

The other two followed him out into the frosty morning air, shouldered their rucksacks, and began the long plod across the glacier to the foot of the icefall. Bruce briskly led the way for several hundred metres and then lurched against a nearby rock, looking rather green. He lent over it, eyes bulging, and threw up several gallons of tea all over the ice.

'I feel much better now,' he announced cheerfully and walked off.

Cathy and Ian stared at each other, shrugged, and followed after him in amused bewilderment.

12:00 – Camp 1

Having reached camp 1, Bruce pulled out his camera to take a team photograph for the Nelson Mandela Children's Fund, the expedition's official charity. He set the camera up, using his ice axe as a tripod, setting off the self-timer and then running back to collapse between Cathy and Ian each time. The pictures captured Cathy watching in amusement, legs elegantly crossed, with her sunglasses and scarf wrapped round her face looking for all the world like Audrey Hepburn. Ian assumed his usual expression of intent seriousness, the vivid white of the zinc sunblock on his lips contrasting with his red sunburnt skin. Bruce sprawled between them, in open, generous posture, looking on contentedly.

'Those should help the charity pledges,' said Ian well satisfied, referring to the fundraising campaign that the Children's Fund was operating whereby the public was invited to contribute money to the Fund, in accordance with how high the expedition climbed on Everest.

As the photography progressed, climbers passed the South Africans on their way down the mountain.

'Now that's nice,' exclaimed Bruce, distracted momentarily from his photography by a vision wearing nothing but full-length red thermal underwear and a harness.

'It must be cosy with you three squeezed into that tiny tent,' called out the vision as she passed.

'Even cosier if you'd join us,' offered Bruce hopefully.

She laughed and went on down.

'Stick to your photography, mate,' advised Ian. 'You're obviously better at that.'

Although the Lhotse Face was obscured by cloud, the cwm and the skies were clear. The climbers realised they were in for a long, hot afternoon and stripped down to thermals, squeezing yet more greasy suntan lotion on to already dirty skins. Bruce unzipped his salopettes to pull off his shirt. Cathy and Ian, seated on their packs and so unfortunately at eye-level with Bruce's crotch, collapsed in smothered giggles.

'Bruce, mate, what on earth are you wearing?' queried Ian, staring fish-eyed at Bruce's underwear.

'Oh, you mean these,' he said, looking down. 'These are my lucky under-rods.'

'Your what?' the others exclaimed simultaneously.

'My lucky under-rods. Been all over the world, these have. Three times to Antarctica, all over the Himalaya. I always wear them on expedition. They are getting near the end of their life, though,' Bruce explained with concern. 'I promised my girlfriend, Sue, that if they made the summit of Everest I'd retire them honourably afterwards. She'll be keen to see the back of them.'

CATHY:

I have been dreading the walk up the Western Cwm and it proves to be everything I feared – long, hot, endlessly uphill, with the moraine of the camp ever hovering on the horizon and never getting any closer. Ian pulls away from Bruce and me, making steady progress. I envy him his strength. I wonder whether I will fall hopelessly behind on the steep slopes of Lhotse.

The damned moraine resolutely refuses to increase in size. There is no way to gauge distance on the white, featureless snowy plain that extends from me to it. I deliberately shut down my focus to exclude my goal and simply concentrate on getting from one marker flag to the next. I randomly number this one I'm standing by, gasping, 20, and then begin a countdown, flag by flag. In the back of my mind I hope to reach the moraine before I count down to one.

I reach 15 and then slump down in the snow, sitting on my rucksack, pulling out a thermos flask of lukewarm juice. Bruce joins me.

'Go ahead if you want,' I say. 'I'm feeling a bit slow.'

'You and me both,' he says with a grin. 'I'm quite happy to let you set the pace.'

Thank goodness I'm not the only one feeling the strain.

I continue counting marker wands, but at last even that gets too tedious. I put my head down and simply concentrate on covering as much ground as possible before flopping down in the snow for a rest.

Finally, with infinite reluctance, the moraine approaches and we begin the last, long slog up it.

Ang Sirke, our camp 2 cook, walks down from the camp to meet us with a thermos flask of warm juice and cups. We collapse gratefully and suck in the liquid after the hot, dehydrating walk.

'It's the last of the great colonials,' exclaims one of the British climbers as he passes us on his way down to base camp.

'At least we're finished, mate,' Bruce calls after him. 'You've still got all that bloody walking ahead of you.'

20:00 – Camp 2

The moonlight cast no light on the great black rock-face that made up the south-west aspect of Everest. Perched on a moraine ridge below the rock-face, the tiny tents made no more impression on the mountain than a footprint on the lunar surface. Outside the tents the night air had dropped well below freezing. Bruce and Ian were snuggled down inside their sleeping bags in the tent they shared, their body heat the only source of warmth. Bruce was wriggling around, trying to find a comfortable position amid the piles of camera gear he insisted on sleeping with, while Ian was engaged in the nightly chore of removing his contact lenses.

'I chatted to some of the climbers we passed going back down to base camp,' Bruce said when at last he lay still. 'A lot of them have just spent some nights up at camp 3 for the first time. It sounds horrible. People were talking about not being able to sleep at all, about battling to breathe, about barely having the energy to drag themselves back down the Lhotse Face. And now they're all scuttling off to base camp as fast as they can to recover.'

'It doesn't seem worth it, does it?' Ian commented. 'They seem to deteriorate more by staying at that altitude than they gain in acclimatisation. I reckon, as with camp 1, we just do a day trip up there and back, and don't sleep there until we have to, until we are actually on the move up to camp 4.'

'Sounds fair,' said Bruce. 'But not tomorrow, I hope. I found walking up the cwm today a bit rough. I could do with a lie-in tomorrow.'

'No, there's no need to go tomorrow,' Ian confirmed. 'The Sherpas need a couple of days to move equipment higher up the mountain. So we'll go up and down to camp 3 the day after tomorrow, then we'll have another day or two's rest back here. Then we'll head for camp 4, and the summit after that.'

They settled back down deep into their respective cocoons, until the only sound was their breathing and the occasional creak of the glacier.

IAN:
I'm very pleased with the way things are going so far. We've come together and re-established ourselves as a climbing team and working unit once more, and we're safely back up at camp 2. This will now be our base for our attempt on the higher reaches of Everest. We've said goodbye to base camp, and hopefully the next time we go back down will be after the South African flag has flown from the top of the world.

30 April
Camp 2

The next day was spent lounging around in camp. The massive bulk of Lhotse dominated the camp at all times, a giant face of glistening ice with a crown of jagged granite rock. The climbers sat on their insulating foam mattresses outside their tents, soaking up the sun like little white lizards and watching the tiny black dots of other expedition members toiling up and down the face.

'They look like insects, the face is so vast,' Cathy said eventually. 'I wonder how they feel.'

'Bloody awful, I expect,' Bruce replied. 'And so will we, soon enough.'

'Thank you for that vote of confidence,' said Cathy, tossing a glacial pebble in Bruce's direction.

'Still, it looks better than the south pillar route. That's a steep piece of climbing,' he said, looking up at the steep, slick corridor of ice that ran to the left of the Lhotse Face and right of the great rock wall that made up the South-West Face of Everest. The south pillar was the route being attempted by the British and Danish expedition led by Mal Duff, and by the Spanish and Swedish teams.

Right of the pillar the ice swept straight up to the sickle-moon shape of the Yellow Band, a curving section of rock named after the vivid colour of its sedimentary composition. Right of that again a line of bulging ice pinnacles, called seracs, swept down in hanging waves from the summit of Lhotse. The ant-like line of climbers was crawling up the left-hand edge of these seracs.

'When this route was first climbed, by John Hunt's boys during the first ascent of Everest, they took a really devious, winding route through those seracs,' Bruce explained, pointing far to the right of the South Africans' intended line of ascent. 'I guess they were seeking easier ground and looking for shelter for the several camps they had to set up. Now climbers take a more direct line, only moving into the seracs to find a shelter for camp 3 at 7 400 metres.'

Bruce and Cathy could just make out the dots of the camp 3 tents halfway up the face, clustered in tiers above each other, depending on where each expedition leader thought they would be in least danger from the avalanches that sweep down the Lhotse Face. From camp 3 the ants crawled off left, traversing diagonally upwards over the Yellow Band and on to the Geneva Spur, the finger of black rock that extended down into the ice-face from the South Col. There the figures disappeared from view as they climbed towards the unknown territory of the South Col at 8 000 metres.

'It's thirsty work just looking at them climbing,' said Bruce eventually. 'Pour us another cup of tea there, love.'

23:00 – Camp 2

That evening the moon presented the Lhotse Face in the purest of silvery whites. The natural beauty of the colours received only glancing appreciation from the climbers as they moved through the icy night from the kitchen tent to their living quarters, or clambered between the pinnacles of the glacier for a last visit to the loo. The chilly beauty of the mountain meant little in the face of the promised warmth of sleeping bags.

CATHY:
I lie alone in the darkness of my tent, my consciousness of the need for sleep propelling me into a state of complete alertness. I spent most of the day observing the Lhotse Face with growing apprehension.

I have always believed myself able to reach camp 2 and 6 500 metres, but to move above that is to move into the great unknown. I am not at all certain of what I will find there, either in terms of the conditions on the mountain or of my own ability to deal with them.

Questions creep insidiously into my sleep-deprived mind. What if it is just too far, too steep, too high? I dread the sick feeling I had the first time I reached 6 500 metres. What will it be like to pass 7 000 metres? Will there be so little oxygen that I grind to a halt? Or will I be so slow that there will be this growing realisation in myself and in the two men that I just do not make the grade, that I need to volunteer or be told to give up, to go down? Good effort, dear, we're proud of you, but really the time has come … Will there be those awkward hours while everyone knows what needs to be said but can't bring themselves to say it?

No, damn it, there won't. I push the ever more demoralising thoughts away, turn restlessly in my sleeping bag, stare at the glow of my watch to assure myself that time really is passing, and wait for morning.

IAN:
Ten days ago I stood on the bottom of the huge Lhotse Face for the first time. I said that it was a good old-fashioned, in-your-face challenge, and I said that soon it would be our turn.

Now that time has come. Tomorrow we will be tested to the limit, both as individuals and as a team. It's show time!

CHAPTER 5

The Waiting Game

1 May
05:15 – Camp 2

'Well, 'ere we go, 'ere we go, 'ere we go! All up and ready for our great day on the big hill, then?'

'Bloody hell, Bruce! It's bad enough getting up at this time and just trying to eat and drink, without having to swallow your nauseating cheerfulness as well,' said Cathy sharply as they sat together in the kitchen tent, drinking tea and nibbling at dry biscuits. 'Where's Ian, anyway?'

'Oh, you know him. Still trying to fight his way out of bed. It's a ferocious battle of mortal combat every morning. Great one for leading from behind, he is,' replied Bruce as he held his hands around the base of the primus stove for warmth.

'Well, as least he's not so revoltingly chirpy.'

When they had finally assembled, the climbers moved slowly away from the camp, treading a path through the pillars of rock and turrets of ice round the edge of the moraine towards the smoother ice of the central glacier. The whole of the Western Cwm was bathed in deep blue shadow and the morning air was bitterly cold. Up until now their attention had focused on the huge face itself, and they'd neglected to consider the distance from the camp to the foot of the face. The glacier once more performed its strange stretching act. Hampered by chilled bodies, stiff muscles and unco-ordinated movement, they stumbled across the hard ice and crisp snow. The Lhotse Face hung in front of them like a giant frosty curtain. As they approached its foot, the shadow seemed to deepen, until the cold penetrated inside their bones. The line of sunlight moved up the Western Cwm from its mouth, creeping forward tantalisingly slowly, as if it would never reach the climbers.

'You all right, youth?' Bruce asked, turning back to look at Ian.

'Yeah, I've just lost my fingers though,' he replied, frantically rubbing his hands under his armpits.

'You seem to have a problem with those hands.'

'Bloody old age I expect,' said Ian, matter-of-factly.

The glacier tilted slowly upwards as they approached its head, until it suddenly fell away abruptly into the bergschrund – the huge crevasse that marked the junction between the head of the glacier and the ice wall of Lhotse. Ian stood hunched over, his gloves still shoved into his armpits to try to warm the numb fingers inside them. Cathy reached for her thermos flask to feel the still hot juice burning down her throat into her stomach, bringing a few moments of warmth. Bruce stamped up and down in the snow to bring the circulation back to numb toes.

'Well, this should warm us up,' he said, looking at the route ahead.

'Some good ice climbing at last,' Cathy commented, cheering up at the thought of swapping the long slog for some serious climbing.

Beyond the crevasse stood a cliff of ice that swept the length of the face and then tilted back to a steady 60 degrees, sliding smoothly up into the sky for the next 1 500 metres. To their right lay a colossal jumble of house-sized blocks, a snow-covered demolition site made up of avalanche debris from the series of seracs that ran up the face. Gravity and cold were constantly at war on the mountain. So much so that as soon as the icy grip eased on any of the rocks or ice blocks frozen into the face, they began the rapid tumble down the slippery slope to land in the debris graveyard by the bergschrund.

To their left the snow was unmarked, testament to the slick ice runnel above it, where the only things left to fall down were rock pebbles frozen into the ice. Smaller than a fist but falling at close to terminal velocity, the pebbles could be as lethal as any avalanche. The climbers would follow a route that wound a way between these two alternatives, moving up the edge of the serac band and staying off the hardest of the ice, but away from the unstable stacking of seracs.

To get on to the face, they had to cross the crevasse that gaped several metres wide in places as it ran all the way across the Lhotse Face from Everest to Nuptse. The trail had taken them to a point where a narrow bridge of snow spanned the drop, providing access to the ice cliff above. The cliff, 4 or 5 metres of vertical ice, was breached by a crack line, sloping diagonally left. With the aid of a rope fixed by the Yugoslavs, the South Africans were able to climb up cautiously, one by one. One hand would run a jumar up the rope, to provide a handhold and a safety catch, while the other fumbled for balance against the chandelier-like ice formations. Boots were kicked against the wall to lodge the metal spikes of the crampons in the ice. All body weight was transferred on to the two spikes, or frontpoints, protruding out from the toe of the boots. Calf muscles strained to hold the weight of the body upright. It was with relief that each climber finally flopped over the top of the cliff on to the steep snow above.

'Wow, isn't this spectacular?' Ian gasped as he looked back down the Western Cwm from their elevated position. 'You can really appreciate the magnitude of this valley from up here.'

Cathy and Bruce looked at one another with raised eyebrows. They felt they knew the magnitude of the valley well enough, having already walked up it twice.

'Are we over 7 000 metres yet?' Cathy asked, moving her head from side to side to try to gauge their height in relation to Pumori.

Ian considered. 'Possibly not quite, but very close.'

'A little higher, I think,' agreed Bruce.

Above them the snow ran up at a steady 60 degrees towards another, smaller ice step. A 9-millimetre line of orange rope provided the safety line, which was attached, at 50-metre intervals, to ice screws or snow stakes. One by one the climbers began to move steadily up the face, one hand running the jumar up the rope, the other on a hip or knee for added support.

The route moved up the face in waves, long sections of steep climbing broken by smaller but precipitous ice steps. The climbers weaved in and out of the edge of the seracs, seeking the safest ground, always watchful for the threat of avalanche from above.

The distance stretched out forever, the miniscule black dots of the climbers rapidly lost in the measureless white expanse of ice. It felt like climbing on a giant treadmill, step after step that seemed to make no impact in the snowy vastness. The only markers were the rope anchor points that appeared at intervals, and were welcomed as an excuse to stop while the jumar was unclipped from the one rope below the anchor point and then re-clipped to the next one above the anchor. Cold hands trapped in huge mitts fumbled slowly to complete the simple but essential procedure. A safety sling was clipped to the anchor at all times during the transfer, for mistakes were all too easy to make.

And then, yet again, the climbing continued.

CATHY:

The climb has become a test of will, of my ability to continue to put one increasingly heavy foot in front of the other, to keep my hand sliding up the rope, to keep moving upwards. But for the first time I am gaining height rapidly. The massive slopes of the South-West Face and of the south pillar sweep down on my left. The cwm slowly assumes its true proportions of a small valley cradled between two huge ridges. Its complex crevassed structure becomes clear as the camp 2 moraines shrink to a tiny rocky strip beside the ice. Finally we clear the barrier formed by Pumori. I remember sitting at base camp watching tiny figures so far above me on the summit slopes of Pumori. I remember years ago so envying friends planning a Pumori expedition, one which never came off. Now I am as high as the summit of that once mighty mountain. And with its dominating bulk passed, for the first time the Himalaya west of us become visible, a view of dozens of mountains, presided over by the massive presence of Cho Oyu, sixth highest mountain in the world.

I pause to drink it all in, the grandeur of the Himalaya, the brutal black rock of the South-West Face of Everest, contrasted against the ethereal icy sweep of the slopes of Nuptse. So beautiful.

And it is really me, here, high up on the slopes of the world's highest mountain.

But there is still work to be done. I continue steadily up the fixed ropes and pull over a steepening rise to find Bruce, seated on his pack, camera in hand.

'Stop there,' he says. 'It's a brilliant background for a photo.'

'Is it going to make me look way hard, Bruce?' I tease. 'It's all right for you guys, a bit of ice in the beard and you look like rugged explorer types.' I still feel a little apart from these men, these mountaineers, with their experience and confidence. As if I have not yet proved, primarily I suppose to myself, that I have the right to be here. But I feel a rising sense of exhilaration. It feels to me like this is the first real day of climbing that we have done so far. And it has been so much easier than my worries last night led me to expect.

IAN:
I pause for a second, my weight resting against the tension of the fixed rope. My heart is pounding with the effort and with excitement. To be on these slopes with Cathy and Bruce! To be on these breathtaking slopes as a team, as our team! Is this the perfect day's climbing? I'm not sure, but it must be close. I know that both Cathy and Bruce will be approaching a new altitude record soon. How thrilled they must be!

Bruce shouldered his rucksack and, with Cathy following close behind, resumed his steady upward progress. Both found themselves glancing skywards increasingly often in the hope of seeing the tents. At last, sheltered beneath seracs for avalanche protection, minute dots of colour appeared. They came closer with agonising slowness, the last two rope lengths appeared to take almost as long again as the entire face below them. The one black South African tent was the lowest of the various camps, to their considerable relief.

It perched nerve-rackingly on the edge of the slope, seated on a little platform chipped out of the near vertical ice. There was no flat ground around it, only the great sweep of the South-West Face of Lhotse behind and the thin air of the Western Cwm in front. The two climbers edged carefully away from the fixed rope towards the tent door. One by one they sank down at the door, cautiously pulling off their packs and tying them to the snow stakes that secured the tent. Then each had to crouch down awkwardly in the low tent entrance, trying not to bring snow in, trying not to put their crampons through the delicate fabric. Only once inside the tent were they safe.

12:00 – Camp 3

'Are you youngsters decent?' asked Ian as he banged on the tent flysheet.

'Unfortunately yes,' Bruce replied.

'Listen, I'm going to carry on back down,' he said, sticking his head through the tent door.

'Are you okay?' Cathy asked, sounding concerned.

'Actually, I've never felt better. That's why I'm going to be off. See you on the Christmas tree.'

Cathy looked at Bruce for an explanation, but he just shook his head and tapped his temple, as the sound of Ian's crampons scraping on the ice drifted away.

IAN:
I'm really pumped up by the morning's climb. The adrenaline is doing a 100-metre dash through my veins. I'm tired and could do with the rest, but I really want the sensation, the natural high, to last just a little while longer. I want to be on my own on this great face, to rub shoulders with the explorers of the past who edged their precarious way up these same silver slopes, ever fearful of what might lie beyond. I feel that this is my day, and I want it to last forever.

CATHY:
Bruce and I, reluctant to leave so soon after so much effort, laze in the tent for a while.

'Well, here we are then,' he says. 'Higher than any mountain in the world outside Asia.' He grins and sticks out his hand to shake mine. 'A new altitude record for both of us.'

His obvious pleasure echoes my own. But the same thought strikes us simultaneously. I can see it written on his face. A long way to go still.

But nothing can destroy my mood right now. I am tired yet exhilarated. I now know I can get to camp 3 in reasonable shape, and should therefore be able to move on to camp 4. And if I can do that, I may just have a chance of having a shot at the summit.

To descend, each climber wrapped the fixed rope around one arm and almost ran down the slope with the rope acting as a friction brake. The ropes were fixed too tightly to allow for abseiling. Besides, abseiling would have been far slower, and speed in the big mountains is everything. They each clipped a safety sling on to the rope, but if they slipped, the safety sling would only catch them when they hit the next anchor point, possibly as much as 50 metres lower down. Moving quickly and facing outwards on the steep slope made it seem even more precipitous than before. The ice steps were particularly nerve-jangling, until gradually they got accustomed to the method of descent.

Finally all that remained was the long haul across the glacier back to the moraine bank where their camp sheltered. The biting cold of the morning was now replaced by a heavy heat that seemed to weigh down on their packs and on their bodies.

20:00 – Camp 2

Ian shifted restlessly in his sleeping bag and then grabbed for the mug of coffee that he'd nearly sent spilling all over the tent floor with his fidgeting.

'Good move, youth,' said Bruce sleepily. 'A wet sleeping bag is just what you don't need after a long day on the hill.'

'I'd forgotten about the coffee,' said Ian. He tasted it tentatively. 'It's cold now, anyway.' He threw it out of the tent door, where it rapidly froze into a brown ice puddle.

'I've been trying to work out how soon we could realistically move to camp 4. I spoke to Ang Dorje earlier and he says that the Sherpas will need three more days to finish moving all the necessary loads up to camp 4, and then they'll need a rest day. So that means we could make a move in four days' time. It's quite a long wait, given that the weather seems to have finally settled. But presumably this is the beginning of the lifting of the jet-stream winds. If Everest follows its normal pattern, we should have a good two weeks of this kind of stable weather coming, and we can pick and choose.'

'What are other teams doing?' Bruce asked.

'The commercial teams all seem to have pulled their clients down to base camp, or below, for a low altitude rest before coming back up in about a week's time. It looks as if they are waiting for the weather to deteriorate,' Ian said with a smile. 'The Swedish, the Spanish and the Yugoslavs are all above us somewhere, taking advantage of the good weather and the full moon. The Norwegian and his 11 Sherpas who were trying to climb the South-West Face have apparently given up and gone home.'

Ian continued to work over the logistics.

'I can get it down to three days,' he announced at last. 'The Sherpas don't want to stay at camp 3. They'd rather go direct from 2 to 4. So if they take their rest day the day we move to camp 3, on 5 May, then we can all meet up at camp 4 the next day. So we can look forward to three days of rest before making the final bid for the summit.'

'I can't imagine,' Bruce wondered, 'why anyone in their right minds would rather go direct from 2 to 4. That has just got to be masochism.'

'They've the strength to do it,' Ian replied. 'And they don't trust camp 3 either. They reckon the position is too dangerous, too avalanche-prone.'

2 May
09:00 – Camp 2

'Your breakfast, Mr Bruce,' said Ang Sirke, smiling and handing Bruce a plate of dubious contents.

'Thank you, Ang Sirke, what is it?' Bruce asked hopefully.

'Breakfast,' came the immediate reply.

'Right, I see,' said Bruce, moving the plate back and forth at different angles in an attempt to shed light on its contents. 'But what was it before it became breakfast?'

Ang Sirke nodded his head and quickly produced an aluminium packet of beans and sausage.

'That's what this was?' Bruce asked, eyebrows raised in disbelief.

'Yes, Mr Bruce,' confirmed Ang Sirke, very pleased with himself.

'Okay. How did an aluminium packet become this?'

Bruce held up the offending plate for everyone to see. By this time the detailed culinary discussion had attracted both Cathy and Ian, as well as the Sherpas.

'I cook, Mr Bruce,' insisted Ang Sirke.

'I dare say you did, but how?'

Ang Sirke gave a in-depth explanation of how he had taken a perfectly good aluminium bag of beans and sausage, and, instead of simply popping it into boiling water, had grilled it over the primus stove, turning it into an unspeakable molten mess.

Already pretty sure he knew the answer, Bruce enquired of Ang Sirke who had explained this particular cooking method to him.

'Ang Dorje,' he announced proudly.

The assembled Sherpas collapsed with laughter at the differing looks on Ang Sirke's and Bruce's faces.

'Ang Dorje, you're fired,' Bruce shouted after the rapidly departing sirdar.

'You see,' announced Ian, 'I told you he could cook.'

'Get lost, Woodall,' smiled Bruce as he set about making his own breakfast.

3 May
10:00 – Camp 2

The climbers lounged in the sun outside their tents, eating cheese and biscuits, and drinking yet another cup of coffee. It was their second day of rest since climbing to camp 3 and back, and as they lay there they watched a small plane circling over the summit of Everest.

'I wonder if that's the crew that is supposed to be filming the Swede reaching the summit,' said Bruce, picking up the radio.

'It must be,' Ian replied. 'I guess that means he's made it.'

Bruce spoke to Philip briefly on the radio and then turned back to the other two.

'It's the Swede's film crew all right, but he didn't make it. He's had to turn back just below the South Summit. Apparently he just couldn't wade through the deep snow on his own.'

'Well, that's the first unsuccessful attempt of the season,' Ian said. 'The Yugoslavs are supposed to be going tonight. It's full moon and the Eastern European climbers always seem to go for full moon summit nights.'

'So, it remains to be seen what becomes of the second attempt,' said Bruce as the plane flew off into the distance.

'Damn, I'm bored,' Ian muttered as he sorted through his collection of tapes. 'Got any good tapes, youth?' he called across to Cathy, who was seated in the entrance of her tent, reading. 'Oh no, forget it. You listen to that weird stuff.'

'Oh thanks,' she replied. 'And Beautiful South and the Cranberries aren't weird? I'll stick to Tchaikovsky and Verdi. Have you got any books, though? I'm reading Ranulph Fiennes's autobiography for the second time.'

Ian disappeared into his tent and rummaged around.

'I've got the second volume of Spike Milligan's war memoirs,' he offered.

Cathy screwed up her face but took the book anyway.

'Better than nothing. Thanks. Anything helps to pass these days of waiting.'

'It's all right. The day's show is about to begin,' Bruce announced. He had been watching the camp of bright yellow tents pitched across the way from the South Africans. 'The Americans have got out of bed.'

The most obvious source of entertainment at camp 2 was the IMAX team, who were making a wide-screen film on Everest. Once again they did not disappoint – their cameraman emerged from his tent wearing what looked like black bell-bottoms and a green hat, complete with feather. He began prancing around the camp with his jacket draped over his shoulders like a cloak.

'I'm not sure if he thinks he's at a party in Soho, or halfway up Everest,' commented Bruce.

But of more long-term value as an object of speculation was expedition leader and film director David Breashears. David, with a multi-million dollar budget at his disposal to make his movie, took his job very seriously. He had descended upon each of the teams at camp 2 to announce that he would be filming higher on the mountain and to request their co-operation. Mal's team had been honoured with a visit, as had Peter Athans's American team. The South Africans waited in suspense to see if they too would be treated to a royal command performance. But to date nothing had come of it.

They were reduced to listening to David's frequent radio calls to the United States. Indeed, they could not avoid listening to them, given the volume at which they were carried out. They always followed the same ritual, with David pacing backwards and forwards across the moraine, shouting into his radio in his broad accent about his latest movie deal, or buying and selling stocks on Wall Street.

12:00 – Camp 2

CATHY:

I get pulled out of my tent to do a short interview for the John and Dan breakfast show on Radio 702. Why me? I'm feeling really grumpy. But everyone else seems like that as well. I sit on the 'radio rock', which is the rock from which we seem to get the best reception, and try to summon up the energy to sound excited about our forthcoming summit attempt. Fairly soon I am convincing even myself.

'Fantastic, Cathy!' says John Robbie. 'Well, thank you very much for talking to us. I think we've all got goose bumps here realising we are sitting in our studio in Johannesburg looking out on a sunny day and you are at camp 2 on Mount Everest.'

I look down the sweeping curve of the Western Cwm to where its mouth is blocked by the afternoon cloud, and then up to the gigantic peaks around me. Yes, there is something to be said for camp 2 on Everest over Rivonia Road in Johannesburg.

I return to my tent to continue reading Spike Milligan and the enthusiasm of the radio call gradually fades.

I'm depressed. I have a headache and feel nauseous. I really want a big hug and to cry on somebody's shoulder. Ian is out of the question and Bruce would probably take it too seriously. I know it is just a passing phase.

IAN:
'Sergeant Major!'
  'Yes sir!'
'The morale of the troops is far too high. Take them outside and mess 'em around a bit.'
  'Yes sir, right away sir!'
I remember my commanding officer's instruction as if it were yesterday. Although a tad eccentric, the logic was clear enough. Idle minds and bodies will find trouble and fault where none exist. We're now about to play an important waiting game, one that, if extended, will tax all our patience and mental reserves. If we're not careful, the simple fact that we're doing nothing could destroy the team. I must watch carefully how I and the others react and, if necessary, suggest we make another trip up to camp 3, even if the conditions are not good enough for us to go on further. Anything, just to be doing something!

4 May
10:00 – Camp 2

Cathy and Ian lay in the warmth of the tent, while Bruce sat on the radio rock chatting to Philip. His voice mingled with the distant but strident tones of the Americans, also on their radio, running up their satellite phone bill.

'What news?' asked Ian as Bruce crawled back into the tent.

'Philip says the Yugoslavian attempt wasn't successful, or, more correctly, never happened. They were due to go for the summit last night but didn't leave their camp 4 due to a dispute with their Sherpas,' replied Bruce.

'So the second attempt of the season has fallen by the wayside,' Ian said. 'The French climber had planned to climb to camp 3 this morning, and then up to camp 4 tomorrow. That would've placed him next in line. But he came over this morning to say that, given the reports of deep snow on the summit ridge, he would like to wait a day and perhaps combine forces with us tomorrow. Unfortunately he has already sent his sleeping bag up to camp 3 with his Sherpas.'

'He's in for a cold night, then, isn't he?'

The two men laughed together at the expense of an Everest climber who had merrily dispatched his one and only sleeping bag up the mountain, only to decide to stay where he was.

'I went over to Mal Duff's team this morning,' said Cathy. 'They say the Spanish have also failed to reach the summit, having had good weather but being stopped by deep snow. They have two climbers ready to go, but they will not try until someone else has reached the summit.'

There was a long pause.

'Well, that leaves us next in line to try,' said Bruce with a twinkle in his eye.

'If the Swede, climbing solo without oxygen, can get most of the way up, we should be able to push the rest of the way,' Ian added.

> IAN:
> Swedish, Yugoslav and Spanish, all have tried for the summit already, and all have been unsuccessful. It's still very early in the season so I guess they'll have time to re-group at base camp and try again. But if we make a summit bid and are unsuccessful, will our small team have the drive and resources to try again?

13:00 – Camp 2

The climbers retreated into their respective tents to begin the process of packing for a possible summit bid should the weather improve and hold. They would never know for sure when they turned in each night whether they would be going climbing the next day or not; that could only be decided each morning when an assessment of the weather could be made. Camps 3 and 4 were by now fully stocked with food and powdered drinks, cooking gas, stoves, tents and oxygen bottles. Some additional equipment from camp 2 would be sent directly to camp 4 with the Sherpas – spare batteries, extra film, down salopettes and gloves, sponsors' banners. The rest would be carried as personal kit – sleeping bags, mats, head-torches, clothing, radios.

Soon the tent floors were strewn with equipment. How much film to take, how many batteries? One spare pair of gloves or two? An extra thermal top? It was a long process in which light and fast was being balanced against heavy but better equipped.

Bruce's radio crackled into life. He found it at last, buried beneath all the camera equipment he was sorting, and answered it.

PHILIP: 'Hi, Bruce, this is Philip. I have a message to pass on to you that came to us via Henry Todd. Rob Hall's team is going to be setting fixed ropes to the summit on 10 and 11 May.'

BRUCE: 'That's very nice for them, Philip, but why tell us? We'll either be well on our way home by then, or have failed with this summit bid and probably still be resting up before the next one. If we fail to go for the summit on the seventh, we won't be trying again for at least another week.'

PHILIP: 'I'll try to get some more info on that. I'll call you back at the usual six o'clock radio call.'

Bruce turned off the radio and turned, puzzled, to Ian.

'What the hell was that about?'

Ian speculated. 'Either they don't want us to be first to summit this season, which seems most unlikely as half that lot seem to have climbed the mountain before anyway, or they're dropping some heavy hints that our timing is out.'

18:00 – Camp 2

When Philip came through for the six o'clock radio call, Cathy, Bruce and Ian were all squeezed into one tent at camp 2 to find out more about the strange goings-on at base camp.

PHILIP: 'I have Henry with me in the comms tent, Ian. He has a message to pass on to you. Please stand by.'

HENRY: 'We've had a meeting at base camp, Ian. The IMAX team will be filming up to camp 4 on the seventh, eight and ninth. Rob Hall will organise to fix ropes on the summit ridge on the tenth, to make it "client-proof", and then Rob Hall and Scott Fischer will move their clients up to the summit over the next two days. My guys will follow after them. Hall and Fischer would like the mountain clear on the tenth and eleventh and were wondering where you guys will be during that time.'

IAN: 'Henry, in all likelihood we'll be at base camp then, either having reached the summit or resting up for another try. But quite frankly, we'll climb the mountain according to the weather, not according to committee decisions taken at base camp.'

The three climbers looked at one another in amazement when the radio call had ended.

'How can they think they can just climb a mountain by committee?' wondered Bruce. 'By all means have a plan, but to start booking summit slots a week in advance seems rather cocky, if not downright arrogant.'

'It must be Rob Hall and his hot line to God,' Ian replied. 'He obviously thinks he can dictate and arrange the weather a week in advance.'

'I've always fancied a shot at Makalu,' said Bruce. 'Anyone got a 1998 calendar? I'd better get in quick and book my summit slot now.'

20:30 – Camp 2

CATHY:

I wriggle into my sleeping bag, rubbing my legs together, trying to get the heat to reach down to my toes. Poor toes, always last to get the good bits and first to get the hard work. I slip my Walkman down the inside of my shirt to warm up the batteries, and rub my pen between my hands to warm the ink. I begin to update my diary, by the light of my head-torch.

I am curled up deep inside the cocoon of my sleeping bag for warmth. This makes it difficult to hold the little hardcover diary at the right angle, keep my head-torch shining on it, stop my pen getting tangled in the wires of my earphones, and still write legibly.

'I am, as ever, nervous about the summit attempt,' I write. 'About the cold, the altitude, using oxygen, the sheer physical demands of the height and the distance. Sometimes I fantasise about being on the summit or about how it would feel to be coming down – never about going up. But mostly I think about it in small chunks – each manageable on its own, even if they are a bit much put together. If I don't get sick, I think I can make camp 4. The ridge above is a completely unknown quantity.'

5 May
06:00 – Camp 2

CATHY:

An insistent beep penetrates my dream-filled mind. I fumble to turn off my wrist alarm and lie still, trying to work out where I am.

Water, why is there so much water running next to my tent? I'm supposed to be at camp 2. How can there be so much water flowing off the glacier? It can't be water.

Too sleepy to think this through, I crawl out of my bag and begin to dress, pulling on salopettes and jacket.

'Wind, there is too much wind! We cannot climb like this. It is no good.' The heavy French accent can only belong to the leader of the French expedition.

'What to do? We cannot climb!'

He seems to take this very personally. I abandon my attempts to pack, and crawl outside. The spindrift is whipping off Everest, Lhotse and the South Col, like an immense white Buddhist prayer scarf. Although it is utterly still at camp 2, the wind sounds like an express train howling past on the horizon.

What to do? Nothing, I suppose.

I stagger over to Bruce and Ian's tent to find them both sensibly still tucked up to the ears in their sleeping bags.

'It's howling up at 8 000 metres,' said Cathy. 'It looks just like the plume we saw coming off Everest when we were still trekking in.'

'I guess the jet-stream winds have dropped back down over the mountain,' said Bruce. 'I suppose it was a bit early in the season for them to lift. Usually they lift from 8 000 to 9 000 metres sometime in the first week of May and then you get two or three weeks of windless weather. We should just wait and see what the weather does.'

'It won't last,' Ian declared. 'The wind will die by lunchtime.'

They could hear the French leader stomping around outside, swearing under his breath and interrogating his Sherpas about what the weather was going to do.

'He can't be happy,' said Ian. 'He's already spent one cold night, what with his Sherpas having taken his sleeping bag up to camp 3. Now he's in for another one.'

Cathy peered out of the tent door.

'It looks like he's off to camp 3 to collect it.'

'Oh well,' said Bruce. 'We may as well go back to sleep then.'

Leaving the men curled up in bed, Cathy crossed to the kitchen tent. It was abandoned except for Ang Sirke, their camp 2 cook, apparently sent by the other Sherpas, who were also tucked up in bed, to make a thermos flask of tea. He looked as grumpy as Cathy felt.

'Not happy, Ang Sirke?' she asked as he handed her a cup of tea.

'No,' he sighed. 'I don't like it up here. On the last expedition I was carrying loads, like the other Sherpas and I think that is easier.'

'Easier than being camp 2 cook?' Cathy asked, puzzled. 'Surely all the carrying is much harder work?'

'Yes, but it is soon over. The others, they get up early, carry their loads and then come back here to sleep. They sleep all afternoon. But I have to work all the time. Up early in the morning to make them breakfast, and then make them lunch and then cook again for supper. All the time I have to melt ice to make water to cook.'

Rather cheered up by the realisation that she wasn't the only one who was depressed, Cathy took her cup of tea back to her tent.

16:00 – Camp 2

'What are we going to do?' asked Bruce. 'Do we go tomorrow or not?'

'What kind of weather report did Philip give you?' asked Ian.

'He said the Nepalese radio weather report predicted winds at about 30 knots for the next couple of days.'

'That's not great. And certainly there's no sign of the wind dying down this afternoon.'

'I spoke to some of the Danish climbers,' Cathy said. 'Over their satellite system they got a good weather report of decreasing winds over the next few days. They reckon they'll go straight from camp 2 to camp 4 the day after to-morrow.'

'Various members of the IMAX team arrived this morning and they, and some of Mal Duff's team, are rumoured to be going higher tomorrow as well,' added Bruce.

'But then again there's the French leader,' said Cathy. 'He came down from camp 3 a few hours ago in a really strange mood, packed up all his kit and continued straight down to base camp. He's convinced the wind has set in for a number of days. And after all, this is the fourth time in five years that he's tried to climb this mountain.'

'So where the hell does that leave us?' Bruce asked.

The three sat in the tent and stared at each other.

'Damn it, let's just go tomorrow, come what may,' said Ian. 'If we wait any longer, we risk getting caught in the queues of the commercial teams.'

'Well, at least it'll get us away from Ang Sirke's cooking,' Bruce ventured.

'Ah, don't be like that,' teased Ian. 'He's doing his best.'

'That's what worries me.'

And all the while the wind continued to howl round the summit of Everest.

IAN:
This waiting is hard on everyone, particularly, I think, on Cathy. She's so keen to be on with the job and the sitting around is really beginning to get

to her. Bruce and me? Well, I guess we adapt a little easier, we can perhaps fall back on our experience of similar situations in the past. That said, there are certainly some mornings when I could definitely use some youthful enthusiasm. But I'll have to get us moving soon. Up or down, it doesn't really matter, but we've worked so hard to mould ourselves into a team that we can't let it unravel through inaction.

CATHY:
Weather is such a frustrating problem, so uncontrollable, so uncertain. We could be the best climbers in the world, with the best-laid plans, and still fail because of the weather. I'd much rather have to turn round because of my own difficulties than because of an arbitrary outside force like the weather. But it is all part of the challenge.

I'm feeling better about being at camp 2, though. Perhaps, like base camp, it just took me a while to acclimatise, mentally as much as physically. I'm beginning to have a chance to look around and see how spectacular it is.

But I would like to get away from it tomorrow. Another night to be spent keyed up for a possible move tomorrow morning.

6 May
06:00 – Camp 2

CATHY:
'Too windy to climb,' Ang Dorje declares authoritatively.

Oh no, Ang Dorje, don't do this to us. I'm up, I'm dressed, fully packed, ready to go, having tea in the kitchen tent. Even Ian has got out of bed.

'Are you sure?' But I know the answer already, I can hear that express train howling above us. We both look up at the plume that still trails away from the mountain.

'Too windy.' He walks off to his tent, clearly going back to bed. The other Sherpas haven't even got up.

I hate these swings of plan, from being all psyched up to move back up the mountain to suddenly being faced with another long day of doing nothing but getting psyched up for tomorrow.

'Ang Dorje says it is too windy to climb,' Cathy told Ian, who was pulling on his boots in the bell of his tent. Ian looked irritated, Bruce resigned.

'I've got stomach problems,' Bruce commented. 'I could do with another day of rest.'

'I'm getting so bored with camp 2,' Ian declared.

Cathy returned to her tent to read bits of Ranulph Fiennes's autobiography for the third time. The others talked and dozed, and watched the Americans on the radio. The consensus was that, as IMAX leader Dave Breashears hadn't talked to the South Africans yet, he wasn't going to. They were clearly too unimportant in his scheme of things.

CATHY:

The hours stretch on, passing as slowly as a disabled snail. We have entered an infinite time warp, of ice and rock and wind, without end.

At last a time arrives that means something, one o'clock, time for the midday radio call.

I take it and Philip passes on the news that Deshun is on the permit. The ministry, unable to get hold of our team at base camp, had faxed the news through to South Africa, from where Philip got a telephone call. I stick my head into Ian's tent to tell him the news. He and Bruce are lying on their sleeping bags, apparently in idle chat.

Ian seems uninterested.

'I'll believe it when I receive a fax from the ministry,' he says. 'As leader I am the only person who can be officially informed.'

He looks at me with that curious closed look he has, when he has pulled his shutters down.

All my tension from the past days swells up in a giant surge of anger. I am speechless with fury. I want to scream at him, to smash those shutters, to force him to acknowledge that the rest of us exist too. But underneath the pulsing anger, a small, calm voice of reason speaks. We are, hopefully, only days away from the summit. This is no time to have a pitched battle with a fellow team member.

In furious silence I withdraw from the tent and stalk off up the glacier. All the things I wish I'd said to Ian hammer through my head. I wander among the rocks and ice pinnacles that stand at the edge of the moraine, kicking at pebbles. I try to understand why one stupid comment should have produced such an irrationally angry reaction in me. What is it that is really worrying me?

I feel marginalised. I feel that I remain peripheral to the team. I know that it is partly spacial, Ian and Bruce share a tent and much of the decision-making happens informally as they lie together, chatting over events. But still I feel left out.

Eventually my patience with my self-pity runs out. But I don't want to go back to my camp, to sit alone in my tent, or to face Ian's complete failure to notice that he has even made me angry. I wander disconsolately across the ice. One of the Danish climbers walks over to join me. I don't know if he senses my mood, but he begins to tell me of some of his problems in reconciling climbing with his life in Denmark.

Finally the gathering snow drives us back to his camp, where we find other members of his team and the Lhotse team huddling in their mess tent. We spend the rest of the afternoon trading stories of climbing round the world, in between speculating about the weather. Everyone is waiting for the wind to die so that they can go climbing.

Official confirmation of the permit came through that afternoon. Deshun joined Philip when he called through on the radio at six o'clock as usual.

BRUCE: 'Congratulations, Deshun. Now you can join us in the suffering up here. But just hold on a minute. Ian wants a word with you.'

DESHUN: 'Thanks, Bruce, I'm so excited. Base camp has become something of a ghost town, with most teams moving on to the mountain. I can't wait to get up there with them.'

IAN: 'Good news, Deshun, well done. But you can't move on to the mountain yet. You have to wait for us. Do you understand?'

DESHUN: 'Roger, Ian. I definitely won't go anywhere without you.'

IAN: 'Good, because although I think you should have no problem getting up to camp 2, and probably higher, you don't have the experience to do it on your own. I invited you on to this mountain and I'm responsible for your safety. You must wait for us to come back down. Roger that?'

DESHUN: 'Roger, Ian. But what if you get to the summit on this push?'

IAN: 'That's not a problem. If that happens, we'll need a few days' rest at base camp, then I'll go back on the mountain with you. Hold on … Bruce says he'll come too. What Cathy does is up to her.'

DESHUN: 'Roger that. I definitely won't try to climb without you guys. I reckon I can probably make camp 2. Anything higher than that is a bonus. But I'm a bit worried by my lack of acclimatisation.'

IAN: 'Well, do what you can around base camp. Do some trips up Kala Pattar and to Pumori base camp. We'll see you as soon as we can.'

7 May
07:00 – Camp 2

CATHY:
Yet another morning and the wind is still blowing, although not as noisily as before. What to do?

This is beginning to be like banging my head against a brick wall. It would be nice to stop. All thoughts of the summit have been replaced by ongoing frustration with the weather. The nervous energy of going to sleep each night without knowing whether the next day will bring the summit chance or just more boring waiting is taking its toll. My enthusiasm is dwindling.

Everything that we can do is done. Now we just wait for something entirely beyond our control. And the longer we wait, at this altitude, the weaker we get. We've been at 6 500 metres for a week now. If we don't get a chance soon, we'll have to go down.

So do I get up or not? I'll wait for signs of movement from the other tent.

09:00 – Camp 2

'Not exactly an alpine start, is it?' said Bruce, sitting in the kitchen tent and chewing his way through a heaped plate of bacon, sausages and beans.

'Well, do we go or don't we?' Cathy asked. 'The winds have lessened, but they haven't stopped.'

'So maybe they're dying down,' Bruce suggested. 'But then again maybe it's the lull before the storm.'

'Great, that's bloody helpful,' Cathy retorted.

'Stuff it, let's go,' said Ian. 'If we don't, we'll get overrun by Rob Hall and his mob. And if we wait much longer, we'll have to retreat to base camp for a rest anyway. Let's see how high we can get.'

Although the decision was made, no one was very enthusiastic about carrying it out. They all moved slowly, the glacier to the foot of the Lhotse Face seeming absolutely endless. Ian stood at the base of the bergschrund, shivering, while Cathy followed Bruce up the ropes. The tasty breakfast churned around, settling unhappily, until Bruce at last deposited most of his just above the bergschrund.

17:00 – Camp 3

Cathy finally crawled into the camp 3 tent, where Bruce was already in situ.

'Be careful,' he fussed. 'Don't bring in any snow. Dust your boots off. With three of us squeezed into here, we're going to have to be tidy.'

'Yes, Mom,' she said and collapsed across his carefully organised tent floor.

'No, woman,' he exclaimed, exasperated. 'Move on to your side. And don't knock over all those food bags. I've piled them carefully.'

'How come I get to sleep with them?' asked Cathy suspiciously.

'Because I get the oxygen bottles and hardware to cuddle up to.'

They both pulled out their sleeping bags and instantly what space remained in the tent was filled with down.

'So where does Ian go?' Cathy asked.

'In the tent bell, at this rate.'

Ian, when he finally staggered in, was pulled into the middle. He lay inert across the billowing pile of down.

'I'd hoped we'd have Cathy in the middle,' joked Bruce as he tried to organise Ian. 'Then at least we could both cuddle up to her. Sorry, old man, but you just don't have the same appeal.'

It was the first time the three had shared a tent, and with three bodies and three sets of equipment, the result was warm but decidedly intimate. They had, by and large, to move one at a time and take care not to dislodge the equipment stacked carefully round the edges of the tent. A subtle manoeuvring was started in order to stay away from the end where the stove was waiting. Somebody was going to end up with the time-consuming process of melting snow and ice to generate the many litres of liquid each climber needed to drink. Ian took the bold move of simply lying across the tent and refusing to budge. Cathy ensured she was trapped behind him at the back end of the tent. Bruce found himself sitting right next to the stove.

'Make us a cup of coffee, won't you, while you're there?' Cathy said with a smile.

CATHY:

Twenty-four hours from camp 4, then 12 hours from the top. Only 36 hours from the summit of Everest, 36 hours from the culmination of the expedition.

I settle down to sleep with apprehension. I'm glad to be sharing a tent with the others, to have us all crammed in together, even if it is a bit of a squeeze. I draw confidence from the company. But I am worried about the altitude. I didn't enjoy my first night spent at 6 500 metres; the thought of one spent at 7 400 metres is far worse. So far I am feeling queasy but my breathing seems adequate. I build up a substantial pillow of rucksack and clothing to try to keep my chest raised. But just as I feared, as I lie down and drift off to sleep, my breathing becomes increasingly shallow.

I jerk awake, unable to breathe, with the terrible sensation of imminent suffocation. I scramble into an upright position, leaning forward over my knees, gasping, forcing myself to take deep breaths, to try to fill my lungs. I understand what's happening to me. It is a typical symptom of altitude, Cheyne-Stokes respiration, whereby breathing becomes irregular and may cease altogether for several seconds. Understanding it doesn't make it any easier to deal with, though.

I try to sleep again, but time and again the pattern recurs. Increasingly I resent the apparent peaceful slumber of the other two. And I long for a quick whiff of the oxygen-enriched air that I know lies inside the orange bottles lying at the side of the tent. But those are meant for tomorrow's climb, not to be wasted on sleeping. I battle on, feeling horribly isolated in my struggle, despite the physical proximity of the others.

'Why don't you sleep on oxygen?' suggests the sleepy voice of Bruce, obviously disturbed by my restless movement in the limited space of the tent.

Happy that someone else has made the suggestion, I pull out one of the cylinders and attach a mask to it. I pull the soft leather over my nose and mouth and taste the strangely tangy oxygen-enriched air. The difference it makes is considerable, and an added and unexpected advantage is that I can now pull the sleeping bag over my head entirely, rather than leaving a breathing hole for a cold nose to poke out of. I sleep better than I have since leaving base camp.

IAN:

I lie squashed between my two friends, but comfortable nevertheless. The lazy days at camp 2 haven't done my fitness any good, and I really took a slapping coming up the face today. But we're all here safely at camp 3, which is infinitely better than being safe at camp 2. Everyone seems to have worked off a little steam during the climb, which was the desired result. Hell, who knows, we may even get a chance to go higher.

8 May
09:30 – Camp 3

'Where're my socks? I know I had a spare pair of dry socks. Ian, are you sleeping on them?' Bruce pushed Ian over to one side while he rummaged around under Ian's sleeping bag.

'No, I'm bloody well not,' Ian replied testily. 'And stop shoving. Now I've lost my contact lens case.'

'Here's another round of tea,' Cathy announced from her cramped perch at the front end of the tent.

'Thanks, love,' said Bruce, grabbing a mug and settling down against his rucksack for a leisurely drink.

'No, you're not supposed to stop,' Cathy grumbled. 'You two have been totally failing in your duty to pack for at least two hours, while I've been stuck with brewing. I can't even begin to get at my stuff while you guys are wriggling around all over the tent. We'll never get out of here at this rate.'

'Nonsense, woman, we're nearly ready. And we need to keep drinking,' said Bruce, peering through the steam rising from his teacup.

'No, we're not,' she contradicted flatly. 'Everybody's half-dressed, none of the sleeping bags is packed, kit is all over the place. For heaven's sake, our Sherpas have already climbed past from camp 2 on their way to camp 4. We'll have a devil of a job to catch them up now.'

'Well, you haven't filled all the thermos flasks with water yet, either, have you?' retorted Ian.

They stared at one another in prickly silence for a moment, then Cathy began to laugh.

'Touché. We're none of us very good at this getting up in the morning thing,' she said.

The pot was back on the boil and she poured herself a cup of tea, snuggling her feet under Ian's sleeping bag. It was so much easier to lie back and enjoy doing nothing, than to keep moving towards eight hours of tough climbing.

The climbers sipped their tea in silence. But slowly the silence was filled by a strange strumming sound. The flanks of the tent began to shiver, the guy-ropes to hum. The three stared at each other, no one wanting to be the first to say the dreaded word.

Eventually Cathy, who was closest to the door, unzipped it and peered out. She got a flurry of spindrift in her face.

'Wind?' asked Bruce gloomily.

'Wind,' she confirmed.

'How bad?'

'Not great. Actually terrible. It's howling across the fixed ropes. You remember sitting in camp 2 watching the flurries of spindrift sweeping across the Lhotse Face? Well, we're right in the middle of that now.'

'Damn, damn, damn,' muttered Bruce. 'Now what?'

'Well, if we're in for another windy spell, there's no point going higher. We'll just use up precious energy and supplies,' said Ian. 'But then again, it may only last an hour or two, and we can't afford to delay that long. Maybe we should just climb through it.'

Cathy peered out again. The Lhotse Face had disappeared in a white blur.

'We don't want to be on unknown terrain in this,' she said. 'It's not just the wind. It's the lack of visibility and the cold. We'll freeze up into little lumps on the fixed ropes. We'll have to wait for it to calm down and decide then.'

As the wind howled, the conversation circled endlessly through the various options, and many cups of tea were consumed. The climbers were sitting in a lazy doze when Bruce suddenly perked up.

'Wind's died. Listen to the silence.'

'You're right,' agreed Cathy, looking out. 'It's a beautiful day. The sun's out and it's completely still.'

'What time is it?' Ian asked.

Cathy fumbled for her watch.

'Noon. A little late to be leaving for a full day's climbing.'

'We'd make camp 4 by dark, just,' said Bruce. 'But it leaves no room for error.'

'And no time to prepare for the summit push either,' Ian added. 'The plan is supposed to be to leave camp 3 early, get to camp 4 just after lunch, pack, eat, drink, then get a few hours' sleep and leave again at 11 o'clock in the evening for the summit. If we leave now, we'll have to push straight on for the summit with almost no rest at all.'

'So we can make camp 4, but we almost certainly won't manage to leave for the summit tonight,' said Bruce thoughtfully. 'That means we have to wait a day no matter what. Now, are we better off waiting here for a day or up at camp 4?'

'No question. We're better off here,' Ian replied. 'Another 700 metres of height is a huge difference. And we'd have to dig into our oxygen supplies as well, and given the effort it's taken to get them up there, we don't want to use the stuff unless we absolutely have to.'

'But what about the Sherpas?' said Bruce suddenly. 'They've presumably made it up to camp 4 and are now sitting around wondering where we are.'

'Damn, you're right. Ang Dorje is going to be furious. They're probably already wondering what sins they've committed in their previous lives to get landed with us in this one.'

Ian thought furiously.

'But the logic still holds,' he confirmed. 'We now have no choice but to wait a day and we're definitely better off waiting here. They should be all right on the South Col. We have enough oxygen in reserve up there that they can use the stuff as much as they need to.'

'I guess we should've gone for it when we had the chance,' said Bruce. 'It's so hard to tell whether you're being sensibly conservative or hopelessly over-cautious.'

The sounds of passing traffic outside led Cathy to peer out once more. She talked briefly to a passing Sherpa.

'We're not the only ones dithering,' she announced. 'You remember the IMAX team arrived at camp 3 yesterday, ahead of us? Apparently they headed back down this morning and are going all the way down to base camp. They must not like the wind either.'

The three climbers looked at each other.

Makalu 8463m
Everest summit 8848m
South summit c. 8750m
Lhotse 8516m
South-East Ridge
Camp 4 on South Col 7980m
Geneva Spur
Yellow Band
Camp 3 7400m
Camp 2 6500m
Camp 1 6100m
Base Camp 5340m
Nuptse 7861m

Lhotse Face

Western Cwm

Khumbu Icefall

Khumbu Glacier

The Route

Everest and the Khumbu Glacier from the west-north-west: the route climbed by the 1st South African Everest Expedition, the same route by which Everest was first climbed in 1953

The team…

Top, left to right: Ang Dorje Sherpa, mountaineer and expedition sirdar; Pemba Sherpa, mountaineer; Jangmu Sherpa, mountaineer. Above: Nawang Sherpa, mountaineer; Ang Sirke, camp 2 cook; Shankar, base camp manager; Ang Mu, base camp cook

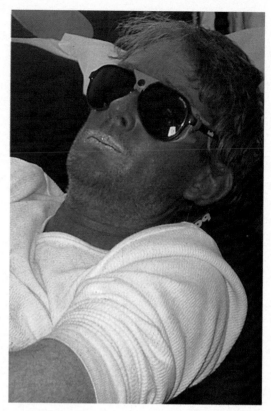

...the team

Clockwise, from bottom left:
Bruce Herrod, mountaineer and
expedition photographer; Cathy
O'Dowd, mountaineer; Ian Woodall,
mountaineer and expedition leader;
Deshun Deysel, mountaineer; Philip
Woodall, base camp technician;
Mr Khatiwada, expedition liaison officer;
Patrick Conroy, Radio 702 reporter

Preparations

Top: The South African base camp: from left to right, the mess tent, kitchen, comms tent, living tents, chorten with prayer flags. Above: The living tents at base camp with laundry laid out to dry. Right: Nawang and Jangmu packing loads to carry up the mountain. Below: The puja ceremony, held in front of the Khumbu Icefall

Tackling the icefall

Top left: Ian crossing a crevasse stylishly, with Bruce behind. Top right: Cathy's first encounter with a crevasse crossing. Above right: Cathy climbing under the ice 'wave'. Below: Ian climbing through the chaos of the icefall

Through the Western Cwm

Opposite page: Figures walking up the Western Cwm towards the South-West Face of Everest. This page, right: Cathy on the radio at camp 2, with the Lhotse Face behind. Below left: Ian (left) and Cathy sorting equipment at camp 2. Below right: Camp 2, with Lhotse and Nuptse behind. Bottom: The upper reaches of the Lhotse Face at sunset

Slow progress on the Lhotse Face

Left: Ian climbing above camp 3.
Top: Cathy (in front) and Ian on the fixed ropes on the Lhotse Face. Above: Cathy (last in line) follows the teams of Rob Hall, Scott Fischer and the Taiwanese up the Yellow Band on 9 May

'I'll try to contact Ang Dorje,' said Ian, rummaging around for the radio. 'We've left radios at each of our camps, so with any luck he'll find the one at camp 4.'

Ian tried to raise their higher camp for a few minutes, and got nothing but the static hiss of radio silence.

'Anyone for more tea, then?' asked Cathy.

14:00 – Camp 3

The long afternoon hours stretched out interminably in front of them. This time there really was nothing to do, nowhere to go. Camp 2 seemed like a holiday camp in comparison to their tiny tent perched so hazardously on the steep slopes. There was no possibility of even going outside for a short walk. Immediately outside the tent's front door the ice fell away down the Lhotse Face. Outside the back door was a small platform, the size of a coffee table, but beyond that the slope slid away again. Above the South African tent, other expeditions' tents clung precariously to other tiny platforms.

With three climbers confined in the two-man tent, any movement disturbed the others. There was nothing to read, no one new to talk to. Nothing to talk about. All topics of conversation seemed to have been used up in the week's wait at camp 2. Just fruitless speculation about the weather, endless tasteless cups of tea, and slowly time passing.

Cathy peered out of the tent, seeking at least visual escape from the grey interior. To the north-east of the camp the monumental ice-face of Lhotse swept up to the rock wall that formed the final barrier of the fourth highest mountain in the world. To the south-west the face dropped away to form the edge of a giant void, the expanse of the Western Cwm. The huge ice bowl, bordered by Everest and Nuptse, opened at the end to provide a glimpse of the distant peaks of the Nepalese Himalaya. They rose, row after row of icing-coated triangles, like a child's drawing of mountains. She watched until the sun set in the mouth of the ice bowl. The icing-coated triangles slowly turned golden and were engulfed by the rising cloud layer.

16:00 – Base Camp

'Pass the tea, then,' said Philip to Deshun, as they sat together in the base camp mess tent, enjoying the usual afternoon drink and biscuits. The tent door was suddenly opened and a young, deathly pale face topped by grubby blond hair peered round the canvas flap.

'Hi, I'm Patrick Conroy, I'm the Radio 702 reporter,' the face said.

He glanced quickly round the tent but didn't see the people he was hoping to find.

'Where are they?' he asked anxiously, before he had even taken his pack off. 'The climbers, where the hell are they? Have they reached the summit yet?'

'It's all right,' said Philip. 'They should make camp 4 today, and should go for the summit tonight. You've just made it. Have some tea and you'll feel better.'

He was concerned by the slight build and wan demeanour of the man, having yet to learn that both were typical of Patrick and hid a considerable level of determination.

'Thank God!' Patrick exclaimed as he sank down into a chair. 'You have no idea of the hell I went through to get here on time. My recurring nightmare was that I would be in some one-shack dump on the way in when the team reached the summit and I would be absolutely the last South African in the world to know.'

As Deshun passed him a mug of steaming tea, the phone rang.

'It's for you,' said Phil.

Patrick staggered across to the comms tent and held his aching head between his hands while he listened to Radio 702 news editor Debora Patta requesting 'two voicers and some actuality as soon as possible, please'. All he wanted to do was sit down and try to reduce his headache, but this was a jolting reminder that he was at base camp to work.

He walked back to the mess tent to retrieve his tea.

'So it's been a bit of a rush to get here, has it?' asked Deshun.

'That's for sure,' he confirmed. 'After our marketing director, Cecil Lyons, spoke to Ian on the phone and confirmed that I could cover the expedition, they had me on a plane within 24 hours. We thought you might summit on the seventh or eighth and even if I pushed myself I would barely get here by the seventh. They were so excited that they put me on the first plane to Singapore, without checking the flight connections to Kathmandu. I had to wait almost two days in the Singapore airport lounge. It was terrible.'

Patrick took a deep swallow of tea to wash away the memory before continuing.

'Then I was trying to get myself to Lukla as quickly as possible, but for three days we were bogged down by the weather. So every day I'd be rushing off to the Kathmandu airport, waiting, waiting, waiting, and no helicopters could get through. Finally, though, we arrived in Lukla where I met two porters coming back down who said the South Africans were two days away from reaching the summit. Then I heard you hadn't reached the summit but were still on the mountain. I was asking everyone coming down the trail from

Everest if they had any more news, but without success. I cancelled all the rest days on my schedule, as I was determined that even if I arrived at base camp half dead, I would at least be there when you lot topped out.

'Crossing the glacier was very slippery, there was a lot of snow and a lot of ice, and we were battling to find a clear route. I wasn't looking around much, rather concentrating on the trail-finding. At one point I looked up and suddenly there was the South African flag a few hundred metres away, flapping in the wind. That was just, yippee! I was jumping for joy, I practically jogged the rest of the way to base camp.'

18:00 – Base Camp

'Come on over to the comms tent and I'll show you the ropes,' Philip said to Patrick. 'We have a radio call scheduled each evening at six o'clock and it's about that time now.'

'Let me just grab my equipment,' Patrick replied. 'I'd like to record some of it, to get some background colour for my news reports.'

Philip picked up the microphone of the radio base station.

PHILIP: 'Hello, camp 3, this is base camp. How're you doing up there?'

IAN: 'Hi, Philip, we're doing very well, actually. We're cursing ourselves for not having forced the wind this morning, though, because it's a beautiful evening up here. Anyway, we'll stay here in camp 3 tonight, and tomorrow morning we'll leave at about seven o'clock for camp 4. That should get us up to the South Col by mid-afternoon, and then we'll leave for the summit at about 11, maybe 12 o'clock in the evening.'

PHILIP: 'Do you think the weather will be better tomorrow, Ian?'

IAN: 'No, not really, but I just feel that we must be due a windless day soon, and our Sherpas are already up at camp 4. I've tried to contact Ang Dorje, Philip, but without success. Could you hold a listening watch for the next hour or so, as you're probably more likely to pick him up on your base station? Then if he comes through, you can just tell him we'll be with him first thing in the morning.'

PHILIP: '10-4. I copy you'll be with him first thing in the morning.'

IAN: 'Yeah, that's fine. Chances are he'll probably wake us up tomorrow morning while we're still here at camp 3, and drag us out of bed screaming, but not to worry. How are the Yugoslavs doing on their second summit attempt?'

PHILIP:	'I've just been speaking to their radio operator. They have three climbers going for the summit this evening. They'll be leaving at about midnight tonight and they'll be hoping to summit at about nine o'clock tomorrow morning. Oh, by the way, Patrick's arrived, the Radio 702 reporter.'
IAN:	'Okay, send our best wishes to the Yugoslavs and say hello to Patrick for me – hopefully we'll speak to him in the near future.'
PHILIP:	'Okay, 10-4. He has an interview later on, so he's doing a bit of recording to get the atmosphere. He has a slight headache, so I've told him just to take it easy and not to make any sudden movements.'
IAN:	'That's a roger, Philip. But he should actually have a big headache. A small headache is nowhere near good enough. For what it's worth, though, we may actually call you at 20:30 to try to get the weather forecast. They've basically been completely crap up to now, but they may get one right.'
PHILIP:	'10-4, Ian. We'll monitor Nepal radio at about 20:15 and then if we can comms again at 20:30 we'll see how accurate they are.'
IAN:	'Roger that, Philip. We have our heart set on going to camp 4 tomorrow anyway, but we'll speak to you later. This is camp 3 out.'

20:30 – Camp 3

PHILIP:	'Hi, camp 3. Anyone there? I've got some great news.'
BRUCE:	'We're all tucked up in bed. What've you got for us?'
PHILIP:	'The Nepalese radio report was vague but fairly positive. But better than that, we got an excellent forecast from the Danish satellite weather system. They predict four days of no wind and clear weather. It looks like this is your window.'
BRUCE:	'Great news, Phil! We'll be going for broke on this one then.'
PHILIP:	'Good luck.'

CATHY:

We settle down for another night at 7 400 metres. I want oxygen but know that there are now only three bottles left, one each for use climbing from camp 3 to camp 4. I am determined to get through the night without any.

The pattern of jerking awake to apparent imminent suffocation repeats itself. As the hours pass it gets worse, not better. Time seems to be slowing down. The thought of a whole night of this fills me with horror, let alone the prospect of sleep-deprived climbing tomorrow. My throat begins to tighten with the lump of held-back tears. That makes breathing increasingly difficult. I begin to panic, the lump grows, the longed-for oxygen becomes ever harder to suck into my lungs. I am caught in a downward spiral but cannot escape out of it. So this is what a panic attack is like. My breathing gets ever more ragged. My windpipe seems to be shrinking by the minute. Soon it will be as narrow as a thread. I'll never get my breath back.

Ian sits up, fumbling for a head-torch. He unzips the frozen tent door and pulls in a bottle from the tent's bell, dumping it between us. The metal is icy to the touch but reassuring. He rapidly attaches a mask to it and pushes it on to my face. My panic subsides as my lungs fill with air. I wouldn't mind an arm round my shoulders to tell me it is all going to be okay, but it seems oxygen is all I am going to get.

IAN:
Tomorrow is a really big day, and we all know it. The whole team up to the magic 8 000-metre mark, the sensationalist's 'death zone'. Wow!

9 May
06:00 – Camp 3

He crawled out of his sleeping bag, rubbing sleep from his eyes, and fumbled for the inners of his boots. He was only going outside for a minute, he didn't need his crampons. Pulling on a jacket, he manoeuvred out of the door of the small tent and moved away to stand on the icy snow. Blinking against the glare of the sun, he peered out over the Western Cwm, past the massive buttresses of Everest and Nuptse, to the distant sentinel of Pumori. It was a beautiful day, a perfect climbing day. As he stared out, he fumbled for his fly.

His foot slipped. Falling over backwards he put his other foot out to regain his balance. But it had no grip on the slick ice. He hit the ice hard and began to slide. Without crampons, without ice axe, he could make no impression on the relentlessly slippery surface. Twisting, tumbling, rapidly gathering speed, he accelerated down the 1 000-metre ice-slide that led to the Western Cwm.

10:00 – Base Camp

Patrick watched fascinated as Philip explained to him the technological wizardry that lay concealed beneath the green canvas of the comms tent.

'You see, when one of the Kodak digital cameras is full of images, Bruce sends it down with someone who is coming back to base camp. I can then plug it into the Apple computer and download the images. And there you have it!'

Suddenly they were both looking at a photograph of Ian posing precariously on a ladder in the icefall.

'It's great for me to be able to see what they're actually doing, and then I can give Bruce a photographic critique over the radio,' Philip laughed. 'He doesn't like that bit very much, though.'

A head peered in at the tent door.

'D'you guys have any climbers up at camp 3?' the man asked in an American accent.

'Yes,' said Philip. 'We had three climbers staying up there last night. They should be on their way to camp 4 by now.'

'So it's not one of your guys who's been killed?' he asked casually.

'What?' Patrick and Philip jumped up together. 'What are you talking about?'

'Some guy took a slide down from camp 3. He was alive when they found him, but he didn't last long,' replied the American.

'But who? From which team?' Philip demanded.

'Sorry, pal, I don't know that. I just thought you guys might know,' he replied.

The head withdrew and Philip and Patrick just stood there and stared at each other.

'It can't be one of our team,' said Patrick slowly. 'Can it?'

CHAPTER 6

Help! Anybody Out There?

9 May
06:00 – Camp 3

'Who's making all that bloody noise?'

Ian sat up in his sleeping bag with a face of thunder. As the team lay in their snug sleeping bags, each waiting for someone else to make the effort of lighting the stoves for morning tea, the stillness of the morning had been broken by shouts from the Taiwanese camp pitched nearby. Somebody was disturbing Ian's precious lie-in and they'd better have a damn good excuse.

'Calm down, old man. You'll give yourself a heart attack. I'll go and see what all the shouting is about,' said Bruce.

'A little peace and quiet, that's all a man asks for,' grumbled Ian as he slid back into the warmth and comfort of his bag.

Bruce stuck his head out of the tent door into the cold morning air to find some Taiwanese Sherpas chattering excitedly and preparing to move back down the ropes. Tragedy had struck.

'Christ, guys, one of the Taiwanese has just fallen down the Lhotse Face,' said Bruce quietly, the blood beginning to drain from his face.

Ian sat bolt upright.

'Do they need any help?' he asked urgently.

'No, they seem to be okay,' Bruce said. 'Their guys are going back down from here to look for him and they have a rescue team coming up from camp 2 as well.'

'How did it happen?' Ian asked, now feeling sorry about his early morning outburst.

'It seems that he went outside for a slash, didn't put his crampons on or clip into the fixed ropes, slipped, and off he went.'

'Do you think that he can survive such a fall?' asked Cathy, who was now sitting up with her arms wrapped tightly around her knees.

The two men looked at one another, then down at the tent floor. Their expression said it all.

CATHY:
I am horrified by the suddenness with which someone has simply ceased to be. And such a stupid way to die, as if it makes any difference what you are doing when you die. But I also feel a curious sense of relief. I know the statistics, that there is on average one death per season on Everest. So it has happened. And not to us, not to anyone we know. Maybe the mountain god will be satisfied now. There will be no more deaths this season.

IAN:
'Mountains don't kill people, people kill people.' I'm not sure that I totally agree with that statement, but certainly in this case it was perhaps more people than mountain. As I sit here slowly sipping my tea it's hard to understand how a climber can forget to clip into the fixed ropes at 7 400 metres, but it is so easy to do. The body is a very adaptable creature. Perhaps too adaptable. After so long in a vertical environment the body becomes used to the steep slopes, the slick hard ice and soft wet snow, and so the risk of complacency creeps in. It can happen to any climber. It's happened to me. Not the complacency of the arrogant, but the complacency brought on by the repetition of high-altitude climbing. We have to concentrate on being safe at all times. We constantly remind each other to be safe. Be safe, Ian. Be safe, guys.

10:00 – Camp 3

'So I'll start on up then?' said Cathy, more as a statement than a question. She was tired of waiting for Ian and Bruce to get ready and there was no sense in putting off the steep climb to camp 4 for longer than necessary.

'Okay, off you go then,' Bruce answered, 'we'll be up shortly.'

Cathy seriously doubted that, but was pleased to get away nevertheless.

'Remember to hold thumbs for the Danish!' Bruce shouted after her, referring to the Danish weather forecast of excellent climbing weather for four days that had everyone charging up the mountain to their respective high camps.

So, shaken by the sudden death of a fellow climber, the South Africans left camp 3 later than they had expected and joined the back of the trail of climbers moving slowly up the fixed ropes towards the Yellow Band. With the welcome onset of some good weather, and the Danish weather bureau's forecast, four of the thirteen expeditions, Scott Fischer's American team, Rob Hall's international team, the balance of the Taiwanese expedition and the South Africans, were on the move. Each hoped to reach the South Col that afternoon and leave for the summit that night.

CATHY:

I find myself walking in the footsteps of Scott Fischer, the giant, blond American leader who is climbing at the back of his string of clients. Each in turn crosses the steep icy traverse to the start of the yellow rock band, a wide strip of smooth, angled rock slabs. The rock-faces are scored with hundreds of tiny white scratches, the marks left by the crampons of numerous climbers. I have begun to use the oxygen bottle that I am carrying. The soft leather mask envelops my nose and mouth, and a tube runs back to my rucksack, where I am carrying the large orange bottle of air. The oxygen-enriched air is tangy, almost like sea air. The difference is noticeable in the steady progress I make and the growing gap between myself and Bruce and Ian behind me.

Scott turns round to photograph me as I climb up towards him on the steep rock slabs. A pity I will never see those photographs, with the great sweep of the Western Cwm below me. As I clear the top of the yellow band and stop to rest, I can see that I am now clearly higher than Pumori, the mountain that had once towered over base camp so impressively. I am slowly escaping the confines of the Western Cwm now. I can see all the way across that valley that was once hidden from us. And I am beginning to see the many mountains that spread out across Nepal.

However, the temperature is starting to drop and I need to keep moving to stay warm. Scott is stopping his clients to bundle them into down jackets and I slowly pass them, one by one, as I traverse my way across the snow slope towards the rocky outcrop of the Geneva Spur. At the foot of the spur my oxygen runs out. I pack the mask into my rucksack and crouch down for a few moments, hands jammed into my armpits, fingers wriggling determinedly as I try to bring blood back to my hands. Little flares of pain run down my fingers as the numbness retreats. Then I begin the awkward climb up the loose rock towards the crest of the spur. To my delight I find that, rather than following the skyline of the spur, the route crosses over it and then traverses gently down towards the great rock expanse of the South Col. The fixed ropes that run along the traverse become increasingly tatty and finally stop altogether. The wind is picking up, and spindrift is beginning to swirl around in the air. I move as quickly towards the tents as I can.

I find all the expeditions' tents huddled together in a crescent moon, as if cowering away from the vast col. The two South African tents make up the furthest point of the crescent. I scramble gratefully into a tent, and burrow my way into down jacket and sleeping bag. Within ten minutes the wind is howling steadily, snow blowing horizontally across the col and visibility is down to little more than 6 metres.

I wait alone in the tent. My sense of time is uncertain, but increasingly I feel sure that Bruce and Ian were not this far behind me. Outside the wind howls, whistling through the guy-lines and hammering against the tent fly. I peer through the flap and receive eyes full of stinging spindrift for my trouble.

What to do? How long to wait? Ang Dorje passes over a thermos flask of hot, milky tea.

'I am worried for the men,' I shout across to him. 'They should be here. Something is wrong.'

He gazes at me impassively and retreats into his tent.

I drink the tea, run increasingly dramatic disaster scenarios through my head and wait. I doze lightly and lose all sense of time. I don't know how long it has been since I arrived. I wait.

17:00 – Geneva Spur

IAN:

'Bloody Danish,' curses Bruce as he hauls himself gasping and blowing on to the narrow shelf and collapses in a heap next to me. 'Where does the route go from here?' he asks pointedly, as there are no fixed ropes to be seen anywhere.

I reply, 'That way, I think,' indicating an area of storm, wind and horizontal snow that looks exactly the same as all the other areas of storm, wind and horizontal snow.

'We'd best try to keep as close together as possible, old man,' Bruce shouts against the force of the wind.

I nod in agreement, not bothering to try to compete with the raging storm. Bruce shows a thumbs-up sign over his shoulder and leads off slowly into the teeth of the storm, and into real trouble. The route to camp 4 and safety is a very narrow one. A slight mistake in any direction could plunge us down the icy south pillar of Everest, but we must keep moving no matter how poor the visibility, because to stop is to die.

We stumble and grope forward metre by dangerous metre. Suddenly Bruce sinks to his knees in the snow and doubles over. I immediately drop down next to him and push my ear right up against his mouth in an attempt to communicate above the noise of the wind.

'I'm completely shagged,' gasps Bruce, 'you'll have to lead from here.'

'Okay, youth, but stay really close.'

Bruce nods. I rise to one knee, as standing upright is impossible, and, squinting into the driving snow, I pick the line of least resistance, although nothing is certain in these conditions. Setting my sights on a visible rock just a few metres ahead, I move forward. Bruce stays on his hands and knees. Realising the situation is becoming critical, I pull off my gloves and start fighting with frozen fingers to tie Bruce's harness to mine to make sure that we're not separated in the maelstrom. That done, I pull away Bruce's snow glasses to look into my friend's eyes in an attempt to judge how far his physical and mental condition has deteriorated.

'We can't go on meeting like this,' Bruce jokes, seeing me gaze meaningfully into his eyes.

'Idiot,' I snap. 'I thought you were dying on me.'

'Not yet, old son, not yet, but you are going to have to get us to camp 4, though. I'm shattered.'

On and on, step by gasping step, we fight our way forward into the white void. Suddenly the snow-covered rocks level out from the 60-degree slope of the traverse off the Geneva Spur to the flat expanse of the South Col. We collapse in the lee of a large boulder in a desperate attempt to find some respite from the forces hurled against us.

'Listen in, Bruce mate, we're on the col. The tents can't be far,' I shout as the wind whips the words back into my face.

There is no response from the large Englishman crumpled against the boulder.

'Bruce, Bruce, listen to me. Wake up, for Christ's sake!' I scream again, shaking him with the little strength I have left.

'Bloody Danish,' replies Bruce with as much of a smile as his frozen mouth allows.

'Listen, we really have to dig in and concentrate now,' I say firmly. 'We can't survive much longer out here and I've no idea where the tents are.'

'What's that over there?' queries Bruce, looking up for the first time and pointing into the distance.

I look across to where he's pointing and to my amazement, in a fleeting gap in the storm, I see the outline of a brightly coloured yellow tent. I know we don't have any brightly coloured yellow tents, but this is a life or death situation, and in these conditions a tent is a tent. So, without a moment to lose, I grab Bruce by the waist belt of his harness and together we crawl on hands and knees towards the little yellow tent and safety.

19:00 – Camp 4

Bruce banged hard against the tent and Cathy hastily ripped open the door to pull him in. His black beard was frosted white, his body shaking with cold.

'We got caught in the storm,' he explained. 'We became totally disoriented and eventually Ian pushed me into the first tent he could find, and went in search of another for himself. I don't know where he is now.'

As he pulled off his damp clothing, Cathy found him dry socks and something warm to drink.

'I was in a tent with Andy Harris, a guide with the New Zealand expedition,' Bruce said through the fabric of his wet underwear, which was getting caught in his beard as he fought to pull it over his head. With a grunt of success and a shower of ice particles from his beard, the offending item was thrown into a forgotten male mess in the bottom of his rucksack.

'They warmed me up really nicely, although they only had hot water to offer,' he continued, while trying to find something warm and dry to wear.

'Any idea what their plans are?' Cathy asked, cowering from the clothing storm that was now raging inside the tent.

'No, they all seem to be waiting for Rob Hall and Scott Fischer to decide whether to go for the summit tonight. I guess it will depend on the weather.'

Cathy was squeezed even further into the corner of the small tent as the front entrance was thrown open once again and Ian stumbled in, helped by Ang Dorje and the force of the jet-stream winds from outside. He immediately collapsed on to the floor, almost kicking over the cup of hot drink that Cathy had been protecting from Bruce's attempts to get changed. She sighed in resignation at the amount of fresh snow Ian had brought in with him and which would soon turn the floor of the tent into a skating rink.

'Dived into Scott Fischer's tent,' stated Ian to no one in particular. 'Looked after me really well. Impressed by his behaviour. Bloody weather.'

He paused. 'Apparently Rob Hall is definitely going for the summit tonight and Scott will probably go as well. His sirdar, Lobsang Sherpa, was saying that the weather will improve.'

He was trying to remove his clothing but seemed unco-ordinated. His speech began to slur, becoming more and more disjointed. It dawned on the others that he was no longer making any sense, that he seemed to be drifting in and out of reality. Suddenly he slumped on to Cathy's lap and lay still.

> CATHY:
> I check his pulse and breathing.
>   'Bruce, he's unconscious,' I exclaim, horrified.
>   Bruce shrugs. 'He's just cold.'

Quickly Ang Dorje and I pull off his boots and damp outer layers, and manhandle the dead weight into a sleeping bag. As Bruce concentrates on warming himself up, I lie next to Ian, rubbing his icy hands in mine and offering him all I have to give, the heat of my body.

I peer down into his face, so small as it lies surrounded by great billows of down sleeping bag. I notice for the first time that his eyelashes, dark near the ends, are red at the roots. The skin around his eyes is so pale by contrast, the skin that has been protected behind his glacier glasses from the harsh glare of the high-altitude sun. He looks so fragile and I feel utterly helpless. Are humans really meant to exist in this environment? No. We may simply trespass here for a little while, but always at our peril.

I search along his wrist for the faint pulsing of his arteries. It is sluggish but steady. I notice when he shifts from unconsciousness to sleep, and he seems briefly aware of me, as his hands tighten round mine. I continue to lie next to him. He is asleep. Bruce too has retreated into the depths of his bag to get warm, and I lie alone, but always conscious of the others. I am glad I am not here by myself. In this environment I feel particularly drawn to touch people, to reaffirm my humanity by sharing it.

Ian opens his eyes, to look into my anxious ones. I notice that his eyes are grey, that he is wearing contact lenses. He reaches up to touch my nose and say thank you. I laugh and ruffle his hair. We move apart. The danger past, we retreat into our personal space.

IAN:
Fight, Ian, fight the cold, fight the mountain, never give in.

I'm so tired, every cell in my body is crying out for sleep. My mind does not belong to me any more, it drifts endlessly back and forth, edging ever nearer to blissful sleep.

No! Don't sleep, Ian, whatever you do don't sleep. Sleep is the silent enemy, sleep is the killer, it'll keep you forever, you'll never wake up.

Be sensible, Ian, you must sleep, you can't keep driving your body this way, you must give it a chance to recover. If you keep fighting now this could be your last, there may not be any reserves after this. Rest and sleep now and live to fight another day.

Don't listen, Ian, you've never given up before, don't give up now!

Sleeping isn't giving up, Ian, it's being smart.

I toss and turn in turmoil. Slowly through the mist I see faces, faces I know, faces I trust. I reach out and they're real.

You're both wrong. I will sleep, but I won't be giving up because I'm with my friends. They will look after me, they'll make sure that I'll wake, for once I'll put myself in their hands. Sleep, sleep, sleep and dream.

21:00 – Camp 4

'Pass the flask over, youngster,' said Bruce, indicating the stainless steel container next to Cathy's legs.

'Christ, Herrod, I don't know where you put all that tea you drink,' Ian commented, shaking his head in amazement. 'You must have a bladder the size of a haggis.'

'It's the English way, old boy,' Bruce replied. 'Besides, the noble haggis is Scottish, and as I'm English I couldn't possibly have a haggis for a bladder.'

'You could've had a transplant,' countered Ian.

Cathy had already put up with weeks of this type of banter and knew that it could go on for hours, if not days, unless it was nipped in the bud. Anyway, the question in hand was the summit of Everest, not bladders and haggis.

'You two seem to have recovered quickly enough,' she interrupted.

Bruce settled his mug firmly between his knees before holding forth.

'Actually, as I was about to explain to Woodall over there, the healing properties of English tea are truly remarkable. I read a study once.'

'It's Nepalese,' Ian interrupted.

'What?' said Bruce, screwing up his nose.

'The tea, it's Nepalese, not English,' Ian stated.

'Yes, I know,' Bruce argued, 'but the principle is the same. For the sake of the discussion tea is tea.'

'Guys, are we going to the summit tonight or not?' said Cathy impatiently. She knew there was no substitute for a direct, serious question.

The tent occupants fell silent for a few moments.

'How do you feel about it, Cathy?' Bruce asked quietly.

'I feel good and strong. Ang Dorje says that the Sherpas want to go tonight, so I think we should go.'

'What about you, Ian?' asked Bruce again.

'To be honest, I'm really tired. I could probably have a bash, but if there's any chance of a rest day, I'd certainly be keen to wait. I'm also not sure how much we can trust this weather. It seems to be improving a little now, but if we have another dose like this afternoon when we're on our way back from the summit, we may not make it back at all next time.'

Everyone went quiet while they thought through Ian's comments.

'I feel pretty much the same,' said Bruce. 'This storm has certainly taken its toll on me. I guess we have to decide whether the storm was just an extreme example of the usual afternoon snowfall or if it presages something worse.'

This was it. The decision. Stay back and miss the summit or press on and risk the weather. Each of them knew it would come to this at some stage of the expedition, but that didn't make it any easier now that it was here.

Bruce broke the silence. 'Listen, let me go next door and have another word with Ang Dorje – maybe he can come up with a suggestion.'

Relief, an opportunity to delay the inevitable. The other two immediately agreed, so Bruce got ready to go across to the Sherpa's tent.

CATHY:

I listen to the circling conversation, edgy and impatient. I feel strong, surprisingly strong, for the day's efforts. Good stuff, that oxygen. I want to go tonight. I fear that every day spent waiting at this altitude will simply weaken me. What if this is the only good night? Tomorrow the weather may change, the winds may rise again. And our chance will be gone. And if we descend and try again later in the season, we will be that much weaker, with that much less energy.

I don't want to go alone, but if Bruce and Ian will not go, I'm prepared to climb with the Sherpas, who also want to go tonight. But I am reluctant to go without the men, after all we have been through together. Is it more important to keep the team together, with the risk that no one will reach the summit, or to split the team to grab a summit chance? I don't know.

As the conversation loops into another round of maybe this, maybe that, my irritation grows. We wouldn't be in this situation if we had left camp 3 earlier this morning. We wouldn't be in this situation if Bruce and Ian hadn't had a macho thing about reaching 8 000 metres without oxygen. If you are not going to use it at all on Everest, fine; but if you *are* using it, use it! Don't create artificial difficulties that only undermine your chances of eventual success.

But then I feel guilty for the thought. I'm the one who was using the stuff up at camp 3. We didn't have enough oxygen left at camp 3 for all of us to use it on the way to camp 4. And I don't want to split the team now, not after everything we've done together. I decide that I will wait 24 hours if the Sherpas also agree to wait. If they don't, I'll think again.

22:00 – Camp 4

Bruce crashed through the tent door and collapsed on his sleeping bag gasping for breath.

'Bloody hell, the air's thin up here.'

He slowly sat up against his rucksack and brushed the ice from his jacket.

'Well?' asked Ian anxiously.

'Well,' Bruce replied, 'Ang Dorje says that the Sherpas would prefer to go up tonight but would wait an extra day with us if we asked them to.'

Cathy nodded in approval and slid back into her sleeping bag. Ian was deep in thought.

'I'd like to wait a day,' said Bruce firmly.

'I'm troubled by this weather,' said Ian, 'I know I'm tired as well, but it's really the weather that concerns me. I think it would make good sense to give the weather the benefit of the doubt and an opportunity to settle down. I think we should wait a day as well.'

'It's settled then,' Bruce confirmed. 'We'll wait here for 24 hours and go to-morrow night at midnight.'

The decision was made.

> IAN:
> Up or down? Red or black? Life is one big gamble. We have arrived at the point of a summit decision as a team. We have faced that decision as a team. We have decided not to follow the other expeditions on the mountain but to climb within our own limitations and make our own decisions. We have now made those decisions and we are still a team. I lie in my warm sleeping bag, listening to the gentle breathing of my team-mates. I'm proud of us.

The South African team dozed on and off through the evening, sleeping on bottled oxygen at a very low flow rate. The wind died in the late evening and, although there was still a lot of cloud about, the spectacular Himalayan star pattern was beginning to peep through in places. At 11 o'clock there was the crunch of heavy boots passing the tents and Bruce looked out to see a very tired Yugoslavian team on the way back from their attempt on the summit. They were turned back by the Hillary Step and had been on the go for almost 24 hours by the time they stumbled back to the safety of camp 4.

23:30 – Camp 4

Bruce, lying on the side nearest the mountain, watched as the other teams left for the summit one by one, first Rob Hall's team, then the Americans with Scott Fischer leading, and finally the Taiwanese.

'Well, everyone's gone but us,' he said to Ian.

The three friends looked at each other uncertainly.

> IAN:
> As the tiny, gleaming head-torches slowly make their way off into the dark-ness in the early hours of 10 May, the unspoken thought is whether we have made a terrible mistake in deciding to wait another day. New Zealand

leader Rob Hall is on the way to his fifth ascent of Everest, the record for any western climber. American leader Scott Fischer has climbed Everest before and is a very experienced and immensely strong mountaineer. Both have decided that the time is right and are going for the top tonight.

All three of us are thinking the same thing. What if this is the only night of the season good enough to climb? What if the winds pick up again tomorrow? What if we have wasted our only chance because we have been too conservative to push on?

At least it's our decision, I say to myself rather unconvincingly. Even if it is the wrong decision. Rather do what we think is safe and get it wrong, and have no one but ourselves to blame, than simply follow people more experienced than us, and then blame them if things go wrong. It's very important that we climb within our own limitations.

Two hours later the winds had picked up again and it was desperately cold. The South Africans drew some comfort from the fact that it was clearly not an ideal night to be climbing to the summit of Everest, and settled back into uneasy sleep.

10 May – Camp 4

Much of the following morning was spent dozing in the tent, eating little but trying to force down cups of tea to stay hydrated. Late that morning the climbers crawled out of the tent to look at their surroundings. The South Col was a flat plain of angular black rocks, bordered by the slopes of Lhotse on one side and of Everest on the other. The third side fell away steeply down the icy slopes that made up the south pillar route and the Lhotse Face. On the fourth side the plain stretched away out of sight but then fell abruptly down the Kangshung Face into Tibet. The various tents were huddled together in one corner of the plain, finding in proximity courage in the face of the empty waste of the col. The sunlit nylon domes in yellow and red seemed bravely cheerful among the black surroundings.

The route up the slopes towards the summit of Everest rose abruptly from the col. A step of crevassed blue ice stretched across its path, followed by a snow plain and then the steep, rock-strewn snow slope that made up the side of the South-East Ridge of Everest. The climbers would have to pick their way carefully up this route to reach the ridge that formed the skyline, and then follow the ridge towards the South Summit, which they could see from camp 4. The true summit itself was hidden behind the South Summit, an unknown distance further. Somewhere up there among the rocks, snow and ice were the three teams that had left in the darkness. Sometime tomorrow the South Africans would be up there as well.

15:00 – Camp 4

By early afternoon Bruce and Cathy were taking some digital photographs and Ian was testing the oxygen regulators for the umpteenth time.

'Many people reach summit, Bara Sahib.'

The team-mates looked up to see the smiling face of Ang Dorje. He was obviously very pleased.

'Conditions very good,' he continued. 'We go tonight?'

There was a moment's silence as the climbers looked at one another, then, seeing the pained and pleading look on Ang Dorje's face, began to laugh.

'Yes, old friend, we go tonight,' said Ian, squeezing his co-leader's arm. 'We go tonight.'

Bruce, Ian and Cathy smiled nervously at one another and then retreated quickly to their tent to begin packing.

Bruce started to sort through the camera gear he wanted to take to the top of the world with him, making sure that his lifelong ambition was to be properly recorded. His pile of equipment swelled and dwindled as he first added more and more bits he might need, and then, considering the growing weight of his rucksack, began to discard excess equipment. Then he would suddenly spot something that he couldn't live without and the pile would start to grow once again.

> IAN:
> I pull out the summit flags that until now have been packed away in the bottom of my rucksack and carefully tie a South African and a Nepalese flag on to each of our ice axes, both ours and the Sherpas. The gaudy colourfulness of the South African flags contrasts with the red zigzag of those from Nepal. Hopefully, within the next 24 hours, Bruce will be photographing our South African Y-fronts flying on top of the world. I force myself not to be too excited, there's still a hell of a long way to go and so much can still go wrong, but when the others aren't looking, I allow myself a quick smile. If only the weather will hold!

> CATHY:
> I sit among a colourful chaos of sponsors' flags, trying to find a balance between fulfilling all our commitments and carrying so much stuff that we never get to the top. A knot of excitement and nerves is building up in my

stomach. At last, we have the chance to go. But we have to leave at midnight, with little sleep, bitter cold and long hours of darkness ahead of us. Finally we can find out what the summit ridge is really like. But we may find out that it is just too much, too hard, too far, too high. Anticipation and fear chase each other round my system as the adrenaline begins to rise.

Why are the other teams taking so long to return? It must be a really long day. But they should be back by now. I unzip my tent door to peer out and find the wind has picked up again and light snow is falling.

'The weather is doing a repeat of yesterday,' I announce.

'Well, doubtless it will clear up in an hour or so, just like yesterday too,' says Ian.

I look across to where he is sitting, surrounded by a brilliant disarray of South African flags. My excitement is rising again, overwhelming the nagging doubts.

15:00 – Base Camp

At base camp the atmosphere was one of nervous excitement. Patrick, Deshun and Philip moved sleeping bags and ground mats into the communications tent and stocked up on hot drinks in anticipation of staying awake all night. In the early afternoon they began to get the news that climbers were reaching the summit. They heard a cheer going up from Scott Fischer's camp, then one from Rob Hall's. People passing by brought news that some of their climbers had reached the top of the world and that others had turned back. Philip and Patrick sat on small unstable camping chairs outside on the glacier, looking up at the mountain and drinking tea while they chatted to pass the time.

'I hope our guys can still make it,' said Patrick. 'I wonder if staying that high for so long won't have weakened them.'

'They should be fine,' Philip replied. 'If they knew they were too stuffed to go for the top on the first night, they'll probably know if they are too stuffed to go tonight.'

'Wouldn't that be terrible?' said Patrick, shaking his head. 'Imagine if all the other teams make it this time round except for us, and then our guys might be too tired to try again.'

'They're a determined bunch. I'm sure they'll go tonight, and hopefully the tracks from today's teams will still be there. That should make things a bit easier for them.'

The late afternoon cold drove the two back into the comms tent. There the conversation turned to talk of their lives back in South Africa, and for a while the hardships of the Himalaya seemed very far away.

18:00 – Base Camp

Suddenly the tent flap was ripped open and Helen Wilton, Rob Hall's base camp manager, stood in the doorway.

'We have a life and death situation on the mountain,' she said, almost in tears.

The two men stared at her in bewilderment.

'Rob Hall's in trouble with Doug Hansen,' she stammered. 'Doug's run out of oxygen and Rob is running out fast. They are near the Hillary Step and very weak. We need someone to get oxygen up to them. We want to know if you can help.'

18:01 – Camp 4

As usual Bruce picked up the radio to make the evening call.

BRUCE: 'Hi, Phil, how's tricks?'
PHILIP: 'Bruce, is Ian there?'
BRUCE: 'Sure, just a second, I'll put him on.'

Bruce passed the radio across to Ian with a deep frown. It had come to be accepted that Bruce did most of the radio calls and he was puzzled by this strange request.

IAN: 'Hello, Philip, this is Ian, what's up?'
PHILIP: 'Ian, we have just been told that Rob Hall and Doug Hansen are descending from the summit near the Hillary Step and have called for help. Their base camp can't reach their camp 4 so they have asked us for help.'

The three team-mates looked at each other in surprise.

IAN: 'Okay, Philip, what do they have in mind?'
PHILIP: 'They would like you to take them some oxygen as they are both running out.'

Ian scratched his head as he tried to comprehend the magnitude of the request. The wind and snow of that afternoon had developed into a full Himalayan storm that was intensifying, with strong winds, extreme cold and snow bringing visibility down to a few metres. The South Africans were at least eight hours' climbing from Rob, even in good conditions, and, having never been above the col before, would not be able to find the route in a storm.

IAN: 'Philip, I appreciate Helen's concern for her team-mates, but I don't think she fully realises what she is asking. Of all the teams up here, we are the furthest away from Rob, and never having been above the col, we won't even find the route, so we have the least chance of finding him in the darkness and storm. Philip, quite frankly, in these conditions we wouldn't get more than 200 metres from camp before we would need rescuing ourselves. Roger so far?'

PHILIP: 'Roger so far, Ian.'

IAN: 'Do we know why they can't get in touch with their own people or any of the other expeditions, as they must all have climbers coming down from the summit who are much closer to Rob than we are?'

PHILIP: 'I'll go over to the New Zealand base camp to try to find out more information.'

The South African climbers waited with their radio on standby.

'My God,' exclaimed Bruce, 'Rob Hall! He's the most experienced man on the mountain. How can he, of all people, be in trouble?'

'I guess he's doing what all good guides do,' Ian replied. 'Staying with a client who got into trouble. Anyway, storms don't choose their victims according to their experience.'

'It sure reminds me of yesterday's little outing, though,' Bruce said, reflecting on how close he and Ian were to the edge in the storm that engulfed them 24 hours earlier.

'Yes,' Ian answered, 'our decision not to go for the summit last night is beginning to look like a good one.'

'What about tonight?' Bruce asked.

'I can't see how we can go for the summit now,' he replied soberly. 'If we can't find our way up to help the others, then we sure as hell can't expect to make a summit bid ourselves.'

'We could go and help if we had someone with us who knew the route,' said Bruce quietly.

'Yes, I know,' agreed Ian, 'I was thinking that myself. If we could follow someone else back to the climbers in trouble, then we could supply the muscle of the rescue.'

'Hell,' mumbled Bruce, 'has anyone ever been rescued above 8 000 metres before, let alone two people?'

'I doubt it,' Ian said, shaking his head. 'Anyway, what do you think? If we can find someone to lead us up the mountain, do you fancy having a go?'

'Should be fun,' smiled Bruce.

Ian looked across at Cathy, who had been very quiet up to now, but she looked both men firmly in the eyes and nodded her agreement.

'Right then,' said Ian, 'it's agreed. I'll tell Philip when he calls back.'

CATHY:

I listen while Bruce and Ian speculate. I find it hard to comprehend the suddenness with which we have been plunged into disaster. What can be going on up the mountain with all those climbers, with Hall and Hansen? Experience is supposed to be your biggest asset. I know the other teams doubt our chances because of our relative inexperience. So how come Hall is out there, possibly dying, and we are being asked to save him? And what do we do?

I remember when we got the radio call from Hall, via Henry, saying he wanted to book 10 May for the summit. And we laughed at his assumption that he could predict the weather that far ahead. The official reason he gave was to reduce congestion. We heard the unofficial reason via the ever-active climbing grapevine, that Hall was saying he didn't want the risk of having to waste time and resources rescuing incompetent climbers from other teams. And now? There is some kind of sickening irony in this somewhere.

IAN:

This could definitely end in tears. We made the decision to delay our summit bid together as a team, and we're stronger for it. But this is different, this is serious stuff. If we're going to see this through to the end, whatever that may be, we're going to need to work together as a team like never before. Basically we are just going to *need* each other. We may even get to like one another! I glance across at Bruce. So strong, but so deceptively gentle. I look across at Cathy. So gentle, beautiful even, but so deceptively strong. Yep, Ian, they'll do nicely. I look down at the summit flags lying so expectantly next to our ice axes. Sorry, guys, maybe next time.

18:30 – Base Camp

Philip was joined at Rob Hall's base camp by some climbers from Scott Fischer's expedition. He found them in intermittent contact with Rob Hall but with no contact with any other climbers on the summit ridge or any of the teams at camp 4. Helen, unable to contact Rob on her radio base station, was reduced to standing on a rock outside her tent, holding the radio above her head with one hand, holding the broken aerial up with the other, and shouting into it. Occasionally a faint voice would emerge from it. Ingrid, Scott Fischer's team doctor, joined the group and, nearly in tears, said she had no contact either with any of her team on the mountain and feared for their safety.

19:00 – Pheriche Village *en route* to Base Camp

The third of the South African Everest support treks was moving up the valley that ran towards the Khumbu Glacier. Having heard rumours that the South African team were moving towards the summit that day or the next, they walked towards the next village, Pheriche, as quickly as possible, in the hope that they might be able to contact base camp by radio.

As soon as the trekkers were settled, camped outside a lodge, Alex Gaudin, the trek leader, sat down on the stone wall that bordered the main footpath through the settlement and turned on her radio. Through the static she could hear Philip speaking, to whom she did not know but it was obvious that there were climbers in trouble on the mountain. Her excitement was instantly overwhelmed by apprehension. She called through on her radio.

'Get off the line!' shouted Philip. 'We have an emergency here.'

'Phil, just tell me, are the South Africans okay?'

'We need the comms. Call back in two hours.'

Philip was gone. Alex was left staring at the radio, her blood chilling in her veins. Surely if the South Africans were okay, Phil would have said so. She left the radio on but could hear nothing more than a hiss. She kept looking at her watch every five minutes as the two hours stretched out interminably. In her mind she ran through all kinds of disaster scenarios. She stared up the trail, but Everest was completely hidden from view. She could only wait.

News spread through the settlement at speed. Already rumours of trouble had come down the trail. One by one the trekkers joined Alex in her vigil on the wall. The French and American doctors from the medical aid post came over as well. The Nepalese residents, some of whom had relatives on the mountain, clustered round. All waited anxiously for news, speculating endlessly with the pitifully little information they had.

19:00 – Kathmandu Headquarters

PHILIP: 'Hello, Kathmandu, this is Philip.'

HQ: 'Philip, what's going on? The ministry's just been informed there are climbers in trouble on the mountain. Are our people okay?'

PHILIP: 'Yes, they're fine, it seems that there are two climbers in trouble, but I just wanted to confirm to you that all our team are safe.'
HQ: 'Thank God.'

15:15 (SA time) – Johannesburg

The phone rang in the Woodall family home in Rivonia. Brenda Woodall picked it up.

PHILIP: 'Hi, Mom, it's Philip.'
BRENDA: 'Hello, Philip, it's good to hear your voice. How is everyone?'
PHILIP: 'We are all fine, but we have a small problem on the mountain. Some climbers are trapped in a storm, and it will be all over the world's press soon. I just wanted to let you know that our team members are safe and well and not involved.'
BRENDA: 'Good heavens, Philip, what's going on? Are you sure Ian, Bruce and Cathy are safe?'
PHILIP: 'Quite sure, they're perfectly safe. I just called so that you won't worry when it hits the news.'
BRENDA: 'Okay, Philip, I understand, but please keep us informed of what's happening.'
PHILIP: 'Yes, will do. Can you phone Cathy's family and tell them not to worry as well?'
BRENDA: 'Yes, of course. What about Bruce's family?'
PHILIP: 'That's okay. I've already done that.'

19:10 – Camp 4

PHILIP: 'Hello, camp 4, come in, Ian.'
IAN: 'Ian here, go ahead, Philip.'
PHILIP: 'Ian, the situation on the mountain is getting worse by the minute. Rob Hall and Doug Hansen are still in trouble and desperately need help. In addition there seem to be another 21 climbers missing as well.'

The team-mates at camp 4 looked at each other in amazement.

PHILIP: 'Hello, Ian, are you still there?'
IAN: 'Roger, Philip. Can you repeat the number of missing climbers?'

PHILIP:	'I say again, figures two one, figures two one. I know it's a lot of people, Ian, but the other expeditions have asked if you can help put together some sort of rescue.'
IAN:	'Okay, Philip, I need you to listen very carefully now.'
PHILIP:	'Roger, Ian, go ahead.'
IAN:	'We have already agreed between the three of us that we will forgo our summit bid tonight and do what we can to help the climbers get off the mountain. Roger so far?'
PHILIP:	'Roger so far.'
IAN:	'We are reasonably well rested and can form the muscle of any rescue attempt from the South Col and are prepared to do so, but the bottom line is that we do not know the route up the mountain. None of us has climbed Everest before and we were intending to route-find our way to the summit as we would normally do on any mountain, but we can't route-find in a raging blizzard. Roger so far?'
PHILIP:	'Roger so far.'
IAN:	'Okay, so what we need is to team up with someone who knows the route. They don't have to take a physical role in the rescue, we can do that; we just need someone who knows which way the climbers are likely to be descending. Roger so far?'
PHILIP:	'Roger, Ian.'
IAN:	'Good, then can you ask the teams at base camp to contact their climbers here at camp 4 and organise us someone to be ready in, say, 30 minutes? Someone who has come down from the summit today would be ideal.'
PHILIP:	'I roger all that, Ian, but we have a problem here at base camp in that none of the teams here has radio comms with the climbers in their camp 4 tents. You guys are the only ones anyone can talk to.'

Ian slowly covered his face with his hands in frustration and gave his eyes a good rub.

IAN:	'Well, I guess there's nothing to be gained by a Spanish inquisition at this stage.'
PHILIP:	'I guess not, bro. Listen, Helen thinks that some of their Sherpas who have returned from the summit may be at their camp 4. They would be ideal to show you the route.'
IAN:	'That's better news, but I guess if you guys can't talk to them then I'll have to go out into the storm and look for them. Can you ask Helen how I can recognise their tents?'

PHILIP: 'Wait one, Ian.'

Ian looked up from the radio and smiled weakly at Bruce and Cathy.

PHILIP: 'Hello, Ian, Helen says that their tents are yellow.'
IAN: 'Philip, every tent up here except ours is bloody yellow. Can't she
              be more specific?'
PHILIP: 'Sorry, Ian, that's the best we can do.'
IAN: 'All right, tell Helen not to worry, I'll do the best I can.'
PHILIP: 'Roger, bro, be safe.'

A request to go outside, that at base camp would have simply meant pulling
on a down jacket and grabbing a torch for a few minutes' walk across the
rocky terrain to the neighbouring tents, took on a very different dimension at
8 000 metres in a howling storm.
  Ian wriggled out of his sleeping bag and began hunting among his equipment for his Goretex salopettes and jacket. Cathy and Bruce, squeezed against
the sides of the tent, lay patiently as he flailed around between them. He had
to fight his way into the stiff salopettes, twisting and turning to put them on
when the height of the roof meant he could barely kneel. Off came the warm
down jacket to be replaced by the cold windproof jacket. He dug around to
find a warm hat and two pairs of gloves, before starting the tortuous task of
pulling on his huge plastic boots. The inner boots were still damp from the
previous day's climbing and it was by now a very cold damp. Toes, reluctantly
pulled out of the sleeping bag and stuffed into that cold damp, began to chill
rapidly. The rigid overboots were a battle to put on with stiff, unco-ordinated
fingers, while the partly frozen laces resisted all attempts to tie them neatly.

    CATHY:
    I'm glad it's not me. The wind is strumming against the guy-ropes of the
    tent like fingers over guitar strings. The tent walls shake as if hit by a giant
    hand. The cold seems to seep through the fabric. But inside we are relat-
    ively warm, relatively safe.
      What are all these other people doing out there? Why have they taken so
    long to descend? And what on earth are we supposed to do about it?
      I suppose I'll go out if I have to. Will I? I'd probably just turn into an-
    other victim of the storm's ferocity within ten minutes. I hope I don't get
    the choice to make.
      I watch Ian wriggling to pull on the last of the protective layers of cloth-
    ing. All those layers that seemed so massive when we first sorted through
    them in the sunshine way down the trail now seem so insubstantial in the

face of the wind. And the figure buried in all the layers of clothing seems even more insubstantial. Be careful, for God's sake. Come back.

20:15 – South Col

IAN:

Fully dressed, I slowly make my way on hands and knees across the tent floor towards the door, and whatever lies beyond. The previous evening's icy experience has given me a good idea of what to expect on the other side of that thin layer of nylon, and going out intentionally into a blizzard at 8 000 metres in the pitch dark is not my idea of a fun night out.

I apologise to Bruce as I unintentionally drag his sleeping bag part way across the floor. He smiles in return and gently squeezes my arm as I edge past him. I nod in reply. Fumbling with gloved hands, I slide down the zip of the tent flysheet and tumble out into the storm.

Immediately I gasp for air. I can't breathe. I can't bloody breathe. The incredible force of the wind has collapsed my lungs, like trying to breathe out of the window of a speeding car, and I tear frantically at my jacket to release the pressure on my chest, but to no avail, the strength of the wind is too great. I begin to lose consciousness. I begin to die.

Turn, Ian, turn your back into the wind. I hear the command, it makes perfect sense, but I can't place where it comes from. If only I can force the logic through to my barely functioning brain. I collapse to my knees, then forward on to my side, lying curled up in the foetal position, at the mercy of the ravages of nature. But with my back to the wind. Somehow the message has got through and slowly the pressure of the wind on my lungs subsides and they painfully begin to suck in huge gasps of the thin, icy-cold but life-giving air.

I must get moving, people in a worse position than me may be relying on our efforts. I try to get my bearings, but looking into the wind is impossible as my face and eyes are immediately scoured by the flying snow and ice particles, and the darkness means that I don't have the customary protection of sunglasses. I hold both hands up against my face and squint through tiny gaps between my fingers in an effort to plan the way forward.

The tents that had once curved away from the South African camp in a crescent leading towards the Geneva Spur have vanished in a pandemonium of noise and ice. The howling, gusting, freezing winds are totally disorienting, but setting my direction as best as I can remember, I jam my hands under my armpits for warmth and, hunched forward against the sting of the wind, move crab-like into the eye of the storm.

Time, distance and direction all seem swept away by the ferocity of the storm. For ease of movement I am not using oxygen so the altitude means a stop every ten or fifteen steps to get my breath back. Yet moving is the only thing that keeps the warmth pumping through my body. Each stop in the fierce winds drains more and more warmth that I can ill afford.

Suddenly a stiff, frozen guy-rope brings me crashing to the ground. Trying to look up into the storm, I fumble forward, running my fingers up the ice-covered rope, feeling for the tent fabric. Even being this close I can't make out its shape and I have to bump into it before convincing myself it's there. The tent's side is vibrating like a drum from the force of the wind, so, placing both hands on the side of the tent, I begin to beat on the fabric with all my strength in an attempt to contact anyone who might be inside.

There is no reply. Taking a deep breath I begin to shout at the tent and pummel its flysheet, but no sooner have the first sounds left my mouth than the winds blow them hopelessly off into Tibet. I'm left coughing and gasping, bent double, trying to force enough oxygen into my tortured lungs.

There is still no reply. Remaining on my knees, I begin to feel along the side of the tent for a possible entrance, but by now the snow from the sides of the tent has soaked through into my gloves and the windchill has frozen them solid. I can't even feel what I'm touching, let alone contemplate opening a zip. The time spent on my knees has cut off the already scant circulation to my feet and frostbite is a very real possibility. So, not knowing whether the tent is indeed empty or whether the people inside simply can't tell the difference between my banging and that of the wind, I have no choice but to leave the tent and begin to look for another. Tent after agonising tent is first located and then left, without any contact being made.

Realising I'm deteriorating fast, I decide to shelter in the next tent I find, no matter what. Seeing one looming in front of me, I collapse before it and bang against the flysheet for all I'm worth. To my amazement it opens and I crawl in, grateful for the sudden warmth and stillness of the interior.

'You all right?'

I was staring into the face of Neil Laughton, a British climber on the Henry Todd team whom I had last seen over a cup of hot chocolate in base camp. I nod in reply, too tired to speak. I look across to the back of the tent and see a pile of wet, cold, tired and frightened Sherpas. Suddenly my radio crackles into life. It's Philip.

PHILIP: 'What is your situation, Ian?'
IAN: 'It's very tough here. It's a bit difficult. We've got driving snow, visibility down to about 10 metres.'
PHILIP: 'Have you located any members of Rob Hall's team?'

IAN: 'Negative. All the tents up here look the same and nobody can hear me knocking above the noise of the wind. Roger so far?'

PHILIP: 'Roger so far.'

IAN: 'Does Rob Hall's base camp know where their Sherpas are on the South Col, because I can't bloody find them?'

PHILIP: 'Negative, negative, Ian. It seems that they're on the way down. We can't speak to them.'

IAN:
I suppress my anger at being sent on a wild goose chase to find the New Zealand team Sherpas who have by now obviously already left the South Col for the safety of the lower camps. Damn! There goes our first possibility of someone showing us the route up the mountain.

IAN: 'Okay. So we can only speak to Rob Hall's base camp manager. Is that correct?'

PHILIP: 'Roger, Ian. We can also speak to Rob Hall as well, though, through a guy on Pumori.'

IAN: 'That won't give us a guide to lead us up the mountain, though. Have you managed to find anyone else who may be able to help?'

PHILIP: 'Yes, Ian, we have contact with Henry Todd, who is not in camp 4 but his climbers and Sherpas are. They have moved up from camp 3 today and should be relatively fresh. If you can find them on the South Col, they should be able to help with a guide.'

IAN: '*Ja,* that's not a problem, Philip, because I'm actually sitting with Neil and his Sherpas at the moment and they're completely shattered and in no position to go out.'

PHILIP: 'Okay, stand by, Ian. Stand by please.'

IAN:
I slide the radio gently back inside my down jacket and reflect on the demise of our second possibility of someone showing us the route back up to the missing climbers.

20:30 – Camp 4

CATHY:
We wait. And wait. And wait.
How long has he been gone? I fumble through the various layers of clothing to find my watch. Only 15 minutes. It feels so much longer.

What has he found out there? People, rescue, perhaps that the missing 21 climbers are actually safely back at camp but just can't contact their base camps to tell them. Or nothing. No people, no help. Maybe even no tents, if he's lost direction in the storm. No, don't think about that.

We may be physically closest to the unfolding tragedy but, in the face of the elements, proximity means very little. We don't talk much. There is little to say, other than to speculate endlessly about what is going on, when we have virtually no information to go on, or worry about Ian. Neither is very helpful. I wriggle restlessly in my sleeping bag. Each position gradually becomes uncomfortable as my tired muscles stiffen up, but to move is to lose precious heat. I need to do something, anything, to wrench my mind away from concern for Ian. Drink, we need to keep drinking.

'Want a cup of something, Bruce?'

I can see from his look that he too is grateful for the distraction.

'So what are you offering, then, woman?'

I give him a cheeky grin. 'Just tea, coffee or hot chocolate. That's about all a man of your age can cope with at a time like this.'

'What? Nonsense. I'm just getting into my prime. A youngster like you would never be able to keep up with me. It takes years of experience.'

We chatter inanely, anything to drown the sound of the wind, to fill the space of Ian's absence. I carefully pour mugs of hot water, tear open sachets of coffee, sugar, cremora, mix it all together. The tepid liquid tastes hot in comparison to the cold around me.

We wait.

20:45 – South Col

Down at base camp the support teams, frantic with worry, desperate to help, but four days' climbing away from the ongoing drama, could do little but radio instructions into a weather chaos that they could not even begin to appreciate. Philip's voice came through again.

PHILIP: 'Hello, Ian, this is base camp, come in.'
IAN: 'Go ahead, Philip.'
PHILIP: 'We think Fischer's team may be able to help. Is it possible for one of Henry Todd's Sherpas to go to Fischer's camp and tell them to turn their radio on, so their base camp can ask them to help you?'

Ian looked across at the Sherpas who had accompanied Neil to camp 4. They were huddled together in the corner, cold and wet and using bottled oxygen continuously. Most importantly, however, they were silent. No cheerful chatter. No quiet discussion. Just silence. They were obviously in a bad way and in no position to go back out into the storm again.

IAN: '*Ja*, Philip, I'm nearest the door, I'll go, it may be the last chance we have of finding someone to show us the route. It'll take me a little while, though, so you'll have to go on standby.'

PHILIP: 'Okay, Ian, base camp standing by.'

Although he had only recently arrived on the col from camp 3, Neil offered to help Ian search for Scott Fischer's camp. As Ian waited for Neil to get suitably dressed for the storm, he wondered how long this storm would last and how many climbers would make it back to base camp when it was all over.

21:00 – South Col

IAN:

'Those two big yellow ones over there look like the best place to start,' shouts Neil, pointing to two large tents on the outskirts of the South Col 'village', his mouth no more than a few centimetres from my ear.

I give a thumbs-up in reply, but I'm not at all sure whether I've already checked them or not. As he leads off into the storm, Neil places his gloved hands over his face, trying to protect his flesh from the viciousness of the wind and snow. After a few metres I recognise a boulder slightly to the right of our chosen path. It's one that I'd used as a reference point when moving from tent to tent. I'm now quite sure that I've already checked the two tents we're heading for and I'm about to alert Neil when I pause to look at the large boulder again. It's definitely the same large rock that I'd used previously, but it seems to be bigger somehow. It's also covered in snow. That's not possible. No snow can stick to the rocks in this wind. Suddenly I realise what I'm looking at and with all my strength I lunge forward, grabbing the back of Neil's jacket, spinning him around, and shout into his ear.

'Christ, Neil, look! There's a climber collapsed on that boulder.'

For a few seconds we both stand transfixed, staring at the figure sitting motionless on the rock with his hands neatly folded on his lap and his chin resting on his chest. The driving snow is covering him rapidly and soon he will be gone from sight.

'He's one of our team,' Neil shouts in astonishment. 'He left camp 3 with me this afternoon but was very slow; I thought he'd turned back.'

There is no response from the frozen figure as Neil and I carry him in a sitting position back to Neil's tent.

'Listen, mate, I'll have to stay here and look after him,' Neil says, once the stricken climber is safely out of the storm.

'Of course,' I agree, 'I'll go on by myself.'

And so for the second time I find myself back out in the storm. Freezing fingers. Empty tents. Frozen feet. More empty tents. Where is everyone? Why can't I find them? Why won't they answer?

Then I hear Philip calling me on the radio. I want to ignore him. My hands are so cold. Stopping to take the radio out from inside my jacket and holding it up into the wind and snow to get a workable reception will drive the cold pain from my fingers, through the bones of my forearms, to explode in my armpits. Get a grip, Ian. We're the only ones with working radios. This might be critical information that needs to be passed on.

Turning my back to the raging snow and wind, I slump to my knees and fumble for the radio.

IAN: 'Hello, Philip, this is the South Col. Come in.'
PHILIP: 'Okay, Ian, I have you. Are you at Scott Fischer's?'
IAN: 'Negative, negative. I couldn't find Scott Fischer's. We're trying to keep ourselves alive up here. Neil and I have just pulled one of their climbers out of the storm. We can't seem to find anybody else right now.'
PHILIP: 'I copy that, Ian. Are you on oxygen at the moment, bro?'
IAN: 'Negative. I've haven't been on oxygen for the last few hours. The problem we seem to have is finding out whether … Christ, I can't even remember his name.'
PHILIP: 'Okay, Ian, I think the best thing for you to do right now is to get back to Bruce and Cathy. You've already been out far too long in these conditions and without oxygen.'

IAN:
Back to Bruce and Cathy? Yes, I must get back to my friends. I am in poor shape, but they will take care of me. Knowing they're there is the only reason I've pushed the envelope this hard. I've tried my best, but now I must get back.

21:10 – Camp 4

'Okay, mate, I've got you.'

Bruce grabbed Ian by the shoulders and supported him as he clambered into the tent, trying as best as he could not to trample on everyone's sleeping bags with his heavy, snow-covered boots.

'Christ, it's death on a stick out there,' cursed Ian as he fought his way out of his waterproofs and into his warm down jacket. Cathy thrust a hot mug of tea into his hand.

'Any luck with finding the other teams?' Bruce asked.

'It was a complete waste of time,' Ian sighed as he pulled and tugged in vain to get his double boots off. 'I couldn't find Rob Hall's or Scott Fischer's camps because all the tents are the same colour, and when I do find a tent the people inside can't hear me because of the bloody wind. It's a total nightmare.'

Ian gave up with his boots and concentrated on drinking his tea as Cathy came to his rescue and pulled the obstinate boots off with a single tug.

'I did find Neil, though,' he continued with a faint smile. 'He looked like a dog's breakfast, but then I guess I do as well.' Ian wasn't comforted by the swift nods of agreement from his team-mates. 'Anyway, we found one of his team out in the storm and managed to get him safely back inside their tent, so I guess it wasn't a complete waste of time.'

'I suppose that leaves us back at square one,' Bruce murmured.

'That's about it. And many more trips outside like that one and we won't be able to supply the muscle for anything, guide or no guide.'

CATHY:
He's too right about that. He's deathly pale under his sunburn and the feet I managed to liberate from his boots are icy cold. The risks of going out on any rescue attempt are huge – frostbite, hypothermia, disorientation and losing the tents, losing life. The concept of 'calculated risk' has just been catapulted into a new dimension. When do you forget about other people and concentrate on saving yourself and your friends?

Still, if we can't find anyone, we won't be going anywhere.

I refill Ian's mug and then squash up against the tent fabric while he wriggles into his sleeping bag. Even so I get elbows in the face and knees in the groin before he is finally settled. He has the down bag pulled right up over his head, with the radio snuggled against his chest. Bruce too is deep in his bag. Back to waiting. But at least we wait together.

21:15 – Camp 4

The friends were caught up in their own thoughts as Deshun's voice broke through on the radio.

DESHUN: 'Hello, Ian, this is Deshun at base camp.'
IAN: 'This is Ian; go ahead, Deshun.'
DESHUN: 'Philip has asked me to let you know that the latest information
            we have is that Rob and Doug are trapped somewhere below the
            Hillary Step. It also appears that Scott Fischer himself is out of
            oxygen and struggling, and lastly a Taiwanese climber and two
            Sherpas are in trouble as well.'
IAN: 'From what you say we have a situation where Rob Hall's, Scott
            Fischer's and the Taiwanese groups are all trying to get off the
            mountain, and there's no one else at camp 4 to help us find the
            route. Is my understanding correct?'
DESHUN: 'Roger. Sadly, that just about sums it up. It's all the news I have.'

It was the only information that anyone seemed to have, so all the South
African radios went on standby as they waited for further developments.

21:45 – Base Camp

Philip waited with a mix of foreign climbers in Rob Hall's base camp. Heaters
were on in the comms tent and everyone huddled close to them, passing
around hot drinks. The mood was tense, especially among those close to Rob,
such as Helen and his senior guides. As the scale of the disaster unfolding high
up became clearer, and the number of missing climbers rose, the support
teams felt a co-ordinated rescue effort needed to be set up. A white board had
been put up in the comms tent at Hall's base camp listing all the climbers and
their whereabouts. Depressingly, over 21 still had to be marked as unknown.

Various other people were hanging around, seeing where they could help.
Patrick walked between the two camps in the forlorn hope of finding out
something they didn't already know. Each time he did so, he followed his own
footprints, which marked the light snowfall covering the glacier, until, at last,
he had beaten his own track between the two camps.

21:50 – Camp 4

Deshun's voice came through the howling winds and flapping nylon that were
the only sounds in the South African tent at camp 4.

DESHUN: 'Hi, Ian, I've just spoken to Philip and he says that the situation is
            becoming more serious. The Taiwanese climber is being carried

by the Sherpas. They seem very strong at this moment, but they don't know how long they're going to last.'

IAN: 'Okay, Deshun, I copy that. Is there any more news on Rob Hall's and Scott Fischer's clients? If any of them are back on the South Col, they could show us the way back up to the Taiwanese and Scott himself.'

DESHUN: 'Negative, Ian, I'm afraid not.'

IAN: 'Roger, Deshun. But base camp must please understand the conditions up here. We have winds, we have driving snow. It's a major blizzard, but if there's anything that we can do, then pass it on down the line and let us know. Remember, we can provide the muscle of any potential rescue if only someone can show us where to go.'

Communications with the South Africans at camp 4 died away as their radio battery weakened. Some digging around under sleeping bags and equipment uncovered the spare battery supply.

CATHY:

I envy the base camp crew. It must be warm and peaceful down there, in comparison to here. When they ask us to pop out to see who else is around, I guess they think of the normal few minutes' walk across the rocky terrain to the next tents, as one would do at base camp. But we are in another world up here.

Yet it can't be easy for them either. Stuck down there, four days' climbing from us with no idea of what conditions are really like, frantic with worry, desperate to help and yet totally helpless. They can issue all the orders they like over the radio. It means nothing to the people up here.

But I'd like to walk into the mess tent, to see Philip's solid, cheerful face, hear Deshun's giggle, have a cup of tea and biscuits and then sit in the sunshine staring up at the icefall. It all seems so far away now, almost as if I'd read about it in a book once.

IAN:

We've made the decision to help our fellow climbers on the mountain, and we'll stick by it. But for how long? How long can we stay up here and still be effective? How long before we become a liability as well? How long before we die? You must watch carefully now, Ian. Watch yourself. Watch Cathy. Watch Bruce. At the slightest sign that any one of us is deteriorating we must get the hell out of here. People have tried to stay on the South Col too long before, and they're still here.

21:55 – Camp 4

Philip managed to get through directly to Ian with the next update from Rob Hall's base camp.

PHILIP: 'Ian, this does look a bit like a disaster. Rescue parties are being organised, though. The idea is to bring down the closest people first and, if possible, organise a high-altitude team for later.'

IAN: 'Roger, I copy all that. But I ask again, what do you mean by a rescue party?'

PHILIP: 'We're trying to get somebody at camp 4 to organise and lead everything from there, so that people don't go out one at a time and get lost on the mountain.'

IAN: 'Roger. That's obviously very sensible, but who is this person going to be?'

PHILIP: 'We're not exactly sure at the moment.'

IAN: 'I'm not surprised, I've been trying to find somebody to do exactly that all night!'

PHILIP: 'Yes, I roger that, Ian. How many Sherpas do you have with you from our team that can help?'

IAN: 'We have four, but what you must understand is that these are Nepalese mountaineers, not paid employees. Each of them will have to make their own mountaineering decision as to whether they are going to take part in a rescue above 8 000 metres.'

With increasing foreboding each group sat down to await further developments, although the climbers at camp 4 knew that all the lists and plans and organisation in the world coming from base camp meant little in the face of the storm on the col.

22:05 – Base Camp

Deshun, Patrick and the liaison officer, Mr Khatiwada, had been huddled next to the radio base station, straining to hear the conversation between Ian and Philip. As the voices faded away, another violent gust of wind swept across the comms tent. For a few minutes, while the tent shuddered from side to side, they wondered whether the material would finally tear.

'I keep getting the horrible feeling that everything is going to lift off and we're all going to be blown to oblivion,' Deshun said quietly. Patrick gave her a squeeze on the shoulder, as much to reassure himself as her. Mr Khatiwada, oblivious of their quiet interchange, was pacing backwards and forwards in the small tent. Suddenly he turned on them.

'How can Philip organise a rescue from here? How can the Sherpas go out in this extremely bad weather with their lives in danger?' he demanded.

'That's what Ian's saying,' Deshun answered quickly. 'They can't be forced to go, they have to volunteer.'

'No, no, it is extremely dangerous and it is better that they do not go out,' said the liaison officer, shaking his head determinedly.

22:15 – Camp 4

Suddenly Philip broke through from Rob Hall's base camp to pass on the latest news.

PHILIP: 'We have communications, very badly though, with Rob Hall's camp 4. The chap up there's name is Stuart. We can't get radio contact with either Rob Hall or Scott Fischer, but people are trying to call them all the time.

IAN: 'That's really good news, Philip. Does he know the way back up the mountain, and is he prepared to show us?'

PHILIP: 'I don't know at this stage. We have a report from this Stuart of lights in the storm, but we lost comms before he could confirm it. The visibility, we understand, is very bad but, if it's possible, could you look outside and see if you can spot any headlights coming down? We've had a report of numerous headlights. Could you check for us?'

Ian went on standby as he and Bruce peered out of the tent into the storm.

IAN: 'Philip, our tents are pitched right on the outskirts of the camp. If anybody could see the lights, we could. To be honest, we can't even see 5 metres with this sweeping snow. Our goggles just snow up within seconds. So we can't confirm that. We'll keep watching and, if lights appear, we'll let you know and go out to meet them.'

PHILIP: 'Thanks very much, Ian. I'm sure you can understand that 21 people still missing is causing a lot of concern down here.'

IAN: 'Yes, roger, Philip, it's a nightmare.'

PHILIP: 'That's for sure, and it'll probably get worse.'

CHAPTER 7

Missing, Presumed Dead

11 May
01:00 – Camp 4

CATHY:

There is a strange, dislocating feeling about being warm, well fed and breathing bottled oxygen, and in the knowledge that one's team-mates are also safe. Somewhere out around us people are fighting for their lives and perhaps even dying because conditions are so appalling. The line between safety and dying is so thin, as thin as the millimetre-thick nylon sheet that makes up our tent.

Our tent is a tiny bubble in a world gone mad. It is as if we are plunged into a Dantean hell as the mountain is raked by howling winds, cloaked in swirling snow, frozen to its very core. It is as if we and our mountain have been ripped away from the earth itself and now swirl distraught through space, caught in a vortex of insanity.

Outside, other human beings, caught on the mountain above us, are dying. But they could be in another galaxy for all we can do for them. We huddle in our little cocoon of warmth and light, temporarily safe, but yet so vulnerable. We expect moment by moment the tent fabric to tear, to be hurled from our haven into madness in a few seconds. Caught on the line between calm and panic, between safety and death, we can do nothing but wait.

Bruce places a torch in the tent door, shining out on to the face of Everest, in the hope that it may act as an indicator of where the tents are in the black and white swirl that makes up the South Col. The biggest problem for the descending climbers will be finding their tents once they are on the col. Ian's earlier experience has proved that.

I lie in my sleeping bag, waiting for the crackle of the radio that will bring further news. Opening my eyes a crack, I can see the light burning in the tent door, like a beacon of hope. But with my eyes closed, the light vanishes, while the noise of the wind does not. It howls on, so much more powerful than our pathetic little light. It is a remorseless, unrelenting killer, all the worse that it can neither know nor care about the suffering it is inflicting on the humans struggling through it.

I doze on and off. Several times the sound of Ian's voice on the radio wakens me, but the news never seems to bring anything but more confusion. Sometimes I wake while turning over and see his silhouette against the tent wall, sitting propped up on his pack, holding the radio, waiting. He never seems to sleep.

01:30 – Camp 4

PHILIP: 'Hello, camp 4, this is base camp, come in.'

The sharp staccato sound of Philip's radio voice floated around on the thin air of the camp 4 tent. Although muffled by the thickness of Ian's jacket, the sound seemed to amplify itself as it bounced and ricocheted off the layer of ice coating everything. Ian struggled to pull the radio out from the bottom of his jacket, not wanting to open the zip for fear of losing the priceless warm air trapped inside his jacket. By the time it was safely retrieved Philip had already called again, a little more anxious this time.

PHILIP: 'Hello, Ian, please answer.'
IAN: 'Hello, Philip, this is Ian. Go ahead.'
PHILIP: 'Is everything all right up there?'
IAN: 'Yes, everything's fine, just a little slow to move, that's all. Any news for us?'
PHILIP: 'Nothing good I'm afraid, bro. We still have all the climbers missing and still can't contact anyone else regularly on the col.'
IAN: 'You're right, that's not good news.'
PHILIP: 'Listen, Ian, I don't know how to ask you this but everyone is in such a state down here. Anyway, Rob Hall's and Scott Fischer's base camps have asked if you will go out again and see if any of their members have made it safely back to the col, and perhaps find someone who can guide you back up the mountain.'
IAN: 'Philip, before I commit myself, is there any indication why I may be more successful finding someone this time than last?'

PHILIP:　　'I hope so, Ian. Helen thinks that Stuart has some of their Sherpas with him.'

IAN:　　　'Helen thinks? Why doesn't she ask him?'

PHILIP:　　'I'm afraid the comms between them are so intermittent and poor that we can't get confirmation for you.'

IAN:　　　'I thought that their Sherpas had left for camp 2 already. They must be there by now. Why doesn't she call camp 2 and ask them whether they left any Sherpas behind at camp 4?'

PHILIP:　　'I'm afraid that we can't reach camp 2 either.'

IAN:　　　'Christ!'

The radios fell silent as a dreadful pause hung over the mountain.

PHILIP:　　'Ian, we wouldn't ask you if we weren't so desperate.'

IAN:　　　'It's okay, Philip, I understand. Give me a chance to wake Cathy and Bruce, then I'll go out as soon as I'm dressed.'

PHILIP:　　'Thanks, bro, everyone really appreciates it. Be safe.'

IAN:　　　'No problem.'

02:00 – South Col

IAN:

Once again I go through the struggle of dressing to venture out beyond the sanctity of our small nylon tent, only this time my boots and jacket are already wet and cold from my previous foray into the storm. My toes go numb as soon as they make contact with the inside of my boots and I know that they're not going to survive another trip outside. I look down at the radio; it's so tempting to tell base camp that my feet are just not up to it. Then I think of my fellow climbers who are fighting for their lives outside, not simply their toes. Oh well, let's hope we can keep the damage down to a minimum.

I finally stumble back out into the wind and driving snow, and, with fingers already frozen solid, begin to open up tents and search for Stuart and his elusive Sherpas. The third tent I visit brings success. Stuart is sitting huddled in the corner of his tent, talking to his base camp. One of his teammates and a Sherpa are lying curled up next to him. All three look completely shattered.

'Base camp told me you were coming over,' says Stuart as I settle inside. 'But I couldn't contact you and tell you not to come. We've no one here capable of going back up the mountain with you.'

'I figured it was a pretty long shot,' I reply, trying to sound enthusiastic. 'Do base camp know?'

'Yes, I've just told them. They think that Scott's team may have some spare Sherpas and have asked me to go out and have a look.'

'We've been through all this before,' I reply, not bothering even to try to sound enthusiastic this time. 'Look, I have to make my way back home anyway, and there's no sense in both of us going outside, so I'll have a look for Scott's Sherpas on the way back to our tents.'

'That would be a great help,' says Stuart, looking somewhat relieved.

Back outside again I spend minute after precious minute banging on tents trying to find Scott's camp, but without success. As I stand up slowly from yet another tent, I find myself completely disoriented. The lack of oxygen and the physical effort of fighting the wind and the cold have finally become too much. I begin to stumble round in circles, searching for any landmark that will re-orient me as to where our small tents may be. My head is spinning and I can't focus my eyes. As I fumble around in the black circling void, the last of the feeling deserts my feet, leaving me with wooden blocks jammed inside my boots, and I know that my toes are frostbitten. Beginning to lose my balance from shaking so violently with the cold, I drop to my hands and knees to continue the search for safety. At last I come across the black mounds of the South African tents and hammer against the fabric of the door with my last resources of energy.

02:55 – Camp 4

Hearing his friend's frantic calls, Bruce ripped open the frozen zip of the tent door and, still flaying with his arms, Ian fell across Bruce and collapsed on to his sleeping bag. He lay motionless on the soft down of his bag, drifting in and out of consciousness. Cathy pulled off his boots and once again manhandled him into his sleeping bag. Her heart sank as she felt the heavy, frozen weight of his feet; without any sign of pain from Ian she knew what that meant. As she lay rubbing his frozen hands, which felt like ice-packs just taken from a freezer, she wondered if he realised that he was frostbitten.

03:00 – Base Camp

Everywhere on the mountain conditions got worse as the night progressed. Philip spent the night at Rob Hall's camp, huddled in between Americans, Britons and Kiwis, all curled up on the floor in sleeping bags. In the South

African base camp the falling temperatures were taking their toll. The generator, never happy with the cold and altitude of base camp, packed up completely and the radio base station was being run off back-up batteries. Patrick had been nursing his recording equipment throughout the evening. The tape recorder had been stuck down the front of his jacket, hugged against his chest, with only the microphone sticking out. But finally even that froze. He and Deshun spent the night on the floor of the communications tent, huddling together in their sleeping bags, unable to sleep.

Deshun had a quick look at the temperature gauge that hung in the tent.

'Minus 38 degrees C,' she told him. 'I've got everything I own on and I still feel as if I'm frozen up to my knees. What can it be like another 3 000 metres higher with the additional windchill?'

They lay in silence for a while, each forming their own mental images.

'You know, when I experienced those heavy winds earlier tonight, I finally realised what people mean when they say 160-kilometre-per-hour winds,' Deshun continued quietly. 'Those winds gave me a reality check. I keep wondering what it must be like on the South Col. I could have been in that storm. I wonder how I'd have coped.'

'Yes, it brings home a lot of things,' said Patrick. 'The danger of climbing, the unpredictability of the weather. And lots of little things, like what if the tent tears, what if the wind blows them right off?'

'So many things keep running through my head,' said Deshun. 'Like how small a person is compared to creation, and how beautiful Everest is, and how terribly deceptive climbing a mountain is.'

'I feel so helpless,' Patrick burst out suddenly. 'I want to do something, to hit something, to make it stop, to help all those climbers trapped up there. But there is nothing we can do.'

'We can keep the comms running,' Deshun replied. 'It's not much, but it might just make the difference.'

05:00 – Camp 4

CATHY:
So warm. Where am I? I love sleeping on oxygen. I can pull the sleeping bag completely over my head, not leaving any space for a cold nose to poke out in search of fresh air. It's so warm.

On oxygen. Camp 4. The storm. What's happening?

I unwrap the sleeping bag from around my head and peer out from sleep-encrusted eyes. Darkness and the ever-present sound of howling wind. I peer at the tiny display of my watch. Early morning. What has happened to everyone? No movement in the tent. Ian seems asleep at last, wedged up against his pack, and muttering to himself. Maybe I can sleep just a little while longer.

IAN:
Am I sleeping or just daydreaming? Is it possible to daydream in the middle of the night? I don't think I'm asleep. I've been trying so hard to stay awake, but maybe I've just slipped off for a few moments, just a few moment's escape, just a few moment's dream.

A dream of helicopters. Helicopters that will pluck us all from the jaws of the storm, and spirit us away to warmth and safety. Helicopters...

05:05 – Camp 4

'No helicopters up here, mate,' said Bruce, mercilessly squeezing the life out of yet another tea bag.

'What's that?' asked Ian as he slowly and painfully tried to ease the cramps out of his back from sitting all night.

'You were mumbling about helicopters, but none could get up here. Their ceiling would be camp 1 at best,' Bruce answered in his typical matter-of-fact style.

'Yes, I know, don't worry, I must have been miles away,' said Ian, shaking his head.

'You'd best forget about helicopters and concentrate on this cuppa,' Bruce said as he thrust a steaming cup into Ian's hand.

'Thanks, youth,' Ian said gratefully.

'How're your feet feeling?' Cathy asked, looking out from behind her oxygen mask.

The two looked at one another for a few moments across the tent and Ian knew that Cathy was aware of his frostbitten feet, he could see the sadness in her eyes.

'Why, what's wrong with your feet?' asked Bruce, glancing up from behind his mug of tea.

'No, nothing at all, they're fine,' Ian quickly answered, casting a glance in Cathy's direction at the same time.

'Okay, but make sure you look after them, old boy, you're no use to any of us with shattered feet,' said Bruce obviously reassured.

'For sure,' replied Ian, relieved and anxious to change the subject. 'What's the weather doing, anyway?'

'As crap as always.'

Cathy and Bruce retreated behind their oxygen masks as Ian started to fumble about, making sure that the charged radio batteries were where he had left them the previous night.

CATHY:
His feet were like wooden blocks when he got back. He's not going to be rescuing anybody like that. And wherever we go from here, he has got a minimum of two days' walking on them before we get back to base camp. That's not going to be fun. And what about the summit?

What about the summit? We can't make a summit attempt now, not in this weather or in all this confusion. So is that it? Are we really going to try to drag ourselves all the way up here once again? And if we do, what about Ian and his feet?

Too many unanswered questions. Just take it one stage at a time. Let's get through the storm first and then worry.

IAN:
My feet are in a bad way. I know it and now Cathy knows it. In time we'll have to tell Bruce, but as there's nothing we can do for them up here at camp 4, there's nothing to be gained by worrying him at this stage. I appreciate Cathy keeping quiet on my behalf, but soon we'll all have to make a decision about the next 24 hours, feet or no feet.

05:15 – Camp 4

'Listen, guys, I've been thinking about whether we should stay up here any longer.'

Cathy and Ian looked out from behind their masks at the sound of Bruce's voice.

'We've already been up here far too long,' he continued. 'I know we wanted to help the others, but that possibility now seems to have gone. The storm shows no sign of easing off, so I think we should give careful thought about getting ourselves the hell out of here while we still have the energy. I've seen some storms in my time, in those three seasons I spent with the British Antarctic Survey, but this one takes the cake. We should get out.'

Cathy and Ian respected Bruce's opinion. He was hugely experienced in these types of conditions and, if he thought they should go down, they probably should.

'I guess you're right, we could be back in camp 2 by this afternoon and in base camp by tomorrow.'

Ian's reply brought immediate reminders of the wonders and luxuries of base camp to the three climbers. Wonders and luxuries that they had banished from their thoughts for so long, lest it cloud their mountaineering judgement.

'I think it's time to go down now,' said Cathy firmly, looking across at Ian.

'Right then, as soon as the sun's up we'll make a move,' confirmed Bruce.

05:30 – Camp 4

PHILIP: 'Hello, camp 4, this is base camp.'

Philip's voice sounded tired and strained, even over the radio, but the climbers were pleased to hear a friendly voice coming out through the darkness and cold.

IAN: 'Morning, Philip, this is Ian, how's everyone at base camp?'
PHILIP: 'Tired and cold, bro, tired and cold. How are you guys getting on?'
IAN: 'About the same really, but not too bad, everything being equal. Any news for us?'
PHILIP: 'Well, Rob Hall and a few climbers are still missing, but it seems that some climbers have managed to make it back to camp 4 during the night.'
IAN: 'That's great news. What about those still missing?'
PHILIP: 'Good news there as well. We have contact with a Sherpa called Lakpa who is on the South Col and prepared to go back up the mountain and show you the way.'

Silence descended on the South African tent standing so defiantly near the top of the world. The three climbers had already decided that their time in the death zone was over and that they would go down as soon as it got light, but now base camp was expecting them to go up the mountain as part of a rescue.

PHILIP: 'Hello, Ian, are you still there?'
IAN: 'Okay, Philip, I roger that. Do you have an estimated time of departure?'
PHILIP: 'Negative, Ian, Lakpa says that the conditions are still too dangerous to go out, but as soon as they improve he'll be ready.'

Ian let the radio sag for a few moments and his head dropped. Cathy and Bruce waited quietly, there was nothing to say. Ian looked up at them, shrugged his shoulders and, while still holding their gaze, picked up the radio again.

IAN: 'Right, Philip, that is good news. Please tell everyone that they can count on our support.'
PHILIP: 'That's excellent, Ian, I knew we could rely on you guys.'
IAN: 'Okay, Philip, just tell Lakpa to give us one hour's notice so we have time to get dressed.'
PHILIP: 'Roger, Ian, good luck and be safe.'
IAN: 'Thanks.'

Ian put down the radio and looked sheepishly at his team-mates.

'I'm sorry, I couldn't say no,' said Ian quietly. 'Look, if you two still want to go down it's okay. I'll ...'

'We started this as a team, we'll finish it as a team,' Bruce interrupted.

'If you stay, then we all stay,' Cathy agreed.

'Thanks, guys.'

The experience was becoming ever more surreal. With their awareness of time confused by the lack of sleep, their senses constantly bombarded by the incessant noise of the wind, and their nerves on edge with worry, the South Africans sat through the storm, waiting for the call that would send them up the mountain.

06:00 – Camp 4

Cathy suddenly heard noises that sounded more like voices than the howling of the wind. Unzipping the tent door, she peered into the maelstrom and saw a torch light in the darkness. She shone her own head-torch out from the tent and the light began to move towards her. Finally the shadow of a figure formed round the light, and a snow-covered body emerged from the storm. Cathy moved over and Stuart crawled into the tent, bringing with him flurries of spindrift.

'Hi, Stuart, what's up?' asked Ian.

'I just wanted to check whether you'd heard about Lakpa going up the mountain when the weather improves,' he answered.

'Yeah, cheers,' said Bruce. 'We've heard. He's going to give us an hour's notice to get ready, then we'll be going with him.'

'That's good. Have you heard about Yasuko Namba and Beck Weathers?' asked Stuart.

'No,' said Cathy, 'never heard of them. Who are they?'

'They're two of my team-mates and they've been seen lying out on the col near the Kangshung Face. Everyone thinks they're dead.'

Cathy, Bruce and Ian looked at each other in horror. They had been sitting for hours and hours in appalling conditions, waiting for a chance to help. Ian had been out in the storm on two occasions to volunteer their assistance to whoever he found. Now two climbers had been discovered, but nobody had bothered to tell the South Africans because 'everyone thinks they're dead'.

'Does "everyone" know for sure that they're dead?' Bruce asked bluntly.

'Yes, I'm sure that's what they said,' Stuart answered.

'So you haven't seen the "bodies" yourself?' pressed Bruce.

'Well, no, actually I haven't.'

'Right,' said Ian firmly, 'it will take Bruce and me about 15 minutes to get ready and then we'll go out and bring them in, dead or alive. Right, Bruce?'

'Too right,' Bruce agreed forcefully. 'Stuart, we need you to take us to someone who knows where they are. We'll never find them on our own.'

'But they're definitely dead,' he argued.

'Then we'll bring their bodies back to camp, it's the least we can do,' Ian said, beginning to lose his temper.

'There's no one who can show you where they are, anyway everyone says they're dead,' Stuart continued lamely.

The atmosphere in the little South African tent had been desperately cold for days, but in the face of this intransigence about helping two fellow climbers, dead or alive, it dropped several more degrees. Stuart began to feel the chill and excused himself to head back to his camp. The South Africans continued to talk unhappily among themselves about the two 'fatalities'. Although they each knew that the magnitude of the storm made some fatalities likely, these were the first actually to be reported dead. It seemed terrible that they should have perished so close to safety. But without a guide the South Africans would have no hope of finding them, so they continued to doze in their tents, waiting for the call from Lakpa.

06:30 – Base Camp

As the first grey light of morning began to penetrate through the gloom of the storm, the winds and snow continued. Reports reached base camp that Rob Hall had found an oxygen supply but that his mask was frozen and he was unable to use it. It seemed that by the early morning of 11 May 15 climbers were unaccounted for. Base camp was now contacting camp 2 to find out if there were any Sherpas or climbers there who could assist with a possible rescue operation, but no one was available to go from camp 2 either.

07:00 – Camp 4

'You awake, youth?' Ian whispered in Bruce's direction.

'Yeah, I'm too annoyed with Stuart to sleep,' he replied.

'I know what you mean. Listen, I'm going to pop next door and check on Ang Dorje and the boys. We haven't heard from them in a while.'

'Good idea. But I'll go, you should be resting those feet of yours as much as possible.'

'There's nothing wrong with my feet.'

'Yeah right,' sneered Bruce, 'and I'm Margaret Thatcher. I know frostbite when I see it.'

Ian smiled to himself. It was a nice thought, but totally naïve of him to think that he could hide the state of his feet from someone of Bruce's cold-weather experience.

'Okay, youth, send the Sherpas my regards. I'll monitor the radio in case Lakpa calls,' he said as Bruce prepared to leave the tent.

07:55 – Camp 4

By the time Bruce returned, Ian and Cathy had made considerable progress in making the inside of their tent more shipshape. The remnants of endless cups of tea and coffee had been plastic-bagged. The festering aluminium containers from their boil-in-a-bag meals had been carefully placed in the bottom of a rucksack so that they were ready for the liaison officer to count when they arrived at base camp. Finally the muddle of clothing that had engulfed the tent over the last few days had now been separated into three distinct piles according to ownership.

'Well, that's settled,' said Bruce as he squeezed into the tent. 'The Sherpas are definitely going down in a couple of hours.' Suddenly he did a double-take and started to look around. 'Hey, sorry guys, I thought this was a South African tent, but I must have stumbled into the Taiwanese camp by mistake.' He started to feign leaving.

'Very funny, Herrod,' said Ian. 'Most of it was your rubbish, anyway. Listen, did you tell them about Lakpa and the rescue party?'

'No, I didn't. They obviously had already made up their minds and were determined to go down, so I didn't think it was fair to complicate the issue for them.'

'No, I agree,' Ian said. 'They must be allowed to make their own mountaineering decisions without any pressure from us. We'll wait here for Lakpa's call on our own.'

08:45 – Camp 4

The storm was slowly beginning to abate, although the winds were still very high. Neil came over to the South African camp looking for batteries for his radio and information, as he couldn't talk to any of his other camps. At the same time Stuart arrived again to discuss the missing climbers from his team, so the five climbers squeezed into the two-man tent and shared news.

Stuart explained that Doug Hansen had now been confirmed as dead, although Rob Hall was still alive somewhere below the South Summit. Andy Harris was thought to have gone over the edge of the Lhotse Face and been killed, and he reaffirmed that both Beck and Yasuko had been discovered on the edge of the Kangshung Face and were presumed dead. Makalu Gau and Scott Fischer were still missing, but all the other clients and Sherpas from all three expeditions were safely back in camp. Everyone was amazed that Rob Hall should have survived the night. Then once more the South Africans, together with Neil this time, tried to persuade Stuart to accompany them to fetch the bodies of Beck and Yasuko, but he refused, feeling the attempt to be too futile and dangerous.

While they were talking, Philip came through on the radio.

PHILIP: 'Hello, Ian, this is base camp.'
IAN: 'Hi, Philip, what's up, any news for us from Lakpa?'
PHILIP: 'No, nothing at the moment. We wondered if you have any news for us.'

Ian looked across at Stuart for his permission to break the news of his dead team-mates. Stuart nodded his agreement.

IAN: 'Philip, I can confirm four people missing, definitely presumed dead. Roger so far?'

CATHY:
Missing, presumed dead.
   Dead.
   This wasn't supposed to happen. This isn't what we came here for, what they came here for. Did they have presentiment, when they left for the summit 36 hours ago, that they had less than two days to live?
   This isn't an epic survival drama any more, where everyone escapes at the last minute with various injuries and some great stories to tell round the dinner table in years to come.
   This is it. Over. Forever.

Ian then went on to give base camp the names of those presumed dead, those still missing, and details of the survivors. For the first time the South Africans began to think of these people as fatalities and victims of the mountain. Climbers who would make the slopes of Everest their final resting place. The mood was quiet and sombre in the South African camp 4 after the casualty report-back to base camp. Stuart left to be on his own, while Neil stayed behind for some tea rather than sit in his tent by himself.

> IAN:
> Four missing, presumed dead. Such an easy thing to say. Such a difficult thing to comprehend. I'm sitting here in the morning of our third day at 8 000 metres on Everest, but I don't envy Philip at base camp. Someone has to break the news to the other teams, so I guess that will have to be him. For once I'm glad I'm on the South Col.

09:00 – Base Camp

Once Philip had received Ian's radio report he wrote two notes, one to Rob Hall's team and another to Scott Fischer's. In them he detailed the death reports that he had just received and then, showing tremendous compassion and sensitivity, took them over to the relevant camps. At base camp there was a sense of shock that four climbers had been killed, but there was also a great sense of relief that so many had made it back alive. Some people still held out hope for Scott Fischer and Andy Harris, because they were both such tough, experienced climbers. Everyone was rooting for Rob Hall too. Many of them had never met him, but they had heard his voice on the radio and they knew his friends in base camp.

The mood was frantic yet very subdued. Everyone was rushing around with chores, talkative about the crisis but, unless they were doing something, they were mostly silent, lost in their own thoughts about the dead, and about how many more climbers would die before everyone got off the mountain safely.

As Philip was at Rob Hall's base camp Patrick was left battling to start the generator, which had finally stopped. Without it they didn't have the power to re-charge any radio batteries, which were vital to talk to the climbers on the mountain. Philip shouted instructions to him over the radio, so Patrick was upgraded to an instant mechanic. He cleaned the spark plug, filled the generator with more kerosene, kicked it, pleaded with it, banged it with a rock, and finally it worked. That done, he plundered the South African's substantial medical supplies to add to those being sent up to camp 2 and those being taken to the medical tents that were being set up on the glacier at base camp.

09:30 – Camp 4

The three climbers were resting, gently breathing from their masks, when suddenly a faint, unidentified American voice broke through on the radio.

CALLER: 'We want you to give your radio to...'

The transmission broke up for a few seconds before continuing,

CALLER: '...on the South Col.'

'What the hell was that?' Bruce asked.
  'It's a really faint signal, it's probably our camp 2 radio,' suggested Cathy.
  'You're probably right,' agreed Ian, 'but that radio was left in one of our camp 2 tents. What's a bloody American doing with it?'

IAN: 'Hello, unknown call-sign, this is the South African camp 4, say again.'

Again the voice refused to identify itself, but insisted that the South Africans hand over their only radio to someone they had never heard of on the South Col. The possibility of handing over their only working form of communication to some strangers, who did not even seem to be part of any co-ordinated rescue effort, was instantly dismissed. Ian refused, and asked who was in charge of the rescue operations at camp 2. He was told that it was Mal Duff and Henry Todd, and so he asked to speak to one of them. Mal took over the radio call and confirmed that the South Africans should hold on to their radio as they had provided all the communications thus far and the camp 2 rescue operation was counting on them for the future.
  Henry Todd then came on the radio and requested that the South Africans do a detailed inventory of the sick and injured at camp 4, as well as a head count. He also asked that they stay on the col as long as possible as they were the most reliable communication link. Bruce volunteered to go out to do the inspection, and was joined by Neil.

09:45 – Camp 4

Alone together, Ian looked up at Cathy and smiled.
  'You okay?' he asked
  'Everything being equal, not too bad really,' she answered.

'I told you I know how to show a girl a good time.'

'Listen, Woodall, next time you place advertisements for women in newspapers make sure you keep them to the dubious personal columns,' Cathy countered with a smile.

Ian laughed to himself. He was quite sure that the team could climb Everest based on their sense of humour alone.

The tent door was pulled open to reveal the tired face of Ang Dorje.

'We go down now, Bara Sahib,' he said pointedly.

Ian and Cathy grabbed their jackets as protection against the strong wind, and struggled outside to say goodbye to their Nepalese team-mates. One by one Ian and Cathy embraced and then said goodbye to Pemba, Jangmu and Nawang, leaving Ang Dorje till last.

'Be safe, Didi,' said a tearful Pemba to Cathy.

'Be safe, Pemba Sherpa,' she replied, squeezing his hand.

As the others were saying goodbye, Ang Dorje pulled Ian to one side.

'Bara Sahib, you come down soon. Too long on South Col. You come down today.'

'We'll see you soon, Ang Dorje,' Ian replied, not wanting to tell his friend that Bruce, Cathy and he may still have to go up the mountain rather than down.

Ang Dorje turned away, shaking his head, then stopped and turned to Ian with his finger raised in admonishment.

'Bara Sahib not go with Lakpa,' he said firmly.

Christ, thought Ian to himself, aren't there any secrets on the South Col? Then realising how stupid they'd been in trying to hide something from the Sherpa grapevine, he burst out laughing and placed his arm around his team-mate's shoulder.

'Don't worry, old friend, we'll be careful.'

Ang Dorje smiled, nodded and then turned quickly away to join the others.

Ian and Cathy stood together in the freezing wind, watching their Nepalese friends head towards the top of the Geneva Spur and safety. They both wondered when it would be their turn to leave this most hostile and unforgiving of places.

10:20 – Camp 4

Bruce was gone for about an hour. Even in daylight with the improved weather conditions, moving from tent to tent was still a tricky and chilling business. He looked in on Stuart and gave the New Zealanders six AA batteries so they could power up their dead radio. He then visited Scott Fischer's team, who confirmed that they were all accounted for other than Scott himself, but refused to give any further information. He was cold and tired by the time he rejoined Ian and Cathy, and desperately in need of tea.

Cathy was slowly sipping her milky tea and gazing out across the South Col, when she suddenly noticed climbers moving past the South African tents.

'Ian, there're five Sherpas heading back up the mountain.'

'Damn, is it Lakpa? He hasn't given us any notice,' Ian asked as he squeezed in next to her to look out.

'I don't know what Lakpa looks like, but they're definitely Sherpas, and they're definitely going back up the mountain,' Cathy confirmed.

'Hell, Ian, what's going on?' Bruce asked. 'Are we going up or not?'

'I've no idea, but I'm about to find out,' said Ian, snatching up the radio.

IAN:	'Hello, base camp, this is camp 4, come in, Philip.'
PHILIP:	Philip here, Ian, go ahead.'
IAN:	'Philip, we've just seen five Sherpas heading back up the mountain, but no one's called us. What the hell's going on?'
PHILIP:	'Well, Ian, I was told down here that two of the Sherpas are going to try to find Rob Hall, while the other three are going to look for Makalu Gau and Scott Fischer. When I asked about your involvement, Ian, I was told that the Sherpas would be faster without you, and that you and Bruce would just slow them down. Sorry, bro, but that's just what I've been told.'

Ian and Bruce looked at one another, their rage increasing in levels proportional to the number of times the South Africans had offered to help the other teams, and the number of times they had been ignored.

IAN:	'Philip, have you spoken to anyone who knows what they're doing, who has confirmed this logic?'
PHILIP:	'Roger, Ian, I've spoken to Henry Todd at camp 2, and he agrees that the Sherpas will be faster without you.'

Ian and Bruce fell silent for a few moments. There were few people whose judgement on the mountain they valued more than Henry's.

IAN:	'Philip, let me get back to you, we're a bit annoyed up here.'
PHILIP:	'Roger, Ian, I understand. I'll be on standby.'

Ian sat looking out across the inside of the tent, still clutching the radio in both hands. Bruce slumped back on his rucksack and pulled his South African beanie over his eyes. Cathy knew that when the men were fuming, it was best to let them fume.

'You know what this means?' Ian said in Bruce's direction.

'Aye,' he answered from under his hat. 'We go down now.'

'Absolutely.'

11:00 – Camp 4

Ian, Cathy and Bruce began to pack up their personal equipment. Staying on to attempt the summit was never even considered. The weather remained windy and bitterly cold and it looked as though it could deteriorate at any moment. Oxygen use over the 36-hour period of the storm had seriously reduced their supply and everyone was beginning to feel the draining effect of too long spent at very high altitude. Besides which, the Sherpas were already well on their way back to camp 2, and the South Africans had promised them an equal opportunity of trying for the summit.

IAN: 'Hello, Philip, this is Ian.'

PHILIP: 'Go ahead.'

IAN: 'We're packing up now to start moving down today. However, I don't want to bail out now if we can still be of assistance in the next couple of hours. Please relay to the rescue team at camp 2 that the South African team must start getting down soon, but if there is anything we can do in the near or immediate future, we will stay behind and do it.'

PHILIP: 'Okay, I copy that. I'm going over to Rob Hall's camp now, I can convey this to Mal and Henry at camp 2 from there, and then update them on the situation.'

IAN: 'We'd like a reply as soon as possible because we have to get the hell out of here ourselves.'

PHILIP: 'Okay, Ian, the round trip takes me about 20 to 30 minutes.'

The three companions sat in the now bare camp 4 tent, rucksacks packed, waiting for Philip's reply.

12:00 – Camp 4

By midday it was clear there was nothing else to be done and Bruce and Ian clambered outside to secure the tents as tightly as possible prior to departure.

Moving around the tent, piling rocks on to the snow valances, they were soon shaking with cold. The wind had picked up considerably in the last hour, with the resulting rapid drop in temperature. Spindrift was sweeping across the col and its steep, deadly edges had disappeared into a grey-white haze. The weather, which had been threatening to disintegrate all morning, had finally broken out into yet another Himalayan storm. Just the challenge of finding their way from the camp to the beginning of the fixed ropes on the Geneva Spur, without falling down the Lhotse Face in the process, was becoming greater by the minute. They quickly retreated to the sanctuary of the vacant Sherpa tent, where Ian tried to thaw his numb hands, his face tight and drawn in pain from his frostbitten feet.

He looked up from rubbing his hands and raised his eyebrows at Bruce who quickly shook his head in response to the silent question.

'We left it too late,' said Ian.

'Aye,' Bruce agreed, 'we should've used the stable early morning weather. It's too risky in the afternoon. We know what it's like to get caught between camps 3 and 4 in an afternoon storm.'

'That's for sure,' Ian reflected. After a few moments he summed up the situation. 'So it's going to have to be first thing tomorrow morning or nothing.'

The two men didn't have to spell out to one another what 'or nothing' meant. If they couldn't get away tomorrow morning, they were in for a very, very long stay.

'I'll get a brew on here,' Bruce said. 'You go and tell the youngster.'

CATHY:
Ian crawls back into the tent in a swirl of spindrift, dragging his pack behind him. 'We've missed the window,' he says. 'The weather's turned bad. We'll have to wait and move very early tomorrow morning.'

Oh, really.

I feel a curious lack of interest in this news, combined with a remote sense of relief that I don't have to get up and put in some eight hours of climbing. So much easier just to sit here …

Christ, I have got to pull myself together. This is how people die, by just sitting around and losing interest, their thinking getting slower and slower. Until they aren't thinking. We've been too high, too long.

I start to unpack my rucksack, concentrating hard on each action, reminding myself why I am doing it.

IAN:
We've come to 8 000 metres to climb to the summit of Mount Everest. The weather has denied us that opportunity. We've decided to stay up here to

help others in trouble. To a greater or lesser degree we've made a contribution towards that. But now we've stayed too long. We face a third night and the beginnings of a fourth day in the death zone. The question is not now whether we should have gone down earlier and saved ourselves. It's far too late for that. It's far more simple than that. If the weather allows us to escape tomorrow, we will live; if it doesn't, we will die.

CHAPTER 8

Escape

11 May
12:45 – Camp 4

Ian called down to Philip to give him the news that they were going to stay yet another night at camp 4. Philip and Patrick were devastated. They were utterly exhausted from the nervous energy and lack of sleep of the last 24 hours and couldn't believe that the climbers were going to spend a third night in that godforsaken place, but Philip hid his concern.

PHILIP: 'Okay, Ian, roger that. Do you have enough supplies up there?'
IAN: 'We have enough for tonight, but we'll have to come down tomorrow, no matter what.'
PHILIP: 'Roger, Ian. Do you have any news on the missing climbers?'
IAN: 'Negative, Philip, I'm afraid that there's no sign of the three missing leaders and I'm beginning to become concerned about the five Sherpas who went to look for them.'
PHILIP: 'Yes, I've just come from Rob Hall's camp and that's a major concern. The Sherpas haven't met up with Rob yet, people are talking to him, he's still coherent, but they haven't reached him yet.'
IAN: 'Well, he's certainly a tough old nut, I'll say that for him.'
PHILIP: 'That's for sure.'

15:00 – Camp 4

Bruce, sick of being squeezed into the side of the tent when sharing with the others, had chosen to take the colder but roomier option of staying alone in the vacant tent. He now came over with some food that he had cooked up. Cathy, although not feeling at all hungry, opened up a packet of chicken casserole and ate her way through it from top to bottom, the first time she had ever finished one of these substantial meals. Having eaten it, she felt neither hungry nor full, just the same as before. Bruce left Ian and Cathy to pack away the empty meal containers while he went back to his 'kitchen' tent, promising to return with chocolate pudding and a thermos flask of hot water.

15:25 – Camp 4

Bruce flew through the entrance of Ian and Cathy's tent.

'Beck Weathers is alive!' he announced.

'What do you mean alive?' asked Ian inanely.

'Alive, I mean alive, as in not bloody dead,' Bruce shouted, throwing his beanie into the corner of the tent in disgust.

'But they told us he was dead,' said Cathy.

'I know what they told us, but he's just crawled back into camp on his own, badly frostbitten, but alive nevertheless.'

The climbers sat quietly for a few moments, reflecting on the implications of Bruce's announcement.

'Oh Jesus, I can't believe we left a man for dead,' said Bruce breaking the silence.

'You know we didn't,' Ian replied soberly. 'Without someone who knew where he was, we never would've found him. You know we would've gone out after him if we could.'

'We should've pushed his team-mates harder,' Bruce argued. 'If we'd got to him earlier, he might not've been so badly injured.'

Ian fiddled with the earphones of his Walkman as he agonised over whether to broach the obvious troubling question with Bruce and Cathy. Finally, deciding that it was only a matter of moments before they worked it out for themselves, he looked up at his two closest friends and watched them briefly before speaking.

'I don't suppose there's any sign of Yasuko?'

The import of Ian's question echoed around their small tent like a thunderclap. If Beck had been alive in the early hours of this morning when the South Africans wanted to go out and bring him in, then maybe Yasuko had been alive as well.

'Oh hell,' said Cathy quietly to herself.

Bruce sank his face into his hands and slowly shook his head back and forth. Ian sat quietly with his own thoughts.

The agonised discussion was to continue long into the afternoon and early evening as the team-mates decided to stay together again for a while.

CATHY:
I wonder what it feels like to know that you were left for dead by your team. Or to have the man you left stumble alive into your tent. Just deep relief that you, that he, survived, I guess. Definitely a miracle.

The mountain forces hard choices on us, unpalatable questions about how far you go for your fellow man before you just get the hell out to save yourself. Questions we would probably never have to face up to, had we stayed in the conventional safety of the suburbs.

IAN:
The human spirit is incredible. Having experienced the conditions through which Beck Weathers had kept himself alive, I sit in awe of the will power of the man. But what of Yasuko? I try to think through the question logically, but it's too depressing. I try to drive away any doubts I may have about whether she could've been saved, but that would be too easy, and life's never that simple. The doubts refuse to budge, they're entrenched, perhaps as reminders for the future.

But Beck is alive, the mountain has returned him to us, but keeps three others nevertheless.

16:30 – Camp 4

Cathy announced 'tea ready' and immediately the two men started to extract themselves from their nests of clothing, sleeping bags, oxygen cylinders and masks. Once successfully unbundled, they accepted the warm liquid gratefully. Seeing that everyone was awake, Ian took the opportunity to bring up the subject of whether they should begin thinking of coming back to camp 4 for another attempt on the summit.

'I think it would be best if we don't make any decisions at this stage,' suggested Bruce. 'I think we should simply concentrate on getting ourselves down to base camp safely, and then take some time out to recover and come to terms with what has happened.'

'Makes sense,' said Cathy.

'That works for me,' Ian agreed, who had been hoping that a decision could be put off for as long as possible to allow his feet enough time to recover.

Their conversation was interrupted by Philip breaking through on the radio.

IAN:	'This is Ian, go ahead, Philip.'
PHILIP:	'Ian, we've received news that the three Sherpas who went to look for Scott and Makalu Gau have returned to camp 4. Have you heard the news as well?'
IAN:	'Negative, Philip, we've not been outside for a while. Did they have any luck?'
PHILIP:	'Yes, Ian, they found Makalu Gau and have carried him back to camp 4. He's very badly frostbitten, but he's alive.'

Ian looked across at Cathy and Bruce and the three climbers smiled at one another.

IAN:	'Any news of Scott, Philip?'

There was a pause on the other end of the radio before Philip replied.

PHILIP:	'I'm afraid Scott's dead, bro. I'm really sorry. He was found with Makalu, but the Sherpas couldn't revive him.'
IAN:	'Okay, Philip, I copy that. Listen, let me get back to you a bit later, okay?'
PHILIP:	'Roger, Ian. Base camp standing by.'

Doug Hansen, Andy Harris, Yasuko Namba, and now Scott Fischer. The three South Africans knew their names. In the case of Scott they knew the man himself. Now they were gone.

12 May
02:00 – Camp 4

IAN:
The wind has always been strong, but now it has a whole new intensity, a whole new rage. I lie awake looking at the thin black nylon above me, stretching and straining under the pressure, the flimsy poles bending and cowering in the face of the tremendous onslaught. I think of the tiny particles of ice being whipped horizontally across the col, any one of which could potentially slice through the nylon of our tent like a razor, flinging us abruptly into the heart of yet another storm. I look across at Cathy. Her eyes are fixed firmly on the roof of the tent as well.

We must get up. We must get dressed, ready for any eventuality. Ready for when our tent blows off into Tibet. I sit up, put on my head-torch and begin searching for my boots and jacket. I should call Bruce next door, alert him to the danger. Don't be an idiot, Ian, I admonish myself. He couldn't possibly hear you above the noise of the wind. Anyway, he's sure to be awake, and with his experience he doesn't need you to tell him how much danger we're in. I squeeze up next to Cathy.

'Do you know where your boots are, Caths?' I ask.

'I'm wearing them,' she answers firmly, her eyes still fixed on the vibrating roof.

Satisfied that we've done all we can, I press my sleeping bag up against hers for mutual comfort, and slowly start running my eyes over every inch of tent fabric, looking for the smallest sign of a tear and potential disaster. Sleep is out of the question.

06:00 – Camp 4

IAN:

I don't know what time it is, but I can see the first light of dawn filtering through the seams of the tent roof. Dawn. This is it. Judgement time. What does the weather hold in store for us? Will it be generous and allow us to escape, or will it continue its rage and keep us forever?

But wait, what's that I hear? Silence? Silence. Pure naked silence. The most beautiful sound in the whole world. I don't care what the weather's doing now. It can be snowing for all I care, because I've climbed in snowfall before. There can be a complete whiteout on the mountain but I won't mind, I've navigated in zero visibility before. All I care about is the silence, the total lack of wind. Without the wind, we can climb in anything. I know now that we're going down.

With renewed energy I pull myself upright in my sleeping bag, only to collapse in agonising pain. A fire has been started inside my feet and is blowtorching its way up my legs. Damn, my feet, I'd forgotten all about them. I grimace again with the pain. I guess they're about to keep me reminded for some time to come.

08:30 – Camp 4

CATHY:

Once I've wriggled into my salopettes and jacket, squeezed over my fleece and thermal layers, I pull on gloves, hat, sunglasses, face mask. No skin is left exposed to be blasted by the freezing wind, back with a vengeance.

I crawl outside and stand up to try to pull my rucksack on to my back. The wind almost knocks me off my feet. It has no respect for some of the most expensive Goretex shell clothing in the world but cuts through it as if it is the most fragile of lace. It cuts through the fleece, through the thermals, through my skin, like a knife through melting butter.

Just a few minutes outside and I'm already shaking with cold. Ian's mittened hands are buried deep in his armpits.

Ian and Cathy walked across to Bruce's tent.

'Come on, mate,' shouted Ian against the wind. 'Let's get the hell out of here.'

A gloved hand unzipped the tent flap.

'Hang on a mo,' said Bruce. 'Just going to take a photo of you two yetis.'

The gloved hands fiddled agonisingly slowly with the controls of the Canon.

'Come on, come on,' Cathy muttered.

'Move it, mate,' Ian yelled. 'We're getting hypothermic.'

As soon as they saw Bruce was out of his tent, they began to walk across the rocky col.

Even with reasonable visibility, finding the route off the col was not entirely straightforward. Ian and Cathy squeezed in next to a giant boulder out of the worst of the wind.

'This is where Bruce and I huddled up when we got caught in that storm on our way up,' said Ian. 'But where the hell do we go now? Having arrived in that storm I don't recognise a bloody thing.'

The rocky slopes of the Geneva Spur spread out both above and below them. There was no sign of a trail.

Cathy tried desperately to remember what the col looked like when she first saw it. A crescent moon of tents, with the South African tents at the furthest tip. But now she couldn't see the tents!

'Up,' she said authoritatively, despite the fact that it seemed more logical to go down.

She began to scramble up the loose, rocky slope, hoping desperately that she was right. She didn't want to do any more uphill climbing than she absolutely had to.

Suddenly she stumbled on to the lighter rock of the trail and turned right to follow it round the bend of the Geneva Spur. She and Ian were now walking into the teeth of the wind, their balance constantly thrown off by the sudden gusts. Ian stopped repeatedly to try to re-warm his hands, while Cathy grew ever colder waiting for him. Bruce caught up with them and quickly saw how cold Cathy was becoming.

'Keep moving,' he shouted. 'It'll be calmer as soon as we drop down off the Spur. I'll keep an eye on the youth.'

09:05 – Geneva Spur

IAN:

Step by agonising step I edge towards the start of the fixed ropes. The pain in my feet is unbearable, but I'll bear it anyway. Simple logic really. As we tiptoe away from the South Col behind the back of the weather, it doesn't matter what damage I do to my feet, or how much they hurt, we have to escape back down, and do it now.

At the top of the fixed ropes I stop to put on my crampons, as we're moving from rock on to ice, but as I try to unclip them from my harness, my fingers won't move, they're frozen solid. Bruce sits down in front of me trying to warm my hands between his knees but eventually gives up and has to put my crampons on for me, clipping my safety karabiner on to the fixed rope at the same time. By this time I have lost all feeling in my feet again, pain or otherwise, they've simply become blocks of cement attached to the ends of my legs. At least they don't hurt any more, for what that's worth.

10:00 – Lhotse Face

As soon as they dropped over the edge of the Geneva Spur into the bowl of the Lhotse Face, the climbers were partly sheltered from the wind. Cathy stopped at every changeover on the ropes and squatted down, hands rammed into her armpits, fingers wriggling frantically, trying to keep the blood circulating.

As they continued down, they first passed two American team members on their way up to help Beck Weathers down, and then slowly caught up with the Taiwanese Sherpas who were assisting Makalu Gau down. Makalu had severely frostbitten hands and feet and was being helped with every step, so the South Africans slowed down to stay a rope length behind the Taiwanese in order not to put too much weight on any one specific rope anchor point.

At camp 3 they were offered cups of sweet black tea by a Sherpa from another expedition. The warm liquid slid into them like petrol into an empty tank. After waiting for an hour to let the Taiwanese pull ahead, they continued down slowly, catching them up again near the top of the bergschrund, and then waited while Makalu was lowered to the floor of the Western Cwm. Once he was safely down, the rest of the Taiwanese threw themselves all at once over the lip of the bergschrund, like lemmings over a cliff. Cathy and Ian glanced at each other and laughed. Then it was their turn to lower themselves cautiously over the edge and sink down gratefully into the snow of the cwm.

As they rested against their packs, searching for strength for the long, boring plod down towards camp 2, Neil appeared above them on the lip of the bergschrund. He was dressed in his bright yellow, J&B logo-emblazoned, one-piece climbing suit, resembling a giant banana posing dramatically on the high edge of the 'schrund.

'Have you ever seen a Royal Marine abseil?' he announced dramatically, as he scorned the help of a friction device to control his descent down the rope and instead wrapped the rope around his body. He stepped masterfully off the edge, the rope sliding round his torso. For a few seconds the situation was under control and his sergeant major would have been proud. But then the rope developed a life of its own, sliding off his shoulder, down his arm and up round his neck. Within moments his left arm was trapped above him with the rope wrapped twice round his wrist, while his legs were flailing frantically, trying to get a grip in the ice. Bruce and Ian, never ones to miss an opportunity, began to rag Neil mercilessly.

'Outstanding!' shouted Bruce.

'Bravo, bravo!' chipped in Ian, starting to stand to applaud, but the sharp pain shooting up his legs made him reconsider, so he just lay back and clapped with his arms outstretched in appreciation.

'Do you think he's been taught to do that or is he just a natural?' said Bruce.

'Oh, a natural, a pure natural,' insisted Ian.

'It must take ages to become that good.'

'Years, years.'

Fifteen minutes later Neil had finally untangled himself from the rope, had his boots on solid snow once more and was coughing hopelessly as he tried to get his breath back, while threatening Ian and Bruce with his ice axe as they pleaded with him for his autograph.

11:00 – Base Camp

Patrick was on the satellite telephone, talking to Radio 702 in Johannesburg.

RADIO 702: 'You've been telling us until this latest disaster how much fun it was to be at base camp. What's the mood like now?'

Patrick glanced round the comms tent, at the chaos resulting from two nights of sleeping there, and at the sombre face of Deshun. He was filing from the inside of his sleeping bag, all wrapped up against the cold. He had seen a lot, and experienced a lot, since his arrival four days before.

PATRICK: 'It's certainly different to what it was a few days ago. Then we were so excited about the different people reaching the summit, and the South Africans really looked good, as if they were going to make it as well. We worked around the clock here on the walkie-talkies, on the radios, trying to get the reports up to date. But the whole mood in the camp has changed now. It's almost as if there's a dark cloud hanging over base camp.'

He took a deep breath and then continued.

PATRICK: 'It started with the Taiwanese climber being killed at camp 3, and then Scott Fischer and Rob Hall were in trouble. They are two of the most popular climbers in this area and very, very well known. Our flag is flying at half-mast in honour of the dead.'

Philip walked slowly into the comms tent. His face looked grey and sunken. 'I've just come from Rob Hall's base camp,' he said. He hesitated, breathed in hard, and continued. 'Rob's not answering his radio.'
Patrick and Deshun stared at him in silence. They all knew what that meant. The second night out at 8 700 metres had been too much for Rob. The great storm had taken a fifth life. The mood of gloom deepened. The first helicopter of the day buzzed over base camp. Everyone assumed it would be a rescue helicopter, but it turned out to be a group of TV journalists filming base camp.
'There's a lot of anger among the other expeditions,' Deshun reported. 'They can't believe that journalists can be buzzing about filming in the middle of this crisis. It seems so callous.'
Every satellite telephone in base camp was ringing non-stop as news organisations from all over the world tried to get details of the tragedy, but each one seemed to be interested only in news of climbers from their own country. Patrick filed reports to Radio 702 but stayed out of the way of the other teams. He knew that the feeling was intensely anti-press.

13:00 – Camp 2

The three slow and desperately tired climbers finally reached camp 2 and slumped down outside their tents, gratefully accepting milky tea from Pemba. As Bruce and Cathy quickly pulled off their heavy boots to release the feet that had been trapped in them for so long, Ian looked at his own extremities with reluctance. He knew that to take off his boots meant confronting the damage that he was sure had been done to his toes over the last three days. At last, he cautiously undid them, pulling the plastic shells off agonisingly slowly to try to avoid hurting the tender toes. The nails of his two big toes were midnight black, with several of the other toes showing signs of damage. Each of the three stared at Ian's feet in silence, wondering what they meant for his chances of another attempt.

> IAN:
> I look down at my toes and my heart sinks. Not perhaps as bad as I had expected, but bad nevertheless, and I still have to walk all the way back down to base camp tomorrow. Will they heal in time? Will there be another time?

18:00 – Camp 2

As the cold evening drew in, Bruce, Ian and Cathy were sitting in their sleeping bags, finishing off the last of the butterscotch pudding. Philip had radioed earlier to tell them about the loss of Rob Hall. So much had happened to the team since they were here last, but none of them felt like talking; they were just sitting there, enjoying the warmth of each other's company before they could finally, for the first time in three days, look forward to a blissful night's sleep.

13 May
07:30 – Base Camp

Patrick watched the medical helicopters coming in one by one. Then he saw the tiny army helicopter that would attempt to retrieve the two climbers from the top of the icefall, Taiwanese leader Makalu Gau and American Beck Weathers, both with severe frostbite. They had been manhandled down the Lhotse Face and Western Cwm by rescue teams, but to lower them through the icefall would be very difficult and extremely dangerous. Nepalese army officer Lieutenant-Colonel Madan was going to attempt to take his helicopter to over 6 000 metres in what would be the highest helicopter rescue ever performed on Everest.

Patrick watched the helicopter flying up over the hummocks of the icefall, and then disappearing out of sight with its turbines whining from pushing itself to the absolute limit. It seemed like a tiny mosquito among the mountains, and just as vulnerable. But a little while later it reappeared and, to great cheers from base camp, flew off down the valley towards Kathmandu.

08:30 – Western Cwm

CATHY:
I plod slowly down the Western Cwm, feeling thoroughly depressed. It is a full two weeks since we walked up this valley. Two weeks in time and an eternity in experience. The mountain is changing as the season progresses. The rising temperatures are revealing more and more crevasses and making the entire mountain increasingly unstable.

I plug into my Walkman, to try to escape my depression. The overture to Verdi's *Nabucco* comes pouring into my head, the glorious music like an audio version of the visual beauty around me. Ian is moving ahead of me, desperately slowly, stopping often to rest. I am glad of the excuse to prolong our time in the cwm.

I drink in the views, the icy magnificence of Everest and Nuptse, trying to imprint each angle on my mind. I am desperately afraid that this is the last time I will see them. I want to try again, so much, so very much.

I am deeply frustrated that we should have been stopped by the weather. I still don't know if I can reach the summit of Everest. But let it be my own limits that stop me, not some external force. Let it be technical difficulty, physical weakness, but not the weather. With my limits still unknown, I want to go out further, in search of them. I am delighted to have reached 8 000 metres. But how much further could I go if I had the opportunity?

Opportunity may be hard to come by. Ian's slow, stumbling gait gives me little confidence. I don't know what Bruce thinks. And there are rumours that the Nepalese may even close the mountain completely after all the fatalities.

I run through all the good, logical reasons not to try once more; I try to put aside my aching gut desire to return, in order to consider the problem rationally. Nothing rings true. The weather may well be the final arbiter, that or the rest of my team giving up. But if the chance is there, I want it.

11:25 – Base Camp

In the icefall the great blocks were beginning to topple over. At one point the safety rope disappeared under a giant chaos of ice, only to re-emerge several metres later. Once down on the Khumbu Glacier, the team found that the glacial melting had changed the appearance of the glacier completely, much of the ice round the camp having disappeared.

But some things were unchanged. Philip was sitting on a giant rock, at the top of the last slope up to the camp. It was a good place to wait because from there he could see almost all the way up to camp 1 and right across to the other camps on the glacier. He thought he could see the climbers weaving their way down through the icefall because their red rucksacks made them so distinctive. It seemed to him in his lone vigil that it took them almost as long to get from the bottom of the icefall to the camp, as it did to get down the icefall itself. As they walked up that last hill, all three looked absolutely shattered and very pale. He walked across to meet them.

'Bruce, my bro, hell it's good to see you,' said Philip on the verge of tears. 'Cathy,' he continued, unable to find any other words but giving each of them a giant hug.

Then he met Ian. The two brothers faced one another again after so much had happened between them.

'Welcome home, bro,' said Philip quietly.

Ian smiled and nodded in return, and they shook hands.

Patrick stood awkwardly behind Philip. He had spent the last four days filing dramatic reports on the status of the South African team, but this was going to be the first time he had actually seen them face to face in Nepal. The last time he had met them was in a restaurant in Rosebank, north of Johannesburg. Now all that seemed so far away.

'Would you like me to carry your pack?' he asked Cathy nervously, trying to be polite.

She stared at the young, slender reporter. She had just spent three nights at 8 000 metres and two days descending Everest.

'I've carried it this far. I think I can manage the last 300 metres,' she replied.

Patrick retreated, feeling rather insulted.

Ian waved a weary greeting in his direction. He looks in a very, very bad way, Patrick thought. He was amazed that Ian had made it back to the camp without collapsing. There is no way they will go back, thought Patrick. They are just too tired. This expedition is over.

CHAPTER 9

Unfinished Business

13 May
15:30 – Base Camp

The three exhausted climbers slumped down next to the mess tent, their faces burnt and haggard, their backs still bent from their heavy loads. Bruce and Cathy watched with anticipation as Ian gingerly removed his plastic boots to reveal his pink and black toes. Shankar brought him a large bowl of warm, salty water and Ian gratefully and gently immersed his feet.

'You look the picture of the sahib relaxed at base camp,' Cathy commented. Then she reconsidered. 'No, actually you don't. No self-respecting sahib would ever allow himself to end up looking that awful.'

'Thanks, youth, but you're no oil painting yourself,' Ian replied defiantly. 'Anyway, this idle banter is all very well, but how am I supposed to get to my tent?'

Cathy fetched Ian a pair of dry socks and Philip shouldered his pack and carried it across the glacier to his tent.

'This is a one-off treat, mind you,' Cathy warned. 'Don't even think of expecting this on a regular basis.'

'What? I thought you'd finally started treating me as befitting a leader of my stature.'

16:00 – Base Camp

CATHY:
I sit down on the floor of my tent, among the chaotic debris I abandoned two weeks ago. A pile of mail lies on the floor, blue aerograms, brown

parcels. I expected to be excited to receive news of home, to catch up on events in South Africa, but I feel a strange reluctance to open them.

I put it off by first unpacking my rucksack and then peeling off the thermal underwear that I have now worn, without interruption, for 14 days and nights. The white top has been reduced to a grubby grey, the leggings a shapeless mass of blue. My skin underneath is pasty pale, but seems to revive after a smart rubdown with some wet wipes.

At last I turn to the letters and slowly tear them open. I find them unsettling rather than comforting. Home seems so far away and news of it so alien, so irrelevant, to the experiences I have just been through. Despite the two days of climbing behind me, I feel suddenly restless, confined by the tiny tent, by the camp.

I wander off down the glacier without plan or direction, and find myself following the standard trail. It has changed dramatically since I walked it last, now tracking the moraine on one side rather than crossing the ice. A lot has changed since I walked it last, including the facts that we have reached 8 000 metres and six people have died. I battle to find a perspective on these two things, turning helplessly in the deep fog of melancholy that engulfs me. I reach an iced-over lake, with giant icicles hanging into it from the surrounding overhanging cliffs. I sit down on a boulder and throw rocks at the ice, trying to break through to the water beneath.

I don't know what the point of this is. It just seems to pass the time.

IAN:
There's a unique feeling about being home, wherever or whatever that may be. My home now is a small nylon tent perched precariously on the rock and ice of the Khumbu Glacier, and I love it. I love the security. I love the gentle afternoon sun filtering through the flysheet, dancing in soft yellow colours off the shining groundsheet and then warming my very sorry and painful toes before being gratefully absorbed by the rest of my tired and aching body. I love the deep, sweet taste of the oxygen-enriched air, and I love the fluffy smell of my toiletry bag sitting so expectantly in the corner. But most of all I love the peacefulness. No wind, no storms, no decisions to be made, just being able to lie back and search for the feeling of excitement that this wild and remote place never fails to evoke in me. To be able to smile quietly with pride and humility as I recall what our little team has faced together, standing united in purpose and spirit, never failing in our duty to one another.

Yes, it's true that my feet are a mess, and there are hard decisions for all of us to make in the near future, but if we are the sum of our actions, I will sleep well tonight. Thankful, proud and well.

20:00 – Base Camp

After supper Bruce and Philip retreated to the warmth of the kitchen with a bottle of red wine and some whisky. They offered both to the Sherpas who were congregated around the kerosene stoves.

'We must have a celebration,' said Bruce. 'Because we have all returned safely from the mountain.'

Ang Dorje first tasted the wine and then the whisky, pulling a face at both.

'No, no, Mr Bruce. This is not good stuff. We must celebrate properly,' he replied.

He fished around in one of the hessian sacks lying against the kitchen wall and pulled out a bottle of semi-opaque white liquid.

'This is what we need to party,' he declared, holding the bottle up for all to see. 'It makes you climb much better, Mr Bruce. A little of this and you will be climbing Nepali speed.'

'No ways, not *rakshi*, Ang Dorje,' exclaimed Bruce, laughing. 'I know what kind of headache I'll get from wine and whisky, but that stuff would knock me out for a week.'

Pemba reached out diffidently for the whisky bottle in order to try the westerners' tastes. He took a deep draught and began to cough and splutter. Muffled laughter came from the Sherpanis who were hovering shyly on the edge of the kitchen. They buried their faces in their multi-coloured wraps, only their sparkling eyes peering out at the handsome Pemba. The women had been making their way up the trail over the last few days to check on the safety of their men after the great storm.

'So, Pemba, what will you be doing after the party ends?' asked Bruce wickedly.

Pemba, abashed, found retreat in the *rakshi* bottle, while Ang Dorje teased the Sherpanis in a rapid rattle of Nepalese. Then he turned to Bruce with a shrug and a sly smile.

'The women come up the trail to look after us. Now we must look after them.'

Philip, meanwhile, had been regarding Ang Mu's kerosene burner with an intent expression. He turned to Bruce. 'So, do you fancy a bacon sandwich? I found some bacon in the hill food barrels while you were away.'

Bruce's eyes lit up. 'Bacon and fried eggs?'

'Bacon, fried eggs and baked beans?' Phil offered.

'Bacon, fried eggs, baked beans and sausages?' Bruce suggested.

'With fried toast!' Phil concluded triumphantly.

Kindred souls in search of a huge, greasy fry-up, they started to rummage through the kitchen for ingredients. The Sherpas watched in tolerant amusement at the foibles of the westerners, as the two men set about frying their precious comestibles on the huge kerosene cooker. Ang Mu watched with puzzled fascination at this strange use of his kitchen.

'Most satisfactory,' announced Bruce indistinctly through a mouth full of 'breakfast'. 'Shame that everyone else has gone to bed.'

'Oh well,' Phil said, helping himself to another slice of toast, 'we'll just have to eat it all ourselves.'

14 May
07:30 – Base Camp

Bruce was woken from a succulent dream of another huge British breakfast by the distant throb of a helicopter. Grabbing his camera, he crawled out of his tent to find Cathy already standing outside, scanning the valley.

'It sounds like a helicopter but I can't see anything,' she said.

They watched the glacier together.

'There it is, coming in just above the valley floor,' Bruce shouted, pointing to his right.

'They fly very low.'

'They have to. We're over 5 000 metres here, close to the height limit for helicopters. You'll see they won't even turn their engines off when they land to collect the casualties.'

They watched as the big Everest Air helicopter circled over base camp before coming to land on the makeshift helipad near the Yugoslavian camp. As they were watching the evacuation, they saw a trail of laden yaks moving past their camp on their way down the valley.

'I guess that's either Scott's or Rob's team moving out,' said Bruce.

'Yes. It's funny to think that within a week at the most they'll be back to hot showers and real beds. Food served on china plates, with all the variety of a restaurant menu. Back with all their friends and family, and all the comforts of first-world living,' Cathy reflected.

'And cars, and bank overdrafts, and pollution, and urban stress,' countered Bruce. 'But there is something to be said for the notion of a hot shower.'

They sat in silence, thinking. They could have all the luxuries of life as well, if they just agreed to pack it in and go home.

CATHY:
Up or down? Mountain or home? Silly question. I've known the answer ever since Bruce first said we shouldn't make any decisions. I was appalled that they could even think that we might not go back. My immediate gut

instinct is to go again. We got so high, coped so well. We've put so much into all this. We can't just walk away now. Not if we have any energy left at all. I try to think it through logically, to see if my gut reaction is not irrational.

The risk – well, that is no worse than it was two weeks ago, despite the deaths. It was always risky. Now it has been brought home to us exactly what the word 'risky' means. It means people die. But the odds haven't got any worse.

The weather – yes, it is unusually unstable but all the more reason that it might change in the next few weeks. Imagine if we all went home and Everest basked in idyllic quiet for the rest of the season.

The hard work – frankly, the thought of climbing once again up the Lhotse Face, across the Western Cwm, fills me with horror. But to turn away now is to negate all the effort I have already sunk into this project.

I want to try again. But do the others?

09:00 – Base Camp

Ian hobbled carefully into the mess tent as the others were making their way through omelettes and toast. The climbers are all looking a lot better than yesterday, thought Patrick, but he realised that that wasn't much of a recommendation as they looked awful then. He was dying to ask Ian what the team intended to do, but he bit his tongue and went back to the last scraps of his omelette.

Ian worked his way silently through several cups of coffee, before lifting his head in that significant way the others had come to know preceded an 'announcement'.

'We, the climbers, haven't made a decision yet about whether or not we'll be returning to the mountain for another attempt. We decided at camp 4 that we would give ourselves a while at base camp to recover and to think through everything that has happened. We will, of course, let you know you as soon as we've made a decision.'

IAN:
Some of the other teams are off home, but they haven't given up. They aren't running away from the mountain. They've just decided it's time to call somewhere else home, and once base camp doesn't feel like home any more, it's definitely time to move on. But it's still my home, and I want to stay. I don't know what Cathy and Bruce will decide. I don't know if I'll be fit enough to go back up the mountain, but for now at least, I'm home.

Later that morning Patrick sidled up to Philip.

'So what do you think Ian's announcement meant?' he asked.

'Oh, I'm sure it means that they're intending to try again,' Philip answered with a grin. 'I can't see Ian, or any of them for that matter, giving up now.'

'How do you feel about that?' Patrick asked curiously. 'Haven't you had enough of the stresses, strains and boredom of base camp?'

'Not at all. I've carved out a routine for myself here. There's so much technical work to do that it keeps me fully occupied. I've never felt bored. In fact I've barely had a chance to read a book since I got here. How about you?'

'Oh, I'd love them to try again. I know a good radio story when I see one and this will be great. But it doesn't seem to me that they're going to make it. They all look so tired, although they perked up wonderfully after a cup of tea yesterday. And the weather seems so bad. I've been chatting to some of the other expedition leaders like Mal Duff and Henry Todd and they're saying it's a very bad year on Everest and it would be better if everyone packed up and went home.'

'Oh no, I hope not,' said Deshun, who had been listening. 'Not now, not just when I can finally join them.' She sighed despondently. 'But there's not much I can do. I'm still fresh, I could go up the hill any time, but I don't know what it's like to have spent all that time up there and then have to decide if you really want to do it again.'

Patrick walked away, little more enlightened than he had been when he woke up that morning. He noticed Bruce sitting on a rock outside his tent, dressed in clean green socks and blue thermals, his mountain clothing spread out around him to dry in the sun. He sat, chin on his knees, staring up at the mountain, unmoving. As Patrick approached him, Bruce looked up and smiled.

'There's no bloody way I'm not going back up that mountain,' he said with a laughing voice but deadly serious eyes.

But what happens if the rest of the team don't agree? wondered Patrick.

The unanswered question hung over base camp all day. That afternoon Patrick spoke to Chris Gibbons on Radio 702 in Johannesburg.

PATRICK: 'The climbers came into base camp yesterday looking very, very tired but in good spirits, and today they're kind of hopping all over the place full of energy. They do seem eager to go back up again, but I don't want to jump to any conclusions.'

CHRIS: 'Patrick, what's the general mood like in base camp at the moment?'

PATRICK: 'The mood is one of exhaustion, really, Chris. Since this Friday all kinds of rescue operations have been going on around the clock, trying to get people off the mountain. We are still waiting to have one casualty air-lifted out of base camp and it seems that he might have to go tomorrow morning. There's a problem with helicopters. Really everyone is exhausted emotionally and physically. A lot of climbers have retreated into their tents, listening to their music and just trying to stay away from the general crowd. Then, at the same time, we have a lot of climbers back in base camp who were slightly injured. Once they've recovered, they'll be making their way back home.'

IAN:
It's decision time, Ian. Our Nepalese team-mates, our base camp support of Philip, Patrick and Deshun, our cooks and kitchen helpers, our porters and yak herders, our families and sponsors back in South Africa, everyone is waiting for our decision. Up or down, the decision has to be made.

Does the expedition have the logistical reserves for another attempt? Yes, I think so. I'd originally planned for multiple summit attempts, although I hadn't expected to spend so long at 8 000 metres, so I think I can work out a logistical plan that will give us another try for the summit. I know that the Sherpas want to try again, but will Cathy and Bruce be keen? My gut feeling is yes, but I can't know for sure.

But what about you, Ian, do you want to go back up that mountain again? I know the answer is yes, I've always known it. It doesn't matter why I want to go back, so I've never bothered to ask myself the question. I guess if I have to ask myself why, then I'll never understand! But will my body, and my feet in particular, allow me another chance? I don't know. I won't know until I go back up and find out.

So, I want to go back up as far as my body will allow, the Sherpas want to go back up, we have the logistics for another attempt, so it's all down to Cathy and Bruce. If they want to go, then we'll attempt Everest together; if they don't, then I'll go on my own with the Sherpas. In either event, we'll still be a team.

16:00 – Base Camp

Late that afternoon Ian called Bruce and Cathy into the communications tent.

'We need to make a decision about what we're going to do,' said Ian sternly. 'We haven't talked about it up until now, but the time has come to discuss it, to think through the implications of what it means to try again, or to give up and return to South Africa.

'Now, I don't know whether you two think we should discuss it together and reach a joint decision, or whether you each want to make your own choice, and then we'll discuss those, and see who wants to do what.'

As Ian continued to talk, he watched them watching him. When he'd finished his 'opening statement', Cathy rolled her eyes at Bruce, who smiled in return: they were both amused by Ian's sudden assumption of the formal leadership role and his complex discussions of the decision both of them had already made.

'I know what I'm going to do,' said Bruce.

'So do I,' added Cathy.

'I'm going back up.'

'Me too.'

Ian looked quickly at both of them, rather startled by their sudden and firm response.

'Right, well, that's settled then,' he concluded. 'I was going back up anyway, even if I had to go on my own, but it's great that we'll be climbing together again. I'll go and have a chat with Ang Dorje.'

> CATHY:
> God, we're committed now. I'm so glad we all wanted to go again. But I wonder if it really is the most sensible thing to do. What if we just spend another week sitting at camp 2 watching the wind howl? Or worse still, toil all the way up to camps 3 and 4 and have to retreat yet again? When we could have gone home and been lounging around in luxury. We must be mad. We probably are. I guess you have to be a bit crazy to want to do this.
>   And we are going to do it! I'm sure we'll get a break. The weather can't continue to be this bad. A window in the weather has to appear sometime.

16:20 – Base Camp

Ian ducked out of the tent after making the decision to go back up the mountain with Bruce and Cathy and saw the five Sherpas sitting pensively waiting on the large boulder outside Ang Dorje's tent. They knew that the decision had been made but were unsure as to its outcome. Seeing the five of them sitting there with such serious expressions etched on their faces, nervously fingering their South African beanies, Ian couldn't resist the temptation to tease them. Putting on the most forlorn and depressed expression he could muster, he walked towards his Nepalese team-mates. As soon as they saw him, the five Sherpas knew that their expedition was over. They would be leaving base camp with the other expeditions and their chance of reaching the summit was gone. To a man they were moved to tears. Ang Dorje stood up and came forward slowly to meet Ian, unable to look him directly in the eye.

Suddenly the collective hangdog expressions of his team-mates were too much for Ian to bear and he began to laugh. The Sherpas looked up for a few moments, confused by the sudden change in their leader's mood. Then, as they realised that they'd been fooled, broad smiles spread across their dark round faces, white teeth flashed in the afternoon sun, and they began to shout and laugh and punch each other with open excitement.

'Bara Sahib very tricky,' Ang Dorje said to Ian, wagging a finger in his face.

15 May
11:00 – Base Camp

The next morning Ian was speaking to John Robbie and Dan Moyane live on Radio 702 about the team's decision to go up the mountain again. The talk-show hosts were fascinated by the psychology behind the climbers' decision.

JOHN: 'Ian, we hear there's some opposition to further attempts on the mountain after the disasters. That some of the people at base camp feel it's not the right thing to do. How do you feel about that?'

IAN: 'To be honest, I've not heard that at all. It wouldn't surprise me though, because, as you can imagine, there's a lot of shock and emotional trauma in base camp. As far as we're concerned, however, we were unanimous in our decision and our base camp support team were thrilled. Our sirdar actually came to me with a sparkle in his eye, waiting for the decision, and when I told him we were going to go up again, he and the rest of the Sherpas were very excited.'

JOHN: 'Ian, having been so close to the disaster of the storm, don't you feel that going back is just tempting fate?'

IAN: 'I think you're tempting fate as soon as you set foot on the mountain. But then again you're also tempting fate as soon as you cross a busy road. So yes, we are tempting fate to a certain degree, but we also came here to do a job. To do a job for our sponsors, for our country, for the Nelson Mandela Children's Fund and, obviously, for ourselves, and we would really like to see it through if we get suitable weather.'

DAN: 'Ian, you say you have a job to do following the disaster of the weekend, but no job is worth your life. Have you thought about that?'

IAN: 'Very much so, Dan. We've lost friends and acquaintances, so it's something we think about all the time. But what would they want us to do? I'm quite sure they'd want us to finish the job, not only for ourselves, but for them as well.'

JOHN: 'When you make your attempt on the summit, you've told us it will depend on the weather. Will you be particularly conservative? Tell us about a possible decision to call off an attempt, even if you are close to the summit.'

IAN: 'Well, it's very much a personal decision as to whether you turn round or whether you press on. Some people do it by the hour. Some people do it by the distance they've travelled. Other people say "We'll go to the top no matter what." It's true that we've got a job to do, but we also have friends and families we'd like to return to. So there's a definite balance between having enough determination to get to the summit, and probably having even more determination to actually forgo it and come back safely.'

John and Dan then spoke to Cathy, still trying to understand how the climbers could face returning to the mountain.

DAN: 'What are your thoughts at the moment, Cathy, after having made this decision, after all the drama, the disasters that we've heard about over the weekend?'

CATHY: 'The tragedy is very sobering. It really makes you think about why you do it and about the kind of risks you're taking. But I think, in the end, it simply leaves us, as a climbing team, with a more profound respect for the mountain. It leaves us very fit and very acclimatised. And having seen some of the very unfortunate episodes of bad luck that have happened to other climbers, I think we'll be more cautious, more level-headed, and that's probably improved our own chances.'

JOHN: 'Isn't it a bit selfish to go ahead if you're going to put your families through all this again?'

CATHY: 'I think this is something that has come to light because Rob Hall and others were unfortunately killed on the mountain, but this is a part of the reality of high-altitude mountaineering. It's a high-risk activity, and no responsible climber would've left South Africa, or any other country, without talking very seriously with their loved ones about it. This is what we did. I talked to my parents and boyfriend about the implications of what I was going to do, how they felt about it, and about the risks I was going to take.

They understood what I was doing. I agree it must be very, very hard for them, but I believe that they do understand what I'm doing, and they support me in giving it another go.'

JOHN: 'Cathy, is the team working well together?'

CATHY: 'Definitely, John. One of the reasons Ian, Bruce and I make such a good team is that everybody is in control of what they're doing themselves, but all the time we're watching out for each other. This is very important, because any of us could get tired or hypothermic very quickly, and so the other two need to be there all the time to help and be aware of what's going on. That's the strength of the South African group compared with some of the commercial expeditions. In the commercial expeditions each person has individually paid a lot of money to join, whereas we're a tight-knit group with a common focus. We're trying to get the whole team to the summit and back, so we're acting and thinking as a responsible unit, not as individuals going for a personal goal.'

CATHY:

Having finished on the radio, I stretch out on a rock to soak up the sunlight. I find the apparent horror of the radio staff at our trying again rather ludicrous. No one would expect climbers never to climb on Everest again. So what difference does it make if it is this year or next? I guess for them the news that people actually die doing this activity comes as a shock. Maybe they thought the talk of the danger was just part of the media hype around the event. So now they seem to find our acceptance of these events incomprehensible. Whereas for us, certainly for me, it had always been a reality. I've faced death on mountains before and with people who were a lot closer to me.

Part of me is excited to have the opportunity to try again, part of me grimly resigned to the effort and discomfort that the attempt will entail. One thing that excites me is that I finally feel an equal part of the team. The storm, for all its tragedies, did us the world of good in pulling us together as a team. Lying jammed together, the three of us in a two-man tent, trapped by extreme conditions, broke down what barriers remained. It increased my trust, both in Bruce and Ian, and in myself. I realise that my isolation was to a large extent my fault, founded in my own uncertainty and therefore my reticence to push myself forward in the company of the others.

I resolve to be pushier in future.

I have been warming up a carefully hoarded Bar One inside my jacket. The trouble with chocolate is that it gets so cold and so hard that it is like biting into a brick. And Bar Ones have been in short supply since the start of the expedition. Now the far less desirable Lunch Bars predominate. So a warm Bar One is a definite catch.

I solemnly unwrap it and eat it in honour of my new resolution.

Patrick was still trying to get the measure of these strange climbing types who lay at the heart of his story. He found Cathy quite unlike the giggly Deshun, who was always ready with a joke and a smile. Cathy was very quiet, friendly to him, but not about to have any great heart-to-hearts with a stranger. She tended to keep to herself.

He felt that Bruce was wary of him at first, sussing out his credibility as a journalist. Then one night Bruce came up to him, after making a phone call to London, and shook his hand.

'Your reports are being put out on the Internet and my girlfriend, Sue, is reading them in London. She's says you're doing a great job.'

Patrick knew then that he'd passed the test.

Ian was the one Patrick spent most time with, as he was constantly approaching him for information. He was also the figure Patrick was most curious about. He found Ian to be a stubborn, focused character. He was a very analytical person, someone who always seemed to be calculating what happens next. He seemed to be a hundred steps ahead of everyone else as he explained the logistic implications of another summit attempt.

'It's more than just deciding to go back up the mountain. It's about food supplies, it's about weather conditions, it's who else is going up, it's oxygen, it's the amount of money we have left. We'd only been expecting to use oxygen for about 36 hours, but in fact we've used it on and off for over 60 hours, so our supplies are pretty thin. Even if we manage to get some more from other teams, it still needs to be moved all the way up the mountain to our top camp. I may be able to buy seven bottles from Henry Todd that are already at the British camp 4, but we may have to sell something in return. We've also used up our supplies of food and gas on the mountain, so I need to do an inventory of what is in base camp as well as the higher camps, and then work out the logistics of moving the additional equipment up the mountain. The medical supplies are in disarray as well.'

16 May
12:30 – Base Camp

Cathy and Bruce sat together outside their tents, soaking in the warm midday sunshine. 'Trekker alert,' announced Bruce, idly pointing to a group of tiny figures stumbling over the glacier in the distance.

They smiled at each other as they watched the group's slow and rather wobbly progress towards them.

'Poor sods,' said Bruce. 'We're so well acclimatised now that I'd almost forgotten what it felt like to be at 5 400 metres for the first time.'

'I wonder if they're one of ours?' Cathy said. 'They seem to be homing in on us.'

'Are we due one?' Bruce queried.

'I think Ian was saying that our third support trek should be here soon,' Cathy answered, stretching lazily and then rolling over to let the sun beat down on her back.

18:00 – Base Camp

Cathy was right, and that evening the climbers and trekkers from South Africa joined together on the glacier for a huge dinner. They crammed themselves into two tents, joined end to end, with a long, metal dining table down the middle, along which an array of metal pots were passed, containing pasta, stir-fry, meat pies, pizza and other high-altitude delicacies. After weeks of being surrounded by English and American people, the buzz of South African accents made Cathy feel rather nostalgic. Maybe she should have decided to go home after all.

The South Africans were joined for dinner by Henry Todd, who was now alone in his base camp as all his climbers had either gone home or back up the mountain.

'They won't make it,' he said of his climbers, his tired eyes peering out from the depths of a huge red down jacket. 'The season is over. The weather this year has been terrible and there's unlikely to be another window in the weather before the monsoon hits us at the end of May.'

'Well, we're thinking of giving it another try,' said Bruce quietly.

'Then for God's sake be careful,' he replied. 'I've seen too many friends lost this season already. I don't think it's worth the risk with this weather. Call it quits and try again another year.'

After the deaths of Scott Fischer and Rob Hall, Henry was now the most experienced Everest leader on the mountain, and his opinion was sobering.

Equally worrying was Ian's absence from the table. He'd been in his tent all day, dozing, battling against a lingering chest infection. Bruce lent across the table to Cathy.

'Have you seen Ian today? Is he coming to supper?' he asked.

'I saw him briefly this afternoon. He looked terrible and said he'd been sleeping all day.' She hesitated. 'It's not a great time to be getting so sick.'

'No, that's for sure. We've ten days left at the most, and we need to be able to move as fast as possible as soon as the weather stabilises. But he's a tough old sod and I'm sure he'll be there when the time comes.'

Ian:
I wrap my arms tightly around my chest, trying desperately to ease the burning in my throat and lungs. Every breath is torture and the thought of an impending cough sends shivers of panic down my spine. The dreaded Himalayan chest infection, unflinching in its determination to drain every ounce of strength from its hapless victim, me! My feet hurt. My chest is on fire. My head is throbbing with fever and I can hardly breathe. Christ, I'm a wreck!

17 May
15:00 – Base Camp

That afternoon Cathy and Deshun sat together in the mess tent, drinking tea, eating butter biscuits and going through Deshun's kit list for her first day's climbing the following morning. Boots, crampons, gaiters, fleece, Goretex, harness, jumars, figure of eight, thermos flask, suntan lotion, hat, glasses, sleeping bag, sleeping mats, gloves … the list stretched on and on, but finally they had covered everything they could think of.

'Have I got everything I need? Where am I going to put it all?' Deshun worried.

'You'll be fine,' Cathy laughed, remembering her own mixture of excitement and nerves the night before her first day on the mountain. 'How are you feeling?'

'Just so excited,' said Deshun enthusiastically. 'I've been waiting for this for so long. I really feel ready now. I can't wait to get off the glacier and on to the mountain.'

'It's funny about the glacier,' said Cathy. 'This morning I took five of the trekkers who were feeling the strongest on a guided tour up to the foot of the icefall. It's the first time I've really stopped to look at the glacier. Previously I've always either walked up it early in the morning, psyched for the icefall and the Western Cwm, or walked down it, totally focused on base camp, just waiting for the glacier to pass so that it would all be over. Anyway, one of the trekkers had a film canister with him that he said contained a message from his dad and that he wanted to leave as high up the mountain as possible. So I offered to take it with me and leave it as high as I could.'

She grinned at Deshun. 'So how high do you think we're going to get, girl?'

'As high as we possibly can!' replied Deshun confidently.

Ian stuck his head into the tent.

'Cut the chit-chat, women,' he coughed, 'I seem to be the only one who ever does any real work around here.'

He quickly ducked back outside to avoid being hit by a variety of biscuits that were thrown in his direction.

'You can talk,' Cathy called after him. 'You've spent the last 48 hours snuggled up in bed.'

'I've been doing all the planning,' protested Ian, slipping back in the tent and pulling up a stool. 'I'm an artist. I need time to contemplate.'

'Yes, right. So what did you come up with?'

Ian shuffled his stool up to the table and pulled out a notebook and pencil from inside his down jacket, before doubling over as his hacking cough swept through him once again. He looked up sheepishly, his face flushed and his eyes streaming with the effort, as he slowly began to regain his composure and then outline the movement plan for the next few days.

'The weather certainly seems to have stabilised down here, so we'll all move up tomorrow from base camp to camp 2. To really know what's happening higher, though, we'll just have to go up there and see, so if it's looking good when we get to camp 2, we'll try to push straight on the next day for camp 3 and then camp 4. If not, we'll wait at camp 2 for it to improve. From camp 2 we only need a 72-hour window to make it to the summit and back, so it's much better to wait there than here.'

Ian then turned to Deshun. 'Are you sure you still want to do this?'

She grinned. 'There's no chance in hell you guys are going to leave me here.'

'Okay, but you'll just have to be careful, keeping a close eye on yourself for any signs of altitude sickness. It's a rushed programme because we don't have a lot of time left before the monsoon arrives, so take it at your own pace and see how high you can get. But don't worry about it too much, we'll always be around if you need help.'

Cathy watched Ian as he talked to Deshun. His face was drawn and sickly pale beneath the sunburnt skin. *If anyone is going to need help, it's probably you*, she thought.

IAN:
Tomorrow morning we leave base camp to go back up the mountain for the last time. It's our final chance of reaching the summit this season. I think the expedition has a good chance of reaching the top. I don't think I've got a prayer. The way I feel right now it'll be a miracle if I reach camp 2, let alone any higher. Still, I'll go as high as I can in support of the others. It's the team effort that counts.

18 May
06:00 – Base Camp

Cathy and Deshun stood at the door of the mess tent, hot mugs of tea cupped in their gloved hands. 'Well, it's a surprise and a pleasure to have a fellow climber actually ready and waiting to go,' Cathy joked to Deshun. 'But don't expect to see the men for a while yet.'

Deshun sipped tentatively at the tea. She suffered from stomach nerves, so hadn't eaten any supper and now couldn't bring herself to look at the breakfast that had been laid out for them. The women were surrounded by a group of shivering trekkers who'd turned out of bed in the bitter chill of the early morning to wish the climbers well in their second summit attempt. 'You can do it,' they were saying, 'make us proud.'

Bruce emerged from his tent just as the women were about to leave.

'I'll stay back to keep an eye on Ian,' he said. 'He doesn't look too good.'

'You'll stay back to have your usual eight cups of tea so you can throw them all up again later,' retorted Cathy.

It was warm handshakes and good wishes all round as the two women shouldered their rucksacks and moved off across the glacier.

07:00 – Khumbu Icefall

Deshun had heard many stories from other climbers about falling seracs and open-mouthed crevasses and fixed rope that came loose when you pulled on it. But no one had told her how beautiful it was, how strangely magnificent.

She had had in her mind's eye a picture of what it would be like to look down into a crevasse, but nothing could have prepared her for actually seeing it. Having been surrounded by the whiteness of the snow, she found the most striking feature of crossing a crevasse all that blackness at the bottom. Looking down, she realised she had no idea how deep it was, how far she would fall. As she stared downwards, she felt her balance wobbling. She stopped in the middle of the ladder to try to regain her composure. Then she pushed herself to go forward, putting aside all thought of the long, long drop.

07:00 – Base Camp

> IAN:
> I look out of my tent and gaze longingly at the two small figures of Cathy and Deshun already well up the icefall and into their climbing, and shake

my head. I've already been through the icefall and back three times during this expedition, but I know this time is going to be the worst. That's if I get through at all. I look across towards the mess tent and see a group of trekkers waiting to say goodbye and wish us well. Damn, I'd hoped to sneak away unnoticed this morning. I guess I should've got up earlier. Swallowing another huge mouthful of cough mixture, I steady myself on shaky feet, and slowly make my way across towards the well-wishers, hoping that the magic of the cough mixture will last long enough to avoid the embarrassment of collapsing in gasping agony in front of the assembled group. The rough stones and boulders of the glacial moraine, together with the weight of my rucksack, the clumsiness of my double boots and the throbbing pain in my feet make the short journey from my tent a nightmare of its own. I crash to the ground twice before Bruce comes to my rescue. As he shoulders my rucksack, he looks me in the eyes and shakes his head.

'I'll be all right once I'm on snow and ice,' I say quietly, but Bruce does not answer and looks quickly away.

The handshakes and good wishes from the group of South Africans who have come so far to wish us well are touching and sincere, and go a long way to cheering me up. The last to say goodbye is Ken, my father. He grips my hand but doesn't resort to words, it's not his style. I know he would rather I stayed behind, but I also know that he's bursting with pride at what we've already done, and what we still hope to do. He has always respected my decisions, as I his, and he's not going to change now, so we nod to one another, squeeze each other's hands for the last time, and then Bruce and I turn away towards the mountain.

The soft snow and hard ice of the lower slopes of the icefall are easier to negotiate than the boulders of the glacier and I begin to find a routine of sorts. One breath, one step, one cough. One breath, one step, one cough. With renewed confidence at making some sort of progress at least, I reach the first of the crevasse ladders and, after clipping into the safety rope, step firmly on to the first rung with my cramponed boot. The raw pain shoots up my leg and I collapse in agony on my hands and knees across the ladder, looking down into the bottomless blue depths of the crevasse. The sudden pain has taken my breath away and I gasp for air, forcing my sick lungs to expand, infection or no infection. The air is mercifully forced in, but then the coughing takes over to force it back out again, and I'm racked with convulsions as the infection fights back. As I slowly regain a semblance of composure, I'm dismayed to see bright red spots soaking into the pure whiteness of the snow, and I realise that I'm bleeding inside. I edge back off the ladder and lie curled up in the snow, arms wrapped tightly around my chest, with tears of frustration pouring down my cheeks.

Go down, Ian, don't be an idiot, you can't possibly make camp 1. Go down now while you still have the strength. I know I must go down, it's the only sensible thing to do. I look back down at the base camp tents, still so depressingly close, and know that I must go back, but I can't. I just can't let my expedition end here. I know that my summit chances are gone, but if I can force myself a little higher, I may still be of some use to Cathy and Bruce when they make their summit bid. I don't know how I'll manage it, but I must go on.

My feet won't take the pressure of the metal ladders, but that's okay because I'll crawl on hands and knees. My lungs won't take the pressure of strenuous climbing, but that's okay because I'll go so slowly that they won't be under any pressure. I can climb through the night to reach camp 2 if I have to. My insides are damaged and bleeding, but that's okay because I can up my antibiotic dose. So I wipe away the tears, take a deep breath, and then slowly edge back out across the ladder.

Just as I'm standing up Bruce arrives, having slid back down the ropes to check on my progress.

'You all right, old man?' he asks, his voice laden with concern.

'No problem, youth,' I reply cheerfully. 'Just stopped for a slash and to adjust my crampons.'

He looks silently at me, as if considering his words carefully, but before he can state the inevitable, I hustle him on.

'Come on then, we can't stand around here all day. The bloody women will get to camp 2 before us if we're not careful.'

And so we move on, Bruce in the lead and me somewhere behind.

Time and again Bruce looks back with his soft, baleful eyes, pleading with me to give up and go back down, and time and again I avoid his gaze and concentrate on one breath, one step, and then one cough.

11:00 – Khumbu Icefall

Deshun rounded another corner to see in front of her another vertical snow wall. And the trail led directly to the bottom of it. Her heart sank. She hadn't expected the walls to be so tough or so numerous. Why don't I have stronger muscles? she thought despondently.

As she stood staring at the wall, she was passed by the doctor from Peter Athans's team, stumbling down using bottled oxygen and assisted by Sherpas. The Sherpas told her that he had fallen victim to acute bronchitis. It was a sobering reminder of just how vulnerable all of the climbers were on the mountain.

She tackled the wall in a furious full-on assault, arms, legs, everything working at the same time. The pack sat like a nagging demon on her back, always pulling her back down.

'Smile, Deshun.'

She looked up to see Cathy sitting at the top taking photographs of her.

'Sod off, I'm tired. Don't make fun of me.'

'I'm not. You're doing really well. And it's a great photo.'

Cathy was impressed by the ease with which Deshun had coped with the icefall. Although she moved slowly and was gradually tiring, she had kept a steady pace.

The two women sat down in the snow above the wall. Cathy pointed out the little tents that made up camp 1. Deshun felt a surge of elation. She was really looking forward to camp 1. And then she looked back down to the tiny tents of base camp. It was a moment of glory for her to see how far she had come. Nothing had prepared her for the toughness, the beauty, the risk of what she had just climbed through.

Cathy started walking again and Deshun rose reluctantly to follow her. To her surprise, the trail took a 90-degree turn and then twisted to go in the opposite direction to the tents. To her horror, she found there was one more giant crevasse, which they had to climb into and then walk along a narrow ridge to escape out of. To have seen camp 1 so close, and then to have this huge detour hit her hard mentally. It seemed forever before she was finally able to collapse next to Bruce and Cathy by the tent door.

12:30 – Camp 1

CATHY:

The midday sun beats down on us through a hazy sky as we lie by the tent. Bruce wants to wait for Ian, who is moving very slowly and is someway behind us. Deshun lies inert, exhausted, beside him.

'If you and Deshun get to camp before us, see if you can send a Sherpa down to help Ian with his load,' Bruce says.

I hate the long walk up the cwm. I don't want to have to wait for Deshun, who is getting slower and slower and beginning to bitch. She did a good job through the icefall but is clearly getting tired. That I don't mind; it's the whingeing that gets on my nerves. Maybe it helps her, but it irritates me. Nobody can help her do this now except herself.

'Tell you what, Bruce,' I say. 'I'll head on up the cwm, you two wait for Ian and then come on up together. I'll send someone down to help Ian. It will be quickest that way.'

I leave before Bruce has a chance to think this through and move away across the undulating snow. Compared to previous trips, the walking is a pleasure. I am fit and acclimatised, the weather is cool. I love being alone in this extraordinary landscape. I power up the glacier, cutting my previous time by half. I feel twinges of guilt for leaving Deshun to Bruce, but those soon fade. She'll manage much better walking at Ian's pace, I tell myself.

13:00 – Camp 1

IAN:

A tent appears through the mist swirling inside my head. Camp 1 or camp 2? I ask myself. I can see Bruce floating outside the tent door and Deshun's feet poking out as well. But there's no sign of Cathy.

'Where's Cathy?' I ask, my voice echoing through my mind.

'She's gone on to camp 2,' comes the distant and faint reply.

Okay, I work out slowly, then this must be camp 1. I'd really hoped that I was further. Never mind, though – camp 1 is progress, and camp 2 is only one number away.

'Come and join us for some juice,' comes the faint voice again.

'No thanks,' I echo back, 'I must keep going. When I stop, it'll be for good.'

I wave in the general direction of the floating figures and then begin to search for my routine once again.

I try to peer through my mental mists, but only general outlines are visible. The magic cough mixture, the antibiotics, the heat of the sun, the struggle for every breath, and the continuous throbbing chest pains make a powerful mixture. One too powerful for me to overcome, and so I try to float with it, swim with it, and if the wind gets up a little, surf with it. But however I manage it, I must follow it to camp 2.

15:00 – Western Cwm

This is dreadful, thought Deshun as she trudged up through the heavy heat of the Western Cwm. She was so tired and so hungry. It had been incredibly tempting to stay at camp 1, but her target was camp 2 and she knew she had to keep moving. Well, you're in the famous Western Cwm on the most famous mountain in the world, she told herself for encouragement.

'If you really have trouble concentrating, count,' Bruce had said. 'It will keep your mind focused on something.' So she counted. I'll get there, she thought. As slow as I might be, I'll get there. Cathy was way ahead by now, even Ian had passed her. Bruce continued to walk with her, to help her through. Conscious of how slow she was, she just wanted to be left alone.

'Get a move on!' exclaimed Bruce at last, exasperated at her snail's pace.

'No, I can't move any faster than this,' she replied testily.

'You'd better start moving your butt if you're going to make camp tonight.'

'Just leave me alone, go on, go on. I didn't say you must walk with me.'

'Deshun, you're too slow. Can you see those bloody things hanging there, they can fall on top of you any minute, anything can avalanche right now.' Bruce was pointing at the great serac bands running across the West Ridge of Everest.

'Yeah, so what if they avalanche? Just go ahead, go ahead. Eff off.'

Once they were clear of the crevassed area, Bruce moved on ahead. The journey up the mountain was one nobody could make for Deshun; she had to find the determination and the endurance within herself to keep going. But she was always in sight of the climbers in front, who kept an eye out for her in case she should run into trouble.

15:30 – Camp 2

'I realised today that my expedition ends here,' Ian said to Bruce as he collapsed in their tent.

'Don't make any hasty decisions,' Bruce replied sympathetically. 'There's a rumour from some Sherpas that one of our tents may have blown away at camp 4. Let's take tomorrow as a rest day, try to find out more about the condition of the tent, and then you should be up to it the day after.'

A rest day? sighed Ian to himself. A rest life more like it!

CATHY:
Seated in the sun outside their tent, putting away yet another cup of tea, I overhear Ian's comment. My frustration deepens. It's all so unfair. Why does he have to be the one not to make it, after all he's put into it? Mentally, he's the toughest of the lot of us, but illness can destroy even the best. After all we went through together in the storm, we really are a tight-knit team now. To lose any one of us is to lose a whole part of what we are.

Bruce has always been easy to get along with, a good friend from the start. But Ian is different. When I first started working with him, on the expedition to Kilimanjaro, he was an unknown quantity. I admired him, I respected him, but I wasn't sure I liked him. But now, having come to know him, after everything we've shared together, I like him a lot.

16:00 – Camp 2

Cathy crawled into Bruce and Ian's tent, bringing coffee and biscuits. She had taken advantage of her early arrival to collect all the gossip from the other expeditions.

'Mal Duff is on his way back down. Apparently he got up this morning, ready to leave for camp 3 and then on for a summit bid, but managed to break a tooth while eating his breakfast. He's been sucking painkillers all day but they haven't helped, so that's basically the end of his expedition.'

'And by such small things are expeditions ended,' commented Bruce. 'What an anticlimax after all that effort! What are the rest of his team doing?'

'Everyone is going down except for the Dane and the Finn,' Cathy continued. 'They got to 8 200 metres a couple of days ago before being blown inside out by the winds and retreating, but they want to try again. Mal also said that he'll close the icefall on the twenty-third, but I spoke to Peter Athans a bit later, and he said that he and Dave Breashears will keep it open if necessary, and we can join them in that.'

Philip came through on the radio with weather news from RAF Bracknell.

PHILIP: 'They say the best day in the near future is going to be the twenty-first, that's three days from now, but even then they are predicting 30-knot winds on the summit.'

The climbers looked at each other. By now they placed little faith in the weather reports, but nevertheless if the report was right, the winds were far too high.

'I'm getting the feeling that this mountain is shutting down around us,' Bruce said glumly.

19 May
07:00 – Camp 2

CATHY:
I wake early. Deshun, who has been tossing restlessly all night, is finally asleep. I slide quietly outside and go to sit in the middle of the glacier to update my diary. I have given up on trying to write and am now using a Dictaphone. From my rock perch I watch the winds sweeping across the Yellow Band, creating swirling feathers of snow dancing across the slope. Occasionally they dip even lower to rake camp 3, and in the background is always the express-train sound of the winds blasting the summit ridge.

I feel an overwhelming sense of *déjà vu*, having spent six days here before, watching exactly the same weather. We may get to the South Col but we won't leave it. I guess our expedition ends here.

09:00 – Camp 2

Cathy returned to her tent to check on Deshun. She was awake but looking very unhappy.

'I had a terrible night,' she said. 'I couldn't sleep. I think it's the altitude. If I feel like this here, I really don't want to risk going any higher, not immediately anyway. I think I'll just spend a few days here and see how things turn out.'

'You must be pretty tired from yesterday,' Cathy said with understanding.

'Gee whiz, yes. It really took it out of me. Mentally too. The cwm is so big and so overwhelming. I didn't expect that. And then I was so unnerved when I passed that guy covered in a blue plastic bag. I had a very eerie feeling. I told myself, this guy is dead, and as I said it I felt such a presence of ghosts around me. When I got to camp 2 I just poured into the tent. I was lying there with all the sweaty clothes that had become cold on my body. I knew I had to move, to get rid of the clothing, but it was so cold. I was having this battle of the minds. I was thinking, okay, what if my body temperature does go up and warm me up sufficiently to dry the moisture? But even as I was thinking it, I knew it was a stupid thought. It was such a relief when I finally got it together to get rid of the damp clothing. I warmed up so quickly after that.'

She smiled suddenly. 'But I made it! And it gave me a slight insight into what high-altitude mountaineering is actually all about. When you read it, it's all fascinating and when you hear people's stories it's all exhilarating and glamorous, but to actually experience it is a totally different thing.'

Deshun drifted back off into a troubled doze, so Cathy climbed into Bruce and Ian's tent, and the morning was spent in the usual idle entertainment. Bruce would tell his 'men only' stories of life in Antarctica, while Ian would compete with 'war' stories from his army days. Cathy on the other hand just settled back, content to laugh to herself as the stories got taller and taller. As light relief, a member of Henry Todd's team came over seeking tea and company. In exchange, he offered the news that Neil and another of their teammates were trapped in camp 3 by the wind. He then sat with Bruce and Ian, taking his turn to swap stories, while Cathy massaged Bruce's feet, reducing him to a state of purring incoherence. Looking out through the tent door, she could watch David Breashears marching back and forth outside his yellow tents, pouring words into his radio. Some things never changed.

11:30 – Camp 2

By late morning everyone had tumbled out of the tent to stretch their legs. Dave was still engrossed in his radio.

'Well, given that he hasn't spoken to us yet, I guess he's never going to,' said Cathy. 'I suppose we're just too insignificant.'

Suddenly Dave stopped, listened into his radio intently and then turned to the South Africans.

'Turn on your radios,' he called. 'Nelson Mandela wants to speak to you.'

The South African team stared at him in stunned silence.

'He's just taking the piss,' said Ian. 'He's got bored with giving Wall Street the run-around, so now he's picking on us.'

'But what if it's true?' suggested Cathy. 'Maybe we should just turn on the radio and check.'

'Why is the president going to be calling us first thing on a Sunday morning in South Africa?' argued Ian. 'If we make the summit, he might want to talk to us, but not before then.'

> CATHY:
> We stand in awkward silence. I want to get on the radio and call Phil, but Ian seems convinced it is just the Americans taking the mickey. It seems so unlikely. Why would the president of the country call up a little mountaineering expedition? I don't know what to believe and vacillate between excitement and uncertainty. Nobody really wants to radio Phil and find out that it's just a joke.
>
> 'We are only a few minutes short of the one o'clock radio call,' says Bruce. 'Why don't we just put the radio on standby and wait for that?'
>
> The minutes stretch interminably. The black box of the radio stands inert on a rock, assuming an awful presence. The silence becomes oppressive.
>
> Spot on time Phil's voice comes through to confirm that the president has indeed phoned and will be calling back in the next few minutes. I can't believe it. What can he have to say to us?

13:02 – Camp 2

Ian walked a few metres away from the tents, searching for the best reception, and then squatted down to wait. He glanced over at Cathy.

'Come here. I'm not doing this on my own.'

She walked over to join him while Bruce listened on one of the other radios. Deshun watched sleepily from her tent.

Just then a voice came through, faint but clear.

PRESIDENT: 'This is President Mandela here in South Africa.'

IAN: 'Good morning, Mr President. Thank you very much for your kind telephone call.'

PRESIDENT: 'I am so happy that you are attempting to climb Mount Everest again.'

IAN: 'Thank you, Mr President. It was not an easy decision but it was a unanimous one. Everybody is very keen to place the flag on top of the mountain if the weather will allow us.'

PRESIDENT: 'I am fully behind you. I have a lot of confidence in you and I know you are going to succeed. The whole of South Africa stands behind you because it is a significant expedition and I wish you all the luck.'

IAN: 'Thank you very, very much, Mr President. I can't begin to tell you how important this telephone call is to us. We've obviously had one or two problems along the way, but we are firmly committed to doing what we came here for and we shall hopefully bring South Africa and yourself full honours.'

PRESIDENT: 'Thank you very much. Convey to all the members of the staff my sincere good wishes for success and we will be waiting with eagerness to welcome you as you arrive at the top of Mount Everest.'

IAN: 'Thank you, Mr President. I can assure you that we will do absolutely everything possible to do that, and to come back safely.'

PRESIDENT: 'Thank you very much. Good luck.'

IAN: 'Thank you very much, Mr President. From the whole team here we really do appreciate your time and trouble to wish us success. This is camp 2 on Everest out.'

President Mandela rang off and Philip's excited voice came over the radio.

'You take it,' said Ian, thrusting the radio into Cathy's hand and walking away.

PHILIP: 'It was completely unexpected. Patrick had been working hard all morning putting out broadcasts to Radio 702, the phone had been ringing quite a lot, and he was starting to get irritated. So when the phone rang this time he answered with a grumpy "yes", instead of his usual "Everest base camp, can I help you?". It turned out to be Priscilla Naidoo from the President's Office. He virtually jumped to attention.'

Philip signed off from base camp so Cathy walked across to join Bruce.

'I'm impressed,' said Bruce. 'I'm very impressed. I can't see John Major doing that. It's funny to see Ian so shaken. He's normally so taciturn.'

'I think he's more affected by the president's support than he's ever been by any of the tragedies on the mountain,' said Cathy. 'But what a completely un-expected bonus!' She paused and then smiled broadly. 'So that's what it takes to get Breashears to speak to us, nothing less than the most famous politician in the world.'

> IAN:
> 'I am fully behind you. I have a lot of confidence in you and I know you are going to succeed. The whole of South Africa stands behind you because it is a significant expedition.'
>
> For the first time since dreaming up the challenge of placing our coun-try's flag on top of the world, I feel the crushing weight of responsibility. The man whom I admire beyond all else has confidence in me, in us, in our little expedition. Are we worthy of such confidence? Are we worthy to carry the hopes of our president? I think not, but perhaps we can take that confidence and use it, nurture it, feed off it, grow with it, and by so doing become stronger individuals, become a stronger team. Yes, that's what we'll do, we'll use it as a crutch, as a guiding light, even as a ladder itself to take us to the top. Yes, that's what we'll do!

18:30 – Camp 2

That night, as the climbers sat together discussing logistics, the mood had changed immeasurably. Ian teased the others about being referred to as 'the staff' by President Mandela, but although they all joked about the call, deep inside it meant a great deal to each of them.

'I'm amazed,' said Bruce. 'You can read all you like, but just in that one radio call, that one phone call from your president, I now know more about South Africa than you've probably ever told me before. I can understand now the sort of drive, determination and camaraderie that you guys have in South Africa, that maybe we don't have in the UK.'

The friends fell silent for a few moments, each engrossed in their own thoughts, and each now determined to climb as high, as hard and as fast as they could. Nothing could stop them now but bad weather.

Ian then went back to discuss the various summit options.

'We've just got to take it bit by bit,' he said, 'and go as high as the weather will allow us. Our first aim should be to break Ian Wood's South African height record, which would be to go over 8 200 metres. We can do that in just a few hours' climbing above camp 4. Then we should try for the South Summit at 8 700 metres. That's higher than any other mountain in the world, including K2, so it's a damn good achievement. But as for the summit, we'll just have to wait and see.'

20:00 – Camp 2

At eight o'clock Philip came through with the evening radio call, still excited at the day's events.

PHILIP: 'The news about your phone call is all over base camp. The other teams can't believe that the president of a country would phone a team on Everest. Several of the Brits swore that even if John Major did phone them, they wouldn't take the call, while at least one of the Danish climbers had trouble remembering who his president was! But for once, I reckon they all envy us for being South African.'

CHAPTER 10

Anticipation at All Levels

20 May
08:30 – Lhotse Face

The enthusiasm and determination of the previous day had taken something of a beating by the time the climbers had slogged up the long stretch of glacier to the foot of the bergschrund in the bitter early morning cold. They quickly spread out, with Ian waiting for the sun to reach the face in order to warm up his hands, while the others kept moving, for standing still seemed too cold an option.

Early on in the morning Cathy and Bruce passed the last two of Henry Todd's team members on their way down.

'We've had enough,' announced one. 'The wind just never lets up and Henry is pulling his whole expedition out.'

'My husband is meeting me in Kathmandu,' said the other with a happy smile. 'I'm glad to go. I've had it with this stupid mountain.'

Cathy and Bruce watched the two dwindle into specks as they moved rapidly down the ropes.

'So another expedition bites the dust,' said Bruce. 'I wonder if they're being more or less sensible than us.'

> CATHY:
> The cwm may have been better than last time, but this slope up to camp 3 is no improvement. With each step I take up the long, steep ice incline I promise myself that it will be the last time I have to do it. It becomes a mental mantra, distracting me from the distance still to be covered.
>
> That one done, and that one done. Never again, and never again.
>
> Each step taken for the last time, or the last time uphill at least.

I will never climb the Lhotse Face again.

I lean over the rope, exhausted from the distance done already, and not amused by the distance still to go. I look down to the miniature figure of Ian, toiling so painfully, so slowly, far below me. God, he's got guts. And bloody mindedness.

Bruce is resting a few metres above me.

'Bruce,' I call. 'Did I ever tell you that in my next life I am going to be a surfer's girlfriend?'

'A surfer's girlfriend? Why?'

'Well, for a start I wouldn't have to do anything more taxing than lie on exotic beaches in a little bikini. He'd spend most of his time surfing so I'd only see him occasionally, and all I'd have to do is tell him how absolutely wonderful he looks out on the waves, and send him out again. It's warm, it's flat, it's at sea level, there is no physical activity involved. It sounds like paradise to me right now.'

Bruce laughs. 'You're too intelligent to lie around on beaches pandering to male egos.'

'But I can learn. All I have to do is bleach my hair blonde, get my boobs enlarged and my IQ reduced, and I'm ready to roll.'

I am convinced that this is the solution. Intelligence, drive, determination and ambition just get you into bloody uncomfortable positions halfway up endless ice-faces. Sun, beaches and lots of oxygen have to be an improvement.

IAN:
I can't believe it's so cold. I'm frozen to the core, but the others don't seem to feel it at all. Even with my damaged toes, I kick my feet into the hard snow as I stamp about below the bergschrund trying desperately to stay functioning, while I wait for the sun to arrive and release me from this frigid hell. I'm sure that it's my overall poor health that's making me so cold, but I take some comfort in the knowledge that, although I'm still a basket case, I have definitely felt a slight improvement over the last couple of days. I watch with envy as Bruce and Cathy power their way up the vertical fixed ropes of the bergschrund and then force their way up and up towards camp 3. Oh well, at least they'll have the kettle on by the time I arrive up there … and arrive I intend to!

The seconds slide by as I watch the morning sun creep over the Nuptse ridge and then race up the dark blue ice towards me, transforming the bergschrund into a glittering spectacle of light and colour, like millions of burning sparklers emerging out of the snow. I stand, face upturned, revelling in the warmth and comfort of this wonderful moment. But I have a day's work to do, and it promises to be a long and hard one, so I turn my attention back to the job in hand.

Clipping in my jumars, I begin to attack the vertical ice wall. Ten minutes of lung-bursting effort and I haven't left the ground. I slump back down in the snow and gasp for breath, sweat pouring through my clothing with the effort. Okay, Ian, not the best start, let's have a rest and we'll try again. Right, back to the ropes. Five desperate minutes later and I collapse once again into the snow, knowing that my thin frame simply doesn't have the raw strength any more to pull itself and my equipment up vertical ropes. I look up into the dazzling sun for help, but Cathy and Bruce are already way out of sight.

The first signs of panic tiptoe their way up my back. If I can't get over the bergschrund, I can't get to camp 3. If I can't get to camp 3, I can't support Bruce and Cathy in their summit bid and my expedition ends right here in the snow. Anger and frustration begin to take over and, with complete disregard for technique, I hurl myself once again at the infernal ropes, only to be repulsed once again with consummate ease.

That's it, I'm defeated, broken even. I have no choice but to return to camp 2. After everything we've been through, I've been stopped by a mere 9 metres of fixed rope. I sink to my knees and beat the snow with my fists in anger and disappointment. Someone or something must be to blame, and, in the absence of any other immediate candidates, the snow will do nicely.

Slowly I begin to collect my thoughts for the lonely walk back to camp 2, shaking my head at the ups and downs of life, and then bursting out in frustrated laughter at the awfulness of my own pun. I glance back up the face for one last look at the unreachable, and see to my amazement a figure standing on the upper rim of the bergschrund about to lower himself down the ropes.

I blink and rub my eyes, but he's still there, and on top of his huge load is a coil of rope. 'Rope *nogal*!' Without a moment to lose, I call to the Sherpa and he lowers me the second rope. In a flash he pulls me bodily up the ice wall and deposits a grinning sahib at his feet.

'Sahib very sick,' he states.

I smile and rub my chest in acknowledgement, but he shakes his head and taps himself on the temple instead, before recoiling his rope and disappearing down towards camp 2.

I don't know who or what sent me that Sherpa, but I do know that I've been given another chance. The expedition isn't over for me just yet. I may still have a role to play. So for no good reason other than I can, I shake myself down and begin the nightmare- and pain-racked journey up to join my friends at camp 3, and I can't get the smile off my face.

13:00 – Camp 3

Once Cathy and Bruce had dug away the newly fallen snow that had been partly smothering the tent, they climbed inside and sat down to brew, swimming their way through cup after cup of tea, with the occasional coffee for some variety and a bit of bacon for sustenance.

Ian eventually staggered in and collapsed between them on to the mounds of down sleeping bags and quickly dozed off, while Bruce kept the stove going. Shortly after Ian's arrival Bruce heard the rustle of the ropes against the snow, indicating that people were moving along them, and stuck his head out the door to see who was coming. By now the wind was up and spindrift was blowing across the Lhotse Face.

'It's our Sherpas,' he said, 'coming down from camp 4. Grab some more tea bags, Cath. It's pretty miserable out there and I'm sure they'll be glad of a brew.'

The Sherpas squatted down on the snow outside the tent, sheltering from the wind inside their jacket hoods, and passed around the cups of tea. They were clearly tired.

'What's the situation with the tents, Ang Dorje?' Bruce asked.

'The one is okay. The other, just the cover is torn. The tent inside is fine,' he answered, his cold fingers squeezed tightly around his warm drink.

'That's good news. Ian, we have a spare tent here, don't we? One that we never pitched.'

'Yeah, it's stored out at the back,' Ian replied sleepily. 'We can just take the flysheet from that when we go.'

'And how's the oxygen, Ang Dorje?' Bruce asked.

'We've brought down 13 empty bottles.'

Ian was beginning to wake up as the discussion turned to logistics.

'So that should leave us 12 bottles on the col, with two and a half being carried up today, plus Henry's 7. About 21 bottles in all, it's tight but it'll have to do. Did you see Henry Todd's bottles up there?'

'Yes, Bara Sahib. They're next to the tents.'

'You all look tired,' said Ian. 'What will the Sherpas want to do tomorrow?'

Ang Dorje shrugged. 'I don't know. They are tired and the weather is not good.'

Ian considered this.

'We'll radio you at six o'clock tomorrow morning, and decide there and then what to do. Okay?'

Ang Dorje agreed and the Sherpas moved off down the ropes.

'If they won't climb tomorrow, we're stuck with either waiting here another day or going down again tomorrow,' said Ian.

The other two received this news in unenthusiastic silence.

'Why don't you get hold of Phil, Bruce, and see what weather updates he has?' Cathy suggested.

14:00 – Camp 3

PHILIP:	'Okay, here's the weather forecast from the IMAX team. 21 May, 25 knots at 7 000 metres, 30 to 40 knots at 9 000 metres, do you copy?'
BRUCE:	'We copy the wind speeds and the heights. Is there any indication of the overall weather pattern?'
PHILIP:	'They have a report that the jet stream will lift and the front will break on the twenty-first.'
BRUCE:	'What does that mean in English?'
PHILIP:	'Your guess is as good as mine.'
BRUCE:	'So we're still experiencing jet-stream conditions. The stuff we've had today is pretty widespread. We can see it closing in over the top of Cho Oyu during the day, the temperature's gone up, and the wind's dropped. It's almost a classic front scenario.'
PHILIP:	'*Ja,* I don't know what it means, Bruce.'
BRUCE:	'Have you got any idea when the IMAX team will go for the summit?'
PHILIP:	'The last information I had, Bruce, was the day after yourself. Dave's going around saying on the one hand that he can finish the movie without reaching the summit, on the other hand he says he has to summit to finish the movie, so I think he's just vacillating backwards and forwards in camp 2 at the moment.'
BRUCE:	'Any news of other teams?'
PHILIP:	'It looks like everyone else who is on the mountain is in camp 2, and they're all either waiting for Breashears to decide, or they'll be going down tomorrow.'
BRUCE:	'Right, the blind following the blind. Are there any indications of three- or five-day advance forecasts at all?'
PHILIP:	'Well, this one here is a three-day forecast. The winds are increasing again on the twenty-third.'
BRUCE:	'Oh yeah. We need that sort of information like a hole in the head.'

The radios fell silent for a few minutes as Bruce changed his radio battery, before Philip moved on to discuss general logistics matters.

PHILIP: 'I was chatting to Henry Todd today about the oxygen situation. He says we've got 38 bottles from him, our original 31 plus the 7 new ones on the South Col. He's confirmed that he's leaving base camp on the twenty-third. I don't know whether you guys will be down by then, but if not, he wants the empty oxygen bottles dropped off in Kathmandu.'

BRUCE: 'I'm sure that won't be a problem. We'll find some way of getting them to Kathmandu and to Henry.'

PHILIP: 'Okay, the concern here is that we need a receipt from Henry to say that we've got all our bottles down from the mountain for the pollution-control people.'

BRUCE: 'I'm sure Henry can send it to us from Kathmandu. Right now I'm more worried about the weather. We'll comms again at 20:30 and see if you can get any joy out of the Nepalese radio weather forecasts.'

CATHY:

I've had it with this mountain. With the cold and effort, and above all with the stupid, stupid weather. Why didn't we just go home when we had the chance? I feel my eyes filling with tears as a flood of self-pity washes over me. I curl up in a ball, burying my head in my sleeping bag, trying not to look as if I'm crying.

Stupid tent. With three of us jammed in it, there is nowhere to go, no privacy, no space. What I would give to be able to get away, just for a few hours! I can feel the atmosphere cool as the men realise what is happening. Damn. How embarrassing!

Mercifully they say nothing. Bruce continues to melt snow. Ian quietly slips an arm across my shoulders. Gradually my breathing slows down.

I feel really hungry now. I sit up, smile awkwardly at Ian, and wriggle round to where Bruce is tending the stove.

'Is there any food going? I'm starving.'

He stares at me in bewilderment. I don't think he's keeping up with the emotional changes of pace.

'What do you fancy?'

'Hmm, chocolate pudding? And coffee?'

'You're weird, woman. I'll see what I can do.'

IAN:

I don't want to think about tomorrow. I'm just thrilled to be here. The weather's never bothered to listen to us up to now, so I see no reason why it should tomorrow. It'll do whatever it bloody well pleases, and after the appearance of my miracle Sherpa, I've seen it all, and I'm simply lying here fascinated and in awe of what this mountain will do to us next.

21 May
05:30 – Camp 3

CATHY:
Once again only 36 hours from the summit. But I've been here before, I've thought this before, and I've been wrong before.

I lie inside the intense warmth and comfort of the sleeping bag, and listen to the wind howl outside, humming against the guy-ropes, slapping against the tent fabric. Oh no, dear God, not again.

At last, bored by inactivity, I unzip the tent flap to find the stove. The stove and pots lie under an inch of snow in the bell of the tent. Peering out of the outer door catches me a face full of spindrift, which then melts against the heat of my skin and trickles coldly down my chest. I rouse the other two with cups of hot coffee and hand the radio to Ian to talk to Ang Dorje at camp 2.

06:10 – Camp 3

Ian switched off the radio and turned to the others.

'Well, Ang Dorje made it very clear that he thinks it will be another day with the winds too strong to climb,' he announced.

'So the Sherpas are staying put,' said Bruce.

'Yes, they are. So what do we do now?'

The climbers lay in the tent, looking at each other and listening to the wind howl.

'I'm keen to stick it out,' said Bruce at last. 'I think we should stay another night here and try again tomorrow. We may not make the summit, but I feel the expedition should end as high as possible. We got up to camp 4 after two nights at camp 3 last time.'

'But we were hardly in a state to move straight on for the summit,' Ian pointed out.

'Yes, but that was because of the storm we were caught in. Cathy was fine, and if we go down now, we may never get this high again.'

'But if we stay here, we'll deteriorate. None of us sleeps well at this altitude, especially Cathy. Maybe we should go down and regroup. Try again in a few days.'

'It's getting late in the season,' Bruce retorted. 'A few days may be all we have.' He paused, looking at Ian. 'So do you think we should go down?'

'I'm just playing devil's advocate,' Ian replied. 'I'm out of the running for the summit. In the end it's you two who are putting yourselves on the line, and the decision has to be yours.'

Both men turned to look at Cathy, who had been sitting silently.

'Well, Caths, what do you want to do?' asked Ian.

CATHY:
What do I want to do? I don't know, I don't know. I'm very unhappy at the thought of a second night at camp 3. When we arrived yesterday we found that the spare oxygen bottle stashed here had mysteriously emptied itself. I managed to fall asleep last night – eventually, after hours of battling to breathe. I can't bear the thought of another long day lying here, another night fighting for breath and then trying to dredge up the energy to climb higher. I think our physical deterioration will outweigh any advantages.

And with no oxygen at camp 3, I have to climb to 8 000 metres without it. I can probably do that, but God knows if I can then keep going higher the next day.

But equally I'm not happy about going back down, not sure if I will be able to find the energy to try yet again, to plod step by step up the Lhotse Face yet again. Having gone down to camp 2, it would be so easy just to keep moving down, to let the momentum carry us down and away from this mountain.

I don't want either choice. I want someone else to choose. I just don't know.

IAN:
I laugh to myself. This mountain is really beginning to make fools out of us, and I can see the signs of strain on Cathy's and Bruce's faces. I have absolutely no way of knowing for sure whether we should stay where we are or go back down, but logically I think going down is best for everyone. Although it must basically be their decision, as they are the most likely summit contenders, I won't be too disappointed to go back down. While it means yet another desperate climb back up to camp 3, it'll also mean an extra rest day at camp 2, which can do me no harm at all. I'm not sure, but I have a feeling that I'm beginning to get my engine back. It's nothing definite, but the first signs are there at least. If so, then an extra rest day that doesn't compromise the chances of the other two is exactly what the doctor ordered.

Besides, I have a return bout planned with a certain bergschrund.

11:15 – Camp 3

'Caths, you know you don't handle sleeping at camp 3 very well,' Ian said at last. 'And now that we've no oxygen left at this camp, you'd have to climb up to camp 4 without oxygen as well. I think you should go down. We'll try to rework the logistics of the oxygen and hopefully we'll get a better chance in a day or two. If not, well, no one can say we didn't try our best.'

'I guess you're right,' she agreed reluctantly. She would just have to dig deep in her reserves and find the energy to climb up again.

'We'll go back down, and, weather permitting, try once more. Give it our best shot,' said Bruce confidently, convinced now of Ian's logic.

Cathy wondered whether it was really worth all the effort. She had a sinking feeling that her best shot had been played out already. By the time they finally reached a decision it was late morning and the wind had died.

11:30 – Camp 3

Bruce called down to Philip to update him on developments.

BRUCE: 'We were getting 60 and 70 knots of wind at five o'clock this morning, so we spoke to Ang Dorje and told the Sherpas to stay put at camp 2. We've seen very few people coming through today. There's been a couple of Sherpas from Henry Todd's group, a lone climber on the ropes below, and some guy walking down in the valley. It might even have been Deshun going for a walk.'

PHILIP: 'Roger, Bruce, it's very quiet down here as well.'

BRUCE: 'We've sat and debated things long and hard this morning. As a summary, we want to give it one more shot, but we want to give it our best shot. It's just a matter of when and how. To have gone up to camp 4 today or even tomorrow morning, I think we would've gone off at half-cock with the weather still so unsettled. So I think what we'll do is tidy up here and then head back down the route to camp 2.'

PHILIP: '*Ja*, 10-4, Bruce. If you go down to camp 2, though, you'll be moving the summit attempt two days ahead. You realise that?'

BRUCE: 'Maybe even three or four days ahead. It depends on how we feel and all the rest. What we'll do is head back down to camp 2 very shortly and regroup there. Ian's still got a little bit of a chest, sort of sitting there and not shifting at the moment. But Cathy and myself are in good shape.'

PHILIP: 'That's good. Look, coming down to camp 2 can only help. Have you got enough medicines and things up there or do you want me to send something up?'

BRUCE: 'No, we're fine. It's just a matter of rest, I think; that's the key component for Ian.'

13:00 – Camp 3

As the team prepared to leave the tents, they heard voices from the ropes below. On realising that it was the IMAX team, Bruce grabbed the initiative and, standing one foot on either side of the ropes, ensured that they had to talk to him. David Breashears was disappointed to find the South Africans still in camp.

'I saw some people moving over the Yellow Band, and I thought it was you,' he said. 'I was rooting for you while I climbed, thinking you had made the right decision to go on despite the wind.'

'We've decided to go back down,' Bruce explained.

Breashears looked dubious.

'According to the weather report, this is the best day we're going to get,' he replied.

As the IMAX team climbed on towards their tents it started to snow.

'If 60-knot winds in the morning and a blizzard in the afternoon is the best weather we're going to get, they can keep it,' muttered Ian.

A quick descent of the Lhotse Face in light but steady snow was followed by a treacherous crossing of the glacier, as the falling snow filled up the tracks and the glare from the white sky distorted distance and direction.

CATHY:
Right decision or wrong one? No way of telling. It is going to be so depressing if the IMAX team summit and we don't. Still, we've gone against the common decision of other teams before and been glad of it. But this changeable weather is deeply demoralising. There is no way of knowing if we've made the right decision in retreating, nor if we'll have the weather, or the energy, to try once more.

Once again it is back to weather-watching, and waiting.

16:00 – Camp 2

Bruce radioed down the news of their safe return to base camp.

BRUCE: 'All three of us, that's Ian, Cathy and myself, are safely back down at camp 2. Deshun's been out for a short walk with Ang Dorje but didn't get very far because of the weather.'

PHILIP: '10-4. How was your trip down from 3 to 2?'

BRUCE: 'Pretty uneventful. We were down quite fast. We passed Breashears and his mob just as we were leaving. They're obviously on their way up, putting faith in the good old British weather forecast. I think he really should know better. No, we were going quite quickly. Ian's quite slow, though. He's got a really bad chest now. I think we're just going to put him to bed for tonight and tomorrow and see how he gets on.'

PHILIP: 'Okay. I understand that the two Danes and the Finn moved from 3 to 4 today. They might try a summit attempt this evening.'

BRUCE: 'Yeah, well, they might well get it right. It's difficult to judge what this weather is actually going to do. Our plan here is to stay all day tomorrow and then on the morning of the twenty-third Cathy and I will move back up to camp 3. Ian's condition is, while not serious, probably serious enough to stop him from doing any really energetic or strenuous climbing.'

PHILIP: 'Is he on antibiotics or anything, Bruce?'

BRUCE: 'I think he's been on everything since he left base camp. It's a very deep, chesty cough and it's beginning to frustrate him quite considerably.'

17:00 – Camp 2

Cathy crawled into her tent to find Deshun dozing in her sleeping bag.

'Wake up, you sloth,' she said. 'We're back.'

'Oh no, you again,' smiled Deshun. 'And just as I was falling asleep. I've been lying awake through the night and only falling asleep at dawn. I've had this terrible headache for days now. It's as if someone is keeping a blunt object against the base of my skull while tightening clamps all around my head. And I have this overwhelming sensation that there is water floating around in my brain. And I feel really nauseous all the time, I just can't eat. I'm going to call it quits and go down tomorrow.'

'With that lot stacked against you, it definitely sounds like a wise decision,' Cathy said seriously.

Deshun smiled weakly. 'To be quite frank, despite all the pain, the thought of having to go all the way back down after gaining all this height is quite dreadful.'

22 May
10:00 – Camp 2

Bruce and Cathy sat in the sun outside the tents, watching Deshun and Ang Sirke dwindle into the distance. The two climbers watched them go thoughtfully.

'Up or down, up or down?' Bruce wondered. 'It's like a game of snakes and ladders.'

'Or being a yo-yo,' Cathy offered.

The lunchtime radio call provided a welcome break in their endless speculation over the weather. Philip's voice came through full of excitement.

PHILIP: 'We've had a really good weather report from RAF Bracknell and it's backed up by the US report. They say the winds are dropping to 20 to 25 knots and the jet stream is finally moving north of Everest. The conditions should be stable for the next few days. It looks like you guys might finally have a window.'

Cathy and Bruce stared at each other in amazement.

'Good God!' said Bruce. 'Maybe our timing is correct after all.'

'Yeah, right. When have the weather reports ever proved accurate?' replied Cathy. 'Still, it would be a pleasant development, since we always seem to be going in the opposite direction to everyone else.'

They looked at each other with suppressed excitement.

'So we go back up to camp 3 tomorrow?' asked Bruce.

'I guess it looks like it,' replied Cathy with a smile.

CATHY:
Although I know the weather reports are unreliable, a good one makes a huge difference to my attitude. I feel as if it's now back to whether we each have the physical and mental resources to go the distance, rather than whether the elements will even let us get out of the tent.

Cathy and Bruce scrambled into the tent to give the news to Ian, who had spent the morning sleeping.

IAN:
'Ian, Ian, the weather's clearing,' I hear Cathy shout excitedly.

'It's true, old man,' says Bruce, 'it looks as if this is our time. We're going back up.'

Of course it is, and of course we are. All three of us.

13:00 – Camp 2

They lay in the tent, each silently contemplating the possibilities of the summit, but they'd thought such thoughts so many times before that their minds
soon wandered.

'This expedition has gone on too long,' announced Cathy. 'All my ribs are
sticking out. You could play a xylophone on them.'

'Ribs, what are those?' Bruce asked as he ran his hands over his well-padded
torso. 'I can't find any such thing.'

'I'm not surprised, given how seriously you seem to have taken the carbo-
loading bit of training before we left South Africa,' Cathy joked.

She regarded him for a moment, noting how his chipmunk cheeks had disappeared, and how his body was slimming down.

'Nevertheless, you have lost a lot of weight,' she continued.

'Oh yes. I keep telling Sue what a fine figure of a man I'm turning into, but
I don't think she's entirely convinced,' replied Bruce.

Cathy returned to the contemplation of her ribs.

'An expedition has gone on just long enough when I end up with a flat
stomach and trim thighs. It has gone on too long when my ribs start to show
and my breasts disappear.'

15:00 – Camp 2

That afternoon Cathy spoke to Chris Gibbons on Radio 702, while Ian slept
once again.

CHRIS: 'How are you, and how are the team?'
CATHY: 'We're all pretty well, given the circumstances. It's the end of the
           season and we've been up here for a hell of a long time. But we're
           feeling good and are keen for one more go at the summit.'
CHRIS: 'You and Bruce at this stage are going on your own. Do you have
           the confidence in your climbing ability and in the mountain?'
CATHY: 'Yes, we do. It's not quite that desperate, though. Four of our
           Sherpas will be climbing with us. They're all very strong, and Ian
           will be in support, probably one camp behind us. So we're still a
           strong team and we have the utmost confidence that, weather per-
           mitting, we should be able to make a very good attempt to reach
           the summit.'
CHRIS: 'And inside yourself, inside the spirit that drives the mountaineer,
           do you have the reserves to go all the way?'

CATHY: 'I don't know. I'll tell you on Sunday. I have the reserves to go a
            long way. But it is a long way and we've never been there. We
            don't fully know what to expect. A lot of good mountaineers have
            turned back on that ridge this season. It's a hell of a big challenge
            and I just don't know.'

That's one of the things I'm up here to find out, she thought to herself.

15:10 – Base Camp

Patrick had been listening as Cathy talked to Chris. Then he was once more
on air to wrap up the interview.

CHRIS: 'I think we have some tremendous people, some tremendous de-
            termination, up there.'
PATRICK: 'Yes! I agree how determined the South Africans are to reach the
            summit, and they've been through all sorts of things. They helped
            out in the general tragedy. They've been caught out in storms.
            They've been miserable, and yet they still have the confidence and
            the determination to say: we're going to go on trying to reach the
            summit until all chance is lost!'

Putting the phone down, he turned to see Deshun stumbling into the camp.
He rushed outside to help her with her rucksack. 'How did it go?' he asked,
passing her a cup of hot juice.

'Horrible,' she replied shortly.

She took a long gulp of juice.

'It was so hot, there was a lot of melting ice and I could hear a lot of water
running. There were huge ice blocks that had fallen over, covering the fixed
ropes. I'd have to unclip from the ropes and climb over them. And I pulled on
one piece of rope and after a few pulls I found I had the ice screw in my hand.'

She sucked up the last drop from her cup and Patrick refilled it for her.

'Ang Sirke was very sweet,' she continued. 'I stopped in icefall more than I
should have because I was so tired, and he kept saying, "We must go, we must
go," and I kept saying, "Please, just five minutes." There was a bond between
us after being together in camp 2 for all those days. He really wanted to see
me achieving.'

'Would you try Everest another year, if you got the chance?' Patrick asked.

She laughed. 'All the way down I was thinking: I am never doing this again,
never, ever, ever. But after a bit of rest I might change my mind.'

She stared back up at the mountain. 'I'll tell you one thing, though. I was sitting at camp 2 and looking up at the South-West Face of Everest, this huge rock face. It felt as if it was falling over right on top of me. Only then did I realise how humungous Everest is. That intimidated me quite a bit.'

15:45 – Camp 2

CATHY:

Bruce wanders across from his tent and sits down next to me. He stares off across the glacier, makes a few inconsequential remarks about the weather and finally gets to the point.

'What are we going to do about Ian?'

I laugh inwardly. I'm sure he's not the only person in the world to have asked that question, only they probably didn't put it that politely.

'You mean about him going climbing?' I say.

'Yes, he looks terrible, sick and exhausted.'

'Well, you know if it was you or me, he'd have packed us off to base camp long ago.'

'Yes, I know. I've tried persuading him to go down or at least to wait here, but he still wants to go up.'

Silence falls. In the back of my mind a niggling worry asserts itself. I know Ian is tough, but does he know when to stop? What if he pushes so far that we have to abandon the summit attempt to get him down? Suppose he collapses halfway between camps 2 and 3. Then what? Does he have a right to push for individual achievement when it possibly endangers the success of the project as a whole? I feel rather embarrassed by these hard-arsed thoughts, but at last I express them to Bruce.

'Oh no, I don't think he'd do that,' Bruce says. 'I think he knows his limits, much better than we do, I guess. Look, why don't you try talking to him?'

'Oh, come off it, Bruce. If he won't listen to you, he's even less likely to listen to me. But I'll try.'

16:00 – Camp 2

Cathy crawled into the tent to find Ian lying sleepily on his down bag.

'So how are you feeling, youth?' she asked.

'I've been better,' he grumbled and began to cough, deep, chest-racking coughs.

She stared at the sleeping bag, at the tent door, at her nails.

'Ian ...' she began.

'Yes?'

'Are you sure you ought to be doing this? You're not in the best of shape,' she said carefully.

He smiled. 'Tell me something I don't know.'

'Ian, do you really think you're going to cope with the rest of this climb? You staggered into camp 2, and crawled up to camp 3. Isn't it time to face up to reality and go down?'

IAN:

I look at Cathy like never before. First she was a team member, then she was a climber. Without me noticing, she became a friend. Has she now become more? I don't know. I'm not sure where this will lead us, but for now she cares, and that's enough.

They truly mean well, but I know my limits. I may not know much else, but I know my limits. I should do, I've been there enough times. I know when I've come to the end of my road but still having left enough in reserve to get back again. But I'm not there yet. I even feel that I may be improving slightly. I may look like hell, but the tank's not empty. So I will go on and up, and I will support my six friends in their bid for the top. Hell, who knows, if I improve enough, the sky's the limit.

18:30 – Camp 2

By the evening the wind had died down and the Western Cwm was completely clear of cloud. The huge ice-face of Lhotse stood glistening at the head of the valley. The team knew the moods of the Lhotse Face so well by now. In the early morning before the sun had penetrated into the cwm it was dark and sombre, the grey-blue of unpolished silver. Once the sun was on it, it became relentlessly, dazzlingly white. As the sun set the colours shifted. Sometimes the whole face turned burnished gold, rich, vibrant gold. At other times, especially when partly shaded by cloud, it turned deep purple in the shadows, with the filtered sun illuminating patches of delicate pink. Where the full rays of the sun just caught the top it created a crown of gold and white. And on a moonless night like this one, it lurked at the head of the valley, a giant shadow, its hugeness emphasised by the gloom.

The team sat together eating soup, rice and roast beef, and waiting for Philip's final weather update.

'I spoke to the Danish climber this afternoon,' said Cathy.

'I noticed you were doing a little serious socialising there,' said Bruce with a wicked grin.

'Nothing of the sort,' Cathy replied primly. 'The fact that he looks like a Greek god has nothing to do with it. This was all in the course of business. He and the Finn did try for the summit again, but they have given up and are going home. It sounds as if he got a little above 8 000 metres before turning round. He said this last attempt had just come too late and that he'd felt much less strong than he had previously.'

'Did you notice that Peter Athans's team have vanished off down the valley as well?' Bruce asked. 'With everybody having gone home, except for the IMAX team and the lone French and Swedish climbers on the South Col, there's no one left but us.'

Ang Dorje brought another thermos flask of coffee and enquired about the time for bed tea in the morning.

'Five o'clock,' said Ian firmly.

There was silence and then an exchange of Nepali between the other Sherpas outside the tent.

'The Sherpas leave at 05:30,' said Ang Dorje meaningfully, before departing.

'I think that burst of Nepali meant: "Tell the lazy sods if they don't get out of bed in time, we're going without them,"' Ian interpreted.

23 May
06:30 – Camp 2

CATHY:
I sit in the kitchen tent, drinking yet another cup of tea. Is this the fourth or the fifth? I can't remember. They all blur into each other, an endless stream of hot, syrupy liquid. I woke up before five, and was ready to leave half an hour later. That was quite some time ago. No sign of life from the male contingent. The 'lazy sods' are as late as ever.

'They are worse than teenage girls getting ready for a party,' I tell Lakpa. He grins and seems to understand. I wonder if teenage Sherpanis are just like all other teenage girls when it comes to getting ready for the boys. Only now I wish the boys would bloody well get ready themselves.

Of all the things we have experienced together over the past weeks, this is what bugs me most. I am a punctual person, but I also appreciate my sleep, especially in the morning. I could have had an extra hour's sleep by now, with no difference to our leaving time. All sorts of more important personality clashes pass me by altogether, solved by some kind of mutual compromise. But this really gets me worked up.

I stalk over to their tent and peer inside. Bruce is fiddling. He has about 11 different pairs of gloves laid out in front of him: fleece ones, wool ones, thick ones, thin ones, red ones, blue ones. And he can't decide which particular combination to take today. For Christ's sake! And Ian is still asleep, sleeping bag pulled over his head, happily off in the warm and cosy land of Nod which I dragged myself from a long, cold hour ago, at his instruction.

I abandon them as a lost cause, steaming off up the glacier. Fuelled by righteous anger, I manage a magnificent couple of hundred metres before the altitude, the cold and the weight of my rucksack deflate my energy. The burst of speed soon wears off.

Bruce overtakes me and is the first up the bergschrund. He deposits most of his breakfast at the top of it before beginning the steep climb to camp 3.

For once, rather than battling cold, we are overcome by heat. My body slows down, and feels immensely hot and heavy with the load and the clothing. What on earth was I wanting a warm sleeping bag for? Now all I need is a cool swimming pool and an iced Coke. It's just too much to feel as if you are about to get heatstroke when at 7 000 metres on Everest, surrounded on all sides by ice.

But the heat isn't the only strange factor. The sky is clear and the mountain absolutely still. Nothing moves. After the weeks of express-train winds that have always sounded in the background, the silence is uncanny.

13:00 – Camp 3

'It's life, Jim, but not as we know it!' Bruce exclaimed as Ian's haggard face pushed through the tent door. As last into the tent Ian was left with the job of brewing up. He crouched by the door, trying to get the stove level on the uneven snow in the tent porch. Each time he put the pot full of snow on to the stove, it tilted crazily to one side or the other, spilling snow. With rising frustration he began to clear out the other junk that filled the porch, putting the rubbish packet right by the door, with his lighter balanced on top of it. Having levelled the snow, he successfully settled the stove.

'Got it!' he announced triumphantly to the others, who were sprawled out behind him. As he turned around to claim his space in the tent, the sleeve of his jacket caught the pot, which tilted over and knocked the rubbish packet. Panic-stricken, he spun back in time to see the little rubbish packet, and with it his lighter, spin down the ice slope, rapidly gaining speed, until they vanished down towards the bergschrund at the bottom of the Lhotse Face.

'Oops,' he said weakly.

There was a long pause.

'Bruce, mate. Can I borrow your lighter?'

'Oh give over,' said Bruce. 'Watching you trying to brew is like watching paint dry. I'll do it.'

He shuffled round to the front door, righted the stove and pan and pulled out his lighter. He spun it a couple of times but could only produce a tiny spark.

'Damn, won't work. Give us yours, Cathy.'

'My rucksack's outside.'

'Well, see if there's a spare one in the food packs.'

Cathy wearily pulled herself into an upright position and began to fumble around. After a prolonged scratching process she finally announced she couldn't find one.

'Well, get outside then, Caths, and get us yours,' said Ian.

'I don't think I'm carrying one,' she admitted sheepishly.

The three climbers looked at each other in consternation.

'And for the want of a nail, the battle was lost,' muttered Bruce as he continued to try to coax a spark from his beleaguered lighter.

No flame meant no heat. No heat meant no liquid. And no liquid, at these altitudes, meant rapid deterioration. They were already dehydrated from a long day on the ice with too few stops to drink. Another night and a day and they would be in serious trouble.

After all their effort, they stood to lose everything for such a small mistake.

'I've got it!' Bruce exclaimed triumphantly as he managed to get a tiny spark to ignite the gas and the stove roared into life.

The three settled down to the serious job of brewing, drinking and eating.

15:00 – Camp 3

A strange beeping noise suddenly filled the oxygen-deprived minds of the tired climbers.

'It's finally happened,' Bruce mumbled from the depths of his sleeping bag. 'The aliens have landed. First alien touchdown on Everest. If we can get the photos, we'll sell them to the *National Enquirer* for millions.'

'Shut up, Bruce, and find the radio,' said Ian. 'Someone's beeping us.'

Ian finally liberated the radio from underneath Bruce.

PHILIP: 'They've done it. They've reached the summit. All of them!'

IAN: 'Slow down, bro. Who's reached what summit, and when?'

PHILIP: 'The Frenchman, the IMAX team and all their Sherpas got to the top of Everest late this morning and early this afternoon, and the

Swedish solo climber finally got there a few minutes ago without
using oxygen.'

IAN: 'That's great news, Philip, they should've left us a good trail. Send
them all our best wishes and congratulations. Did they report any
difficulties?'

PHILIP: 'Not that we've heard of. Now you've just got to get yourselves
up there.'

IAN: 'We're trying, bro, we're trying. The weather looks good and
we'll give it our best shot, that's for sure.'

Bruce pulled out his thermos flask of lukewarm juice and silently filled the
three mugs, giving one to each of them.

'A toast,' he declared. 'To those who were successful today and to our success two days from now!'

They all drank in silence.

24 May
05:00 – Camp 3

Cathy woke at dawn. She rolled up on to one elbow to survey the two blue
down sausages that lay, unmoving, next to her. She tried shaking Bruce first.

'I'm sleeping until six,' he declared. 'I've been looking forward to it all
night.'

Cathy ignored the dubious logic of this and turned her attention to Ian. He
simply pulled the sleeping bag over his head in silent protest.

She looked out of the tent flap to find perfect weather, no cloud, no wind,
just hundreds of mountains basking in gentle sunshine. She began to brew up.

09:00 – Lhotse Face

On the long, steep haul up to the Yellow Band the South Africans passed
David Breashears and his team on their way back down. The three climbers
offered their congratulations to the American and he wished them luck in return. As the two teams chatted away, Dave warned the South Africans that
they would pass the bodies of Scott Fischer above the South Col and of Rob
Hall near the South Summit, a sobering reminder of what lay ahead.

'Odd lot,' Bruce commented as the Americans moved on down. 'Above
7 000 metres they turn into normal, pleasant human beings. Below 7 000
metres they become all strange.'

'I'm sure the world would be a far better place if all Americans lived above 7 000 metres,' replied Ian sarcastically, his aversion to Americans well known.

14:00 – South Col

The team finally moved over the top of the Geneva Spur and on to the traverse towards their top camp. It was completely clear, and for the first time they had a chance to appreciate the size of the col. It swept up on the left into the rock-dotted snow slopes of Everest. On the right it was drawn up into the rocky ridge that ran towards the summit of Lhotse. And in the distance it disappeared towards the great drop down the Kangshung Face of Everest into Tibet.

All the tents had gone, except for the two black South African tents that huddled together in the midst of the vast rocky expanse. Pemba had found some abandoned prayer flags and was busy stringing them up, providing a burst of colour against the black and white of the mountain. To the west, mountain after mountain protruded from a low-lying blanket of cloud. Otherwise the weather was clear and still.

15:00 – Camp 4

The climbers piled into the tent and began heated negotiation over bed space.

'I'm not being squeezed into the tiny coffin in the corner, like I was last time,' announced Bruce.

'It's not our fault if you're bigger than we are and take up more space. Sleep on my side if you want, if you can find place between the oxygen bottles and food bags, which for some reason always end up in my space,' offered Cathy.

'Or try the middle,' said Ian. 'Try being squeezed between two other climbers so that you end up with elbows in both sides and no space at all.'

Eventually Bruce consented to stay where he was.

They found the seven bottles left by Henry, and checked all the bottles to make sure they worked and were compatible with their oxygen regulators. Bruce and Ian found some half-full bottles abandoned by the IMAX team to use that night, so as not to break into their own supply. Then they started sorting out personal and communal equipment to take to the top. Ang Dorje joined them to talk about the arrangements for the summit bid. Three of the four Sherpas had climbed up to the col that day, but Nawang had remained at camp 2, having decided he did not feel strong enough to make a summit attempt. But he was keen to climb up to camp 4 the next day in a support role.

17:00 – Camp 4

As they worked, the sun slowly set, turning the cloud blanket golden, with row after row of shimmering peaks protruding from it. Cathy and Ian contented themselves with looking out of the tent door occasionally to monitor its progress.

'Now, of course, if we'd had a professional photographer with us,' said Ian, 'he would be out there taking dozens of photographs. A once-in-a-lifetime opportunity to watch the sun setting from 8 000 metres on Everest.'

'It's looking really beautiful,' reported Cathy, head stuck out of the tent door. 'All golden and sparkly. But it won't last long.'

Bruce muttered something under his breath and ignored the others.

'There's not much you or I can do with our little compact cameras,' Ian continued. 'But a real photographer, who knew what he was doing, with a proper camera? He could take some stunning shots. But I guess we'll just have to go back to South Africa without them.'

Bruce swore to himself and, grabbing his jacket and Canon, fumbled his way out of the tent.

'That wasn't very nice,' Cathy commented as, from the warm depths of their sleeping bags, she and Ian watched Bruce stomp off across the col.

'He'll thank us in the long run when he comes back with some stunning photographs.'

And Bruce did indeed come back raving about the beautiful views and berating the others for being too lazy to get out of the tent and look for themselves. They smiled and said nothing.

18:00 – Camp 4

As the evening radio check drew near, Bruce turned to Ian.

'Would you mind if I make the call?' he asked. 'I've been looking forward to this one all expedition.'

Ian just nodded and smiled.

BRUCE: 'Hello, Philip, this is camp 4.'
PHILIP: 'Hi, Bruce, how's everything?'
BRUCE: 'Well, Phil, it's nigh on perfect, so I have the pleasure of officially informing you that the South African Everest expedition will be leaving for the summit tonight.'
PHILIP: 'That's wonderful news, Bruce. Is Ian going as well?'
BRUCE: 'Roger, Philip, all six of us will be going.'

PHILIP: 'Okay, Bruce, I'll let you get some rest now. Everyone down here
             wishes you all the best.'
BRUCE: 'Thanks, Philip, we'll call you again just before we leave.'

18:30 – Base Camp

By the time Bruce radioed base camp to confirm that the team would definitely go, the support team were already well into their preparations for another long night. They'd moved sleeping bags and mats into the comms tent,
and prepared a small kitchen stocked with thermos flasks of tea and coffee.
Philip organised spare filtered kerosene for the generator, got the log books
ready, and worked out the order in which the various authorities needed to be
notified if the team reached the summit. Patrick spent the afternoon filing pre-
recorded 'voicers' to Radio 702, which they could play during the early hours
of the morning while waiting for news of the team.

The whole of base camp was very keyed up, following the successful summit bids of the previous day. They were excited and confident, yet also quite
nervous. The memories of the disastrous storm during the previous summit
attempt were always present.

And this time the South Africans were alone on the mountain. There would
be no one to help them.

14:30 (SA time) – Johannesburg

Brenda Woodall, who knew the team were high on the mountain but didn't
know exactly what their plans were, had been waiting by the phone all day. As
it rang she hurriedly picked it up.

PHILIP: 'Hi, Mom, it's Phil.'
BRENDA: 'Philip, how are you? What's happening on the mountain?'
PHILIP: 'Bruce, Cathy and Ian and three Sherpas are going for the summit
             tonight. The weather's great and their chances look good. We'll
             phone you with news as soon as we have any. Please spread the
             word to Cathy's family and friends.'
BRENDA: 'I will, Philip. Wish them luck for me and tell them to be careful.'

Brenda put down the phone and then sat for a few minutes to calm her beating heart. The long days of waiting had been hard on family and friends in
South Africa. There had been raised hopes before, and tragedies as well. Now

it seemed that the final wait was on. She telephoned her daughter, Jane. She could do with some company through the long hours of the night.

19:00 – Camp 4

'We'll wake at ten, and try to be gone by eleven, okay?' said Ian firmly.

'No problem, Ian,' smiled Cathy. 'I think the problem is going to be trying to get to sleep, not waking up.'

They both settled down in their bags, wearing their inner layers of clothing, thermal long johns and a thermal long-sleeved top, with fleece salopettes and some kind of warm, close-fitting shirt or pullover over that. The thermal layer had not been taken off since they left base camp a week ago. Into the bag with them went gloves, hats and socks, so that they'd be warm when the time came to put them on, and, most importantly, their insulated inner boots, which would otherwise freeze, making them impossible to put on again.

Bruce continued to sort through his equipment.

CATHY:

Oh my God! It's really beginning to happen. This time we are really on our way to the top. Will we make it? Will we all make it? If someone drops out, who might it be? If someone doesn't make it back, who might it be?

No, that won't happen. It's all perfect, at last. If we can just find the strength in ourselves to take advantage of the chance. I wish this was two weeks ago, when I felt that much stronger. But I'm feeling quite good now. So close … and yet so far to go still.

How on earth am I supposed to sleep? Butterflies are breeding in my stomach and my mind is racing in circles. But I must sleep. I need sleep. There isn't going to be much of that for the next 24 hours.

Bruce is still fiddling, with his camera gear, with his overboots, with all those bloody pairs of gloves. Just like last time, his pile of equipment gradually swells until suddenly he realises it has got too big and he starts to discard things ruthlessly. Until he spots something he cannot live without.

Go to sleep, mate. You'll need it.

22:00 – Camp 4

Ang Dorje's hand was pounding against the tent door, a thermos flask of tea ready to be passed in to the climbers. It was time to get ready. In between cups of tea, working in a sleep-deprived daze in the small pools of light cast by their head-torches, they struggled to dress for the cold night's work ahead. They pulled fleece jackets on over their clothing and began to struggle into down suits. The suits consisted of down salopettes with massive down jackets on top. It would be the first time they'd used the suits, the first time they'd had to climb in such extreme cold that they were necessary.

'Bloody hell,' Bruce muttered as he wriggled and twisted to try to get the down salopettes up over his rump, 'this is going to be like climbing in a sleeping bag with arms and legs cut in it. I feel like a Michelin man.'

'We'll never find you a Michelin man up here,' Ian quipped.

Ignoring Ian's awful attempt at humour, Bruce finally succeeded in getting the braces of his salopettes untwisted and correctly buckled, and then pulled on his jacket. Cathy started to laugh.

'You look like a giant blue snowman.'

Once the laborious process of dressing was over, gloves and hats had to be found and put on in the correct layers, thermal inner gloves, fleece or wool mittens over that, finally covered by Goretex mittens; then for the head, fleece or silk balaclavas with woolly hats pulled on top. Feet were already encased in warm socks and insulated inner boots. Now the inner boots had to be forced into the rigid, plastic outer boots, the frozen laces had to be tightened and tied, and last the nylon gaiters had to be pulled up and zipped closed over the bulky down legs of their climbing suits.

Climbing harnesses had to be pulled on over the giant boots and the waist straps buckled over the many different layers of clothing. Thermos flasks had to be filled with hot juice; oxygen sets checked and attached to bottles in the rucksacks. Sunglasses stored safely for easy retrieval at sunrise, a last check for cameras, spare batteries, extra film; a bar of chocolate secreted in an inside pocket so that, when the time came to eat it, it wouldn't be frozen solid.

This all seemed to take an age.

IAN:
Many roads and open doors, and a few dead ends, have led us to this moment. A few years ago we as South Africans were not welcome in Asia. A year ago this idea was simply the foolishness of one person. A couple of months ago we stood at the bottom of the mountain and for the first time saw the magnitude of our undertaking. Two weeks ago our fellow climbers were succumbing to the ravages of the great storm. Just a few days ago I was physically incapable of climbing out of bed. But now, at this very moment, we stand ready to make our final bid for the summit. And we are ready, individually and collectively. I'm proud of us. I'm proud of the little South African flags that have waited so patiently on our ice axes for their turn. I can't wait!

25 May
00:10 – Camp 4

At last they pulled themselves out of the tent, and stood in the clear, crisp night air. It wasn't as cold as they anticipated, and it was completely still. Bruce was busy sorting out Jangmu's head-torch, which had mysteriously decided not to work. Pemba was still fiddling with his oxygen bottle.

'We must leave, we must go,' Ang Dorje urged as he fidgeted in an agony of anticipation.

Above them the mountain loomed, a huge shadow of a darker shade of black, set against the night sky.

CHAPTER 11

09:52

25 May
00:12 – Camp 4

'Camp 4, camp 4, this is base camp.'
  Bruce grabbed the radio.

BRUCE:	'Phil, it's nice to hear your voice. We're just leaving. A bit of a mess sorting out the oxygen and the crampons and all the rest of it, but I guess we're on the move, mate. There's no need to stay open for us. We'll try to call you after six o'clock in the morning.'
PHILIP:	'Okay, Bruce. It's 13 minutes past 12 and I have two messages for you. The visibility down here is 20 to 30 metres using head-torches, and the temperature is zero degrees. There are no clouds, but there's a thick mist and fog.'
BRUCE:	'Yeah, that's great. That's good news, actually. That means conditions are quite stable.'
PHILIP:	'The second message is from the French team. They report danger between the South Summit and the Hillary Step. In the last 200 metres there is a snow overhang on the right-hand side. Do not put any weight on the overhang.'
BRUCE:	'Yeah, I copy that. That's pretty standard on that section so we'll bear it in mind. Thanks for that.'
PHILIP:	'Okay, Bruce, we'll let you get on your way. Everybody down here wishes you well, and it looks like you've got excellent weather for it. Just do it.'
BRUCE:	'Fingers crossed, mate. It's not going to be easy, but we'll give it our best shot.'

PHILIP: 'Right, we'll have the radio on, Bruce, so if there's a problem, give us a shout. Base camp is clear and standing by.'

BRUCE: 'This is camp 4 heading for the summit. Cheers now. Bye.'

As Bruce signed off, Pemba and Cathy were already heading across the rocky plain towards the ice step with Ian, Jangmu and Ang Dorje following closely behind, each climber moving in a tiny, individual pool of yellow light cast by their head-torch. As they disappeared into the darkness, each was reduced to a minute star in the inky blackness of the moonless night.

00:30 – South-East Face

CATHY:

I trudge slowly over the uneven surface of the col, and then move on to the hard blue ice of the ice step below the face. Bisected by narrow slots, some partially concealed by snow, the step requires concentration, which I have to dredge reluctantly from my sleepy mind and unco-ordinated body. I feel so slow, so heavy, disoriented from the lack of sleep, stiff and cold. As I move awkwardly up the steepening snow slopes, I trawl through my mind for every possible excuse for turning round and crawling back into the warmth of my sleeping bag: illness, altitude sickness, too slow and don't want to hold up the others. Unable to think of one that will convince Ian or Bruce, or, for that matter, myself, I keep moving. Thinking of excuses becomes a mental game, to distract me from the slog of the climbing.

I dread a night like I had reaching the summit of Kilimanjaro. There too we had left at midnight and climbed through those long, dark hours of the early morning. Although consisting of little more than unpleasant walking on loose scree slopes, it was exhausting and bitterly cold. I remember being desperate to stop for a rest, huddling down behind a rock seeking protection from the wind, and realising rapidly that the only way to keep warm was to keep moving. A devil's bargain, when rest and warmth became incompatible. Somewhere in those long hours, when it seemed as if the sun would never rise again, I decided to withdraw from selection for the Everest expedition team. I reckoned that if climbing Kilimanjaro could be this unpleasant, I didn't want to spend three months on Everest in similar discomfort.

But then a slim line of red had appeared on the horizon, and I immediately felt stronger. All thoughts of giving up dissipated with the darkness. Now, recalling Kilimanjaro, I steer my thoughts away from another long, cold night.

IAN:
I love this job. A beautifully still night at 8 000 metres on the highest mountain in the world. A unique mental and physical challenge lying ahead, and
a great team of friends with which to share the experience. I look quickly
around, revelling in the outrageousness of our situation. Hell, this is really
living, I feel so alive, there's truly nowhere else in the world that I'd rather
be than here. I've always thought that South Africans are ideally suited to
big-mountain climbing, because although we may not be the brightest
things on two legs, we never give up, we just switch off and buckle down to
the job in hand. So congratulating myself on being a South African, I give
myself a good slap in the face and set my sights on the climbing ahead and
begin to stomp into a routine that I hope will take me where no other South
African has ever been before.

02:20 – South-East Face

Once past the ice step the climbers moved up snow slopes, which became
steeper and steeper with every step, followed by a short section of tricky fixed
ropes up a snow gully. Above that the terrain changed to bands of loose rock,
sprinkled with snow. The climbers wound a devious route across ledges and
up unstable breaks in the rocky bands, with the insecure surface calling for a
degree of thought difficult to dredge up in the early hours of the morning.
Pemba climbed on steadily in front, stopping occasionally until Cathy caught
up with him. The headlights of the others were spread out on the slope below
them.
   The night sky was clear and pitch black. Occasional sheets of lightning on
distant horizons turned the sky momentarily electric-blue and the hundreds
of peaks of the Himalaya stood silhouetted in jagged black grandeur, before
disappearing again into darkness. The small circles of light formed fragile bub-
bles of purpose and direction in an otherwise limitless landscape. The only
sounds were the rasp of breath drawn through oxygen masks and the crunch
of snow underfoot.

03:00 – South-East Face

Pemba stopped once again, this time to fiddle with his oxygen set. Cathy
moved up slowly to stand by him.
   'No oxygen,' he blurted out, his voice on the edge of panic. 'It doesn't
work.'

Cathy tried to focus her attention on his oxygen set, to concentrate through the fog of sleeplessness and altitude. She checked the various indicators slowly and meticulously, assuring herself that the bottle was full and the oxygen flowing. She realised she must be missing something, but what?

The figure below moved up steadily to join them and she saw to her surprise that it was Ian and not Bruce. She waved a gloved hand at Pemba's oxygen cylinder and Ian leant over to inspect it. The oxygen was flowing so it had to be the regulator.

'You've got it on a 1-litre-a-minute flow rate, instead of 2 or 3,' said Ian, playfully punching their Nepalese team-mate in the ribs. 'No wonder you aren't getting any air.' With a quick twist of the valve he adjusted the regulator. Pemba nodded his thanks and gave Ian and Cathy a firm thumbs-up before turning his attention back to the mountain.

CATHY:
We climb on up the steep slopes of shattered rock and loose snow. Even though Pemba is ahead of me and Ian close behind, I feel intensely alone. No one else can know what I feel now, no one can help me find the strength to do this. We are higher than all but a few mountains in the whole world, but still this one looms above us, disappearing into the inky night. I am frightened. The snow slope seems so steep, yet not steep enough. It is too precipitous to walk up easily, yet not vertical enough to plunge my ice axes into properly. Below me it falls away into yawning blackness, the void both concealing and emphasising the drop down to the South Col.

I am acutely aware of how much height I have gained in the last three hours. To fall now would be to fall all the way down, to roll and bounce and scream, smashing into rock and ice, before landing on the rocky col, still, broken, like a rag doll.

I am frightened.

I am aware of Ian's presence a few steps below me. I take comfort in that nearness, although I will probably never tell him that. I consider telling him that I am scared. But there is no point. There is no way out of this. Even to give up means returning down the treacherous ground I have come up. And it is always harder to descend. This high there is no rescue. For me to freeze with fear only endangers the others.

And besides, I am not that afraid. I have not put in months of effort, weeks of slog, to give up 12 hours from the top. I just want to share my feeling. I compromise and imagine telling Ian, while not actually doing so. I fear that he would not understand, that he would read my admission as weakness. I know it is not. It is acceptance of who I am, knowledge that I can be both frightened and capable simultaneously.

As I am battling my private demons, the snow has been changing from grey to salmon to faint pink. While I move upwards, the first false light of dawn illuminates the line of the eastern horizon. Slowly the red smear spreads sideways and then reaches up into the sky. As the sun rises from the horizon so far below us, the mountain turns vivid pink. The plateau below is striped with pink, orange, blue and purple. The deep valleys on either side of the mountain fill with dark blue shadow. The South Col appears out of the darkness, reduced to a little black postage stamp between Everest and Lhotse, the tents invisible. The yellow orb slips smoothly into the pale sky, and light and life and confidence return with it.

Now that the night has passed, I am surprised by how short it was, and how warm. The sweat is trickling down my back, stewing in the warmth of my massive down jacket and salopettes. In the end it was easier than Kilimanjaro. I clamber on to the ridge that we will turn to follow to the summit. The junction is marked by a dozen orange oxygen bottles with the names of David Breashears and the IMAX team emblazoned on their sides. I sink down in the snow beside Pemba, resting gratefully against my rucksack, and watch Ian toiling up towards us.

04:00 – South-East Ridge

Ian pulled off his oxygen mask.

'Remind me to ask Herrod if he still thinks that slope really isn't all that steep,' he said, referring to a comment Bruce made the night before.

'I thought the summit pyramid was supposed to be straightforward,' said Cathy. 'I didn't enjoy that climb at all. It needed some thinking about.' She hesitated before continuing. 'I'm tired, and frightened.'

'Why?' asked Ian. 'Frightened of what?'

She hastened to explain.

'Not now so much. But coming up that steep slope with the huge drop.'

Ian grinned at her.

'I'm proud of you.'

Taken aback by this unexpected reaction, Cathy could think of nothing to say in response.

The three climbers looked out over the Himalaya, the black and white mountains now glorious in pink, purple and gold. The sombre pyramid of Makalu dominated the view, a massive mountain of classic proportions, fifth highest in the world. To the left, the deep valley of the Kangshung Glacier reluctantly emerged from darkness. On the horizon, the squat form of the giant mountain of Kangchenjunga, third highest, reigned supreme.

CATHY:

I find a deep sense of satisfaction in looking out over so many mountains, and being apparently equal with some of the biggest. The long slog through the dark has yielded its reward, a giant leap in height, concrete evidence that we are making progress and might actually be able to complete this challenge.

But then I turn to look upwards. Above me the long snowy ridge winds up towards the South Summit. A tiny line traces its way up it, the footsteps of the Americans and French from two days previously. And the main summit is still hidden, the path to it still elusive, the big unknown in our assessment of our ability to reach it.

Pemba, eager as ever, begins to move up the ridge. Aware of the cold and stiffness seeping through my body, I start to follow him, with Ian close behind. I find it distinctly depressing to have Ian following me so closely, given his poor physical condition over the last few days.

I sink the shaft of my ice axe into the soft snow and bend over it, arms folded across the head, to rest. Ian moves on past me. It is rather like losing a race to a snail, I think dismally as I watch him plod steadily upwards. We both seem to be moving incredibly slowly. I assume it is some time in the mid-morning, but the effort of locating a watch under the numerous layers of clothing and gloves seems too great. I mark time by the gradual rise of the sun.

I battle through the soft snow, sinking up to the knee with each step, my axe shaft plunging into the snow as if it were butter. The steps left by others crumble away under the new weight. The resulting progress up the ever-steepening ridge is slow and painstaking. In a few places tattered remnants of fixed ropes lie in the snow, their anchor points uncertain and their history unknown.

I become aware of a giant pyramid of blue, running across the cloud and the peaks of the Nepalese Himalaya. I stare at it in puzzlement for a moment before realising that it is the shadow of Everest, cast by the rising sun. I stop to photograph it, thinking it is so beautiful ... and so big.

IAN:

I can feel the power surging through me. The climbing is superb, the situation dramatic, and the view breathtaking. The concept of the challenge is perfect in its simplicity. To keep going higher and higher, until we have to stop or start going down into Tibet. It's the raw simplicity, the ability to focus on one overriding goal without any complications, that drives me now, and I look forward expectantly to the next step, and the next, and the next.

06:00 – South-East Ridge

'We're above 8 500 metres,' Ian called down to Cathy.

'How do you know?' she asked, before realising that he couldn't hear her through the oxygen mask. She fumbled with mittened hands to pull the mask off and then repeated the simple question.

'We've cleared the top of Lhotse,' he replied, gesturing towards the black bulk of rock on their left.

They looked towards the giant mountain that had dominated their walk-in to base camp. The mountain that had loomed over their trips up the Western Cwm and their days at camp 2. The mountain whose slopes they'd so diligently and so repeatedly climbed, counting each step done, cursing each step still to take. And now the giant was below them.

It was another landmark attained and passed, but still the bulk of Everest towered over them, the endless, undulating slopes up to the South Summit blocking all thought of what lay beyond.

08:00 – South Summit

IAN:

I hoist myself up on to the top of the South Summit of Everest. At 8 700 metres Pemba and I are standing higher than any other mountain in the world. Only the summit of this mountain is higher, by 148 metres. But can we still go higher? I'm not sure. I'm feeling strong but I don't know what time it is. I don't know how long I've been climbing. That's the issue, how long I've been climbing, not some arbitrary time of the day set by people who've never been up here. But the later it is now, the longer I've been climbing, the closer I'll be to my limit and the less I'll have in reserve. Notwithstanding how strong I'm feeling, by the look of the sun we've been climbing too long and we'll probably have to settle for the South Summit.

Ian thought that the possibility of reaching the summit had probably gone, but as the two friends were sitting there in the snow, higher than any other human beings on earth, Pemba grabbed his arm excitedly and pointed to his own watch.

'Very good time, Bara Sahib, very good time.'

Looking at Pemba's watch, Ian quickly realised that he'd been fooled by the sunrise, not appreciating how early the sun had risen at this extreme altitude. They hadn't been climbing as long as he first thought so they should still have the reserves to make the summit in good time. He opened up the radio to call

The great storm

Above left: The South Africans' camp 4 on the South Col, with the summit pyramid of Everest behind, as the storm of 10 May gathers. Above right: Ian relaying news of the storm down to base camp. Below: Cathy and Ian leaving the South Col on 12 May, passing the storm-damaged tents of other teams

Aftermath of the great storm

*Opposite: Ian descending down the
Yellow Band on 12 May. This page, top:
A helicopter landing at base camp to
pick up storm casualties. Right: Bruce
and Deshun crammed into the camp 1
tent on their way to camp 2, 18 May.
Below left: Bruce, Cathy and Ian (from
left to right) ready to climb on from
camp 2. Below right: Ian checks the
damage to his feet at camp 2*

Final attempt

Above: Ian ties South African flags on to iceaxes in preparation for leaving for the summit. Right: As dawn breaks on 25 May, the climbers are high on the snow slopes above the South Col. Below: Bruce calls base camp on the radio on 24 May to tell them the team leaves for the summit at midnight

So near, yet so far

Left: Ian climbs up the Hillary Step on the summit ridge, photographed from the South Summit. Pemba is on the slope above him. Below: The shadow of Everest lies across the mountains of Nepal

The summit

Top: Cathy appears over the last rise before the summit of Everest, with Lhotse behind. Above left: Ian (left) and Cathy on the summit, flying the South African and Nepalese flags. Above right: The entire base camp crew celebrates the summitting with San Miguel beer. Left: Ian walks away from the summit

...and after

Top left: Ian below the Hillary Step, just before he falls off. Top right: Ian and Cathy on their arrival back at base camp on 27 May. Right: Cathy and Ian with the celebratory cake at base camp. Below: The last photograph taken of Bruce, as he climbs up the South-East Ridge. Pemba descends behind him

The Bruce Herrod memorial

Top left: The lama conducting the Buddhist memorial ceremony. Top right: Philip, Ian and Cathy (left to right) next to the memorial to Bruce. Right: The stone placed in the Bruce Herrod memorial. Below: The memorial, lying in the shadow of the great mountains of the Himalaya

down to base camp. Philip, who'd been dozing by the base station, jumped up, startled.

IAN:	'Philip, I'm not exactly sure what time it is, but I'm sitting on the South Summit with Pemba at the moment.'
PHILIP:	'Okay, Ian. It's eight minutes past eight, it's 08:08. Are you having a bit of a rest up there?'
IAN:	'I wasn't actually sure what time it was, I wasn't sure whether to carry on, or to stop at the South Summit.'
PHILIP:	'I think you can afford a few minutes for yourself up there. Have you seen any of the others?'
IAN:	'Cathy's about 20 minutes to half an hour behind me, although 20 minutes on the ridge isn't actually that long. I think Bruce has given up. I haven't seen him for a couple of hours, so he's either turned round or he's just sitting waiting somewhere. I'll tell you what, though, this ridge is a lot steeper than I'd expected.'
PHILIP:	'Roger that, Ian.'
IAN:	'Okay, Philip, I'd better sign off now. I haven't had a look over the top yet to see what the Hillary Step and the rest of the ridge is like. I may not risk it if I don't like what I see.'
PHILIP:	'Okay, 10-4, Ian. Call us whenever you like. It's eleven minutes past eight now so you're still in good time.'

Ian and Pemba started cautiously down from the South Summit towards the narrow ridge leading to the dreaded Hillary Step, the great boulder that breaks out of the snowy summit ridge. They were telling each other to be careful, Pemba in Nepalese and Ian in English.

IAN:
I stand at the bottom of the South Summit, looking at the narrow sliver of snow leading towards the Hillary Step, just the width of one footprint and with terrifying vertical drops on both sides. On the left the huge expanse of the South-West Face, and on the right the incomparable Kangshung Face. No room for error here, Ian. A single slip, a single stumble, and it's good-night Irene. Hell, maybe we should have brought a rope with us after all. Still, I've come this far!

But before I can move anywhere I have to pass the silent, still figure of Rob Hall lying curled up in the snow. We'd been told he was resting below the South Summit, but I'd expected him to be on the South Col side, not here on the summit side. Anyway, that's all history now, I can't change what has happened, but I can pay my deepest respects to a fellow climber taken so tragically by the mountain. As I stand here for a few quiet moments, I recall the horrors of the storm that Rob fought so bravely for so long. I try to imagine what type of man, what type of guide, stays with his ailing comrade, rather than make a bid for safety on his own. Would he be alive now if he'd left his client? I guess nobody will ever know.

I nod my respects to a brave man before re-focusing my attention on the climbing yet to be done. The traverse across to the step is mountaineering exposure at its most extreme, and as I edge my way across I tremble and shake with nervous excitement.

Suddenly I hear Cathy's voice behind me and, turning, I see her standing on the top of the South Summit.

CATHY:

As I cross a miniature yellow band, several feet of the same yellow rock found on the Lhotse Face, I experience a growing feeling of suffocation. A quick glance at my regulator shows me that my oxygen bottle is empty. I sit down in the snow to change it for a fresh one, to remove my by now unbearably hot down jacket, and to rest. I leave the empty bottle to collect on the way down.

By the time I am moving again Pemba is out of sight and Ian is disappearing up the twisting ridge. I move in my own miniature universe, where the only sound is my body straining in activity, and the only sight the few steps directly in front of my feet, the next few steps to be taken.

Achingly slowly, the South Summit approaches. I block it out, watching only the two steps in front of my feet, saving a look upwards for the occasional treat, to convince myself that I am actually making progress. I climb on with grim determination, all my effort focused on reaching the South Summit. All thought of what is beyond it has been pushed into the background.

I wonder how far ahead of me Ian and Pemba are. Am I moving hopelessly slowly? I imagine standing on the South Summit and seeing them in the far distance, somewhere near the summit, realising that I can't make it. I imagine standing on the South Summit and Ian yelling to me to turn round, saying that it is too late, too far for me. And I imagine myself telling him to get stuffed.

At last I clamber on to the top of the South Summit of Everest. 8 700 metres, not bad going, I whisper to myself. Higher than any other mountain in the world. Higher than K2. I feel an amazing sense of disbelief that it should actually be me who has achieved all this. But can I go further?

I look on to the ridge that runs towards the true summit. In a few shocked seconds I absorb several salient facts. It is a classic mountain ridge, knife-edged, corniced, twisting gently up over a series of rises. I instantly recognise the rock step on the ridge as the Hillary Step and realise that it isn't as fearsome as I had imagined. I notice the doll-like figures of Pemba and Ian approaching the step, and see they aren't as far ahead of me as I had feared. I take in the precipitous nature of the ridge and the immense drops on either side of it and dismiss them as do-able. And I realise that although the summit is still not in sight it can't be too distant.

From deep within me incredible excitement wells up.

I can do that, I can climb that ridge. I have the energy and the ability. For the first time in the entire expedition, standing on the summit of Everest manifests itself for me as a concrete possibility, rather than just a wishful daydream. All the weeks of uncertainty, of bad weather, of ill health are swept away in the awesome realisation that the goal lies so tantalisingly close.

08:45 – Summit Ridge

'Ian,' Cathy yelled, and watched as he turned cautiously towards her. 'Ian, I'm going on.' It was a statement, not a question, but she was still relieved when he waved enthusiastically in agreement.

'Be careful,' he called. 'Any sign of Bruce?'

'No. He and the two Sherpas seem way behind.'

She paused for a few minutes to photograph Ian as he tackled the Hillary Step, and then moved down towards the start of the ridge.

IAN:

So this is it, the infamous Hillary Step. The vertical section of rock that repulsed the strong Yugoslavian team a couple of weeks ago. I don't like rock climbing, I never have, but if I want to reach the summit of Everest I have no choice. As I'm contemplating the best way of tackling the climb (there wasn't really any serious thought of me not climbing it), Pemba comes up behind me and with a few deft moves skips his way to the top of the step. Damn, I hate rock climbers, I mutter to myself as I step off the psychological safety of the snow ridge and begin to scrape my crampons on the warm, hard rock. It isn't a pleasant sight, but after 20 minutes of panting, cursing and some rather peculiar moves, I eventually deposit myself in a steaming heap next to Pemba on top of the step.

'Bara Sahib better ice climber,' he understates as I estimate how much I'll get for his gold tooth if he ever describes my 'step performance' to another living soul.

I'm anxious to move on, on towards the summit. It's not far now, just a matter of some 50 metres. Pemba has already moved ahead, but I quickly catch him up and squeeze past as he balances on the narrow snow ridge. On and up, on and up. I can feel the waves of excitement and anticipation well up inside me. Then there it is, the dash of beautiful colour marking the summit of the world. My eyes begin to run and cloud over with emotion. I turn to shout to Pemba, but he's already seen the top and has taken out his camera to record the moment a South African reaches the top of the world for the first time.

Life is so precious, and for human beings on this earth so short, but I can still compress my entire 40 years of life into this moment, this one moment of being higher than any other human being on earth, and I do!

09:50 – Summit

Ian slumped down in the snow a few metres below the summit and took off his oxygen mask. The last few metres could wait a few minutes, he thought, while he got his breath back. He planted his ice axe in the snow beside him. He had at last realised a dream that had been born long ago in a damp London bedsit. The South African flag was flying on top of the world.

He pulled the radio out of his rucksack.

'Ian calling base camp.'

09:51 – Base Camp

Patrick and Deshun were sitting on the blue barrels in the comms tent finishing off the last of their breakfast when suddenly Patrick jumped to his feet as he heard a faint voice crackling through the base station radio.

'Call Philip, call Philip, Deshun,' he shouted excitedly.

'Who is it?' she asked.

'It's Ian,' he replied.

'Where is he?' she asked again.

'I don't know, but call Philip quickly.'

Philip hurried in and grabbed the radio.

PHILIP: 'Hi, Ian, this is base camp. Come in.'

As Philip spoke, the satellite phone rang. Patrick hit the record button on his tape recorder and then dived for the phone.

Ian's voice came through distant and crackly.

IAN: 'We have 09:52 and the Nepalese and South African flags are fly-
            ing on the summit of Everest.'

09:52 – Summit

> IAN:
> I speak the words with a feeling unlike any other. I allow the sensation to
> flow through me, to become part of me. I want to drown in it, hold on to it
> forever, to be able to recall it at will, to be able to take it with me wherever I
> go. To parcel it up and give it to my children and grandchildren. I don't
> know whether to laugh or cry, so I do both.

09:53 – Base Camp

At receiving the news the base camp crew broke out into wild cheering.
'Well done, guys, well done!' Philip yelled as he felt the tears welling up in
his eyes.
'Well done, Ian. Fantastic!' called Deshun as she hugged Patrick.
Shankar came running into the tent at the sound of Ian's voice. He grasped
the situation in a single glance and ran back outside to grab the tins of San
Miguel beer that he'd been chilling on the ice of the glacier. He and all the
other staff crowded into the tent, passing around the beers in celebration.
Patrick had answered the phone to find it was the producer of the Radio
702 morning news programme.
'Hold on,' he said. 'There's a broadcast coming through, they're somewhere
on the mountain.' Then he began to shout. 'They're on the summit! They're
on the summit! Put me on the air! Put me on the air now!'
In a moment he was live on the Jeremy Maggs show, and with the adrenaline pumping he began to file reports. The radio station had prepared an hour-
long lead-in package to run up to the climbers reaching the summit, but had
not even begun it, never having expected the South Africans to reach the top
so early. The various talk-show teams had been betting on whose shift the
summit would fall in. Now Jeremy Maggs had the honour and it was one of
the most exciting moments of his broadcasting career. The news went out at
six o'clock in the morning in Gauteng, to friends and family, to insomniacs
and early birds, to depressed rugby fans who had just watched the All Blacks
thrashing the Springboks.

10:00 – Summit

As Ian spoke into the radio, he noticed Pemba waving his ice axe gleefully in the air and pointing back along the way they had come. Looking up, Ian saw a small figure standing on the lip of the snow slope below them, and a broad smile spread across his face.

IAN: 'If you hold on about ten minutes, Philip, you're about to have a third.'

PHILIP: 'Is Cathy on her way?'

IAN: 'Roger that. She's just on the last little serac. She'll be about ten minutes.'

PHILIP: 'Okay, Ian. Sit down, take some oxygen. Wait for Cathy. Give us a call then. Don't tire yourself out.'

IAN: 'No, I'm fine. I'm fine.'

PHILIP: 'Okay, we're standing by for you. We're standing by for Cathy.'

IAN:

Soon we'll be three. A challenge worth doing is a challenge worth sharing, and there is no one on earth whom I would rather share this moment with than my team-mates, because without them I wouldn't be here myself. Cathy will soon join Pemba and me on top of the world. Who'd have thought it? One can never be sure, but after that first day in the icefall, which seems a lifetime away now, Bruce and I agreed that we certainly wouldn't bet against her making it. I'm so happy for her, so proud of her.

10:05 – Summit

Pemba, meanwhile, clambered on to the summit for the picture made a classic by Tenzing Sherpa almost 43 years ago. Straddling the summit, with one leg in Tibet, the other in Nepal, Pemba held his ice axe aloft, with the Nepalese and South African flags fluttering in the gentle breeze. His face was split by an enormous grin and the sunlight glinted off his golden tooth. Then he photographed Ian proudly holding the South African flag above the summit of the world. As he looked out around him, Ian identified seven of the world's highest mountains, all over 8 000 metres – to the east Lhotse, Makalu, Kangchenjunga, to the west Cho Oyu, Shisha Pangma, Manaslu and Annapurna. He was higher than all of them.

Pemba then grabbed the radio, and in a long, animated spiel of Nepali told Shankar and all the other South African base camp staff the dramatic details of his ascent. He then called his friends at the Swedish base camp, and those at the Taiwanese base camp. Quickly realising that there were still another 11 base camps to be called, and only limited battery resources, Ian retrieved the radio from Pemba and waited to give it to Cathy when she arrived.

06:10 (SA time) – Johannesburg

Back in South Africa the families of the various climbers were waiting, anxious for news. Ian's mother, Brenda, and his sister, Jane, had been sitting by the radio since four o'clock that morning. Suddenly they heard Patrick's excited chattering, and then Ian's voice, scratchy but distinct, speaking from a place so far away from Johannesburg. Jeremy Maggs then called Brenda on the telephone.

JEREMY: 'Congratulations, how do you feel?'
BRENDA: 'Oh, I feel wonderful. I think it's such a great achievement. I'm sorry Bruce is not with them. I do wish him well. I hope Cathy is there very, very soon. I'm sure so many people are listening and I think it's a wonderful achievement.'
JEREMY: 'Brenda, could you explain to us how you have felt over the past couple of weeks as your son embarked on this expedition which had become so dangerous, so many people have died on the slopes of Mount Everest? Has it been very difficult for you as a mother watching her son, listening to his exploits?'
BRENDA: 'Yes, it has. It has, Jeremy. It's been very difficult. But, you know, it's something that they want to do, and then you mustn't stand in their way. This is something that they want to do and so they must go ahead and do it.'
JEREMY: 'When he comes back to South Africa, and obviously we're all praying today that they will make that descent safely as well, what's the first thing you're going to say to him?'
BRENDA: '"Do you need a cup of tea?" I think. He loves his cup of tea. A big hug, and then a cup of tea. And when he's ready, he'll tell us all about it.'

10:10 – Kathmandu

Brenda immediately phoned Ian's father, Ken, who was just leaving the hotel in Kathmandu to fly back to South Africa.

'Daddy, there's a telephone call for you,' called the Nepalese hotel manager, using the name by which Ken is affectionately known in Nepal. Looking quickly at his watch to see if there was time to take the call before leaving for the airport, he slipped into the manager's office. A few minutes later he emerged with a slight, suppressed smile.

'No problem?' asks the manager anxiously.

'No problem at all,' answered Ken. 'My son's just climbed Everest.'

08:50 – Summit Ridge

CATHY:

I move down the short steep slope to the start of the ridge. I notice a set of orange oxygen bottles piled by the track. And something else, a long, blue shape. I realise with shock it is the body of Rob Hall. But here? From all I remembered of the events of the storm, I expected him to be lying on the other side of the South Summit.

But now it is the crossing of the ridge that claims my attention. It is slow, cautious work. The trail runs just to the left of the knife-edge of the ridge, staying below the cornices that hang over the Tibetan side, while staying above the unstable dinner plates of rock a few feet down on the Nepalese side. The only flat ground is the footprints left by previous climbers. I move up the ridge almost as if I have put on mental blinkers, seeing only the two footsteps ahead of me. With each step I sink the shaft of my ice axe into the snow on the uphill side, using the head of the axe to provide a handhold. It is a little like walking along an undulating plank. Not particularly difficult, as long as you ignore the fact that there is a 2 500-metre drop on one side, and a 3 000-metre drop on the other.

Despite my concentration, other thoughts and memories wander through my head. It is ten years and half a world away from orientation week at Wits University in 1987. I knew then that I hated all physical activity, or what I knew of it in the form of school sport. Nevertheless, I enjoyed the outdoors, although I knew nothing of the sport of climbing. I had spent the week wandering around the university, looking at all the different clubs on offer. I had watched with disbelief the figures in old khaki shorts and shocking pink lycra scaling the library wall, and listened to the pitch from the Mountain Club chairman. I was not convinced, and was more interested in joining the Exploration Society. But on the very last day, with the abandon born of spending my father's money, I decided to join the Mountain Club as well.

Little did I know then where I would be ten years later.

My steady progress along the ridge is broken by the sudden rock wall of the Hillary Step. I stop short, trying to re-focus mentally from snow to rock. The first section is relatively easy, involving some cautious scrambling up and round big blocks. Then a careful traverse across loose scree brings me to the foot of an awkward, angled chimney. The floor is unstable rock and snow, the chimney just wide enough to wriggle up with a pack on. I work my way up it, suddenly conscious of the burden of the bulky clothing, the big oxygen set, the enormous boots and crampons. Jammed awkwardly near the top, I contemplate the tangle of ancient fixed rope that hangs down the back of the chimney. The creeper-like mass consists of bits of all sizes and colours, much bleached bone-white from years of extreme weather. Manoeuvring past it without getting it tangled around my rucksack, crampons or ice axe is as much of a challenge as negotiating the wall itself. Finally I grab a huge bundle of it in one hand and pull, wriggle and flop my way on to the summit of the block.

Again, odd memories float through my mind. I remember the first rock climb I ever did, Donderhoek Corner in Upper Tonquani, all of grade 12. A classic chimney thrutch, it was an unprepossessing beginning. The second was Hawk's Eye, a daring 13. Although I coped well with the wall, it took quite some talking to get me to climb over the nose of the Hawk's Eye. I quite enjoyed the climbing, was less impressed by the amount of flaming Sambuca being thrown down everyone's throats, and was far from convinced that this was an experience to be repeated. However, I was impressed by a young and handsome blond called Mike Cartwright. And given that the only place he could be found on the weekends was in the kloofs, I decided to give this climbing lark another go.

Once above the Hillary Step the ridge widens slightly, still corniced and very steep on the Tibetan side but slightly gentler on the left, before the steep drop of the South-West Face. I realise with amusement that although the exposure, and the danger, is far greater here than on the slopes lower on the mountain, I feel no fear, only exhilaration. I can see straight down the South-West Face of Everest into the Western Cwm, down to the tiny camp-site over 2 000 metres below me, our camp 2. We have come a long way since then, and a longer way still from home.

I've been moving alone along the ridge for some time. Pemba and Ian are out of sight ahead, the other three climbers somewhere behind. Although I mostly concentrate on the few steps in front of me, blocking out the vast empty spaces surrounding the ridge, occasionally I allow myself the luxury of looking out across the myriad of snowy peaks below. With no one else in sight, and no signs of human existence visible below, it is like being the last person alive on earth, having the whole of a magnificent planet to myself.

I feel humbled, aware of how frail and fragile the humans are dotted on the side of this huge edifice of snow and rock. I am also frustrated. The ridge undulates gently. Each crest looks as if it might be the final one, but as I drag my weary body on to the top I find another one slightly higher, slightly further on. The ridge seems to run on interminably in front of me. I feel like the *Flying Dutchman* trying to round the Cape, or as if I might be on a snowy treadmill, a ridge that runs forever with no conclusion, and I am condemned to walk it for eternity.

I've anticipated the false summits, recalling reading about them in Stacey Allison's account of the first American woman's ascent of Everest. I try to suppress all expectations, to deal with the ridge step by step, rather than face the inevitable disappointment expectation of the summit would bring.

My mind wanders once more, seeking escape from the mental boredom of the slow, plodding ascent. I recall my first great pronouncement on my climbing career. It was made halfway up a small, loose and aloe-strewn rock-face in Wilgepoort. I was following the route with a friend, Linda Waldman. I told her that while I liked climbing, I had no interest in learning to lead rock routes. She agreed. Within a few months we were both leading.

My next great pronouncement came after a friend hauled me up a 300-metre rock-face at Blouberg. The first few hours I enjoyed, but then I was ready to go home. Unfortunately we were only halfway up. I announced that I was interested only in walk-ins under half an hour, and climbs of 50 metres or less. Over the next few years I climbed big walls all over the country, from Blouberg, to the Drakensberg, to the Western Cape, and then moved on to 600-metre rock walls in the Alps.

My third great pronouncement was that, although big walls were great, you wouldn't catch me dead mountaineering. Too high, too cold, too dangerous ... Little did I know.

I move slowly up yet another small rise and on to the top of it. And stop short, aware of two figures and a sudden blaze of colour. Ian and Pemba are seated in the snow with something behind them that to my puzzled gaze looks rather like a ruined tent. After hours in an almost monochrome world of blue sky, white snow and black rock, the medley of red, yellow and green is disconcerting. Then Pemba turns and sees me. A huge grin spreads across his face and I notice his gold tooth glinting in the sunlight. He stands up and begins to wave both arms and his ice axe in the air.

That's it, I think. That is the summit of Everest.

For the second time today I am filled with an incredible sense of excitement. At last I know that not only am I capable of climbing Everest, but that I have actually done it. Only ten more metres. I never imagined it would get to this.

The last slog up the final slope seems interminable. I am very tired, stopping to rest every four or five steps. I clamber slowly towards the dash of colour, which becomes a pile of prayer flags covering a metal tripod.

Ian speaks into the radio: 'And then there were three.'

Philip's voice comes through in a chatter of excitement.

I sink down on to my knees beside Ian and hug him, barely able to feel the man beneath the piles of clothing we are both wearing. I turn to hug Pemba, acutely conscious of the pleasure of being able to share the moment with friends and team-mates. I am glad that I am not here alone.

10:10 – Summit

Ian thrust the radio into Cathy's hand. Pulling off her mask, she was aware of the immediate drop in oxygen as she breathed in the ambient air and began to pant. She realised she'd be fine for a while but dared not stay off the bottled oxygen too long. She spoke into the little black box in her gloved hand.

CATHY: 'Hello, base camp, can you hear me?'

Everyone offered her their congratulations.

CATHY: 'I did it. I don't believe it. I am actually there. It's amazing.'

PHILIP: 'Cathy, sit down, take a break, take some oxygen and we'll call you back in a minute. Your mother is on the phone at Radio 702. Call us back when you've caught your breath.'

IAN: 'Roger, we're on standby.'

PHILIP: 'Okay, any sign of Bruce, Ian?'

IAN: 'Negative.'

PHILIP: 'We'll give you five minutes to catch your breath and if you don't mind we'd like to do some patching.'

IAN: 'Roger, but please make it quick because we don't want to get chilled. We want to get out of here.'

PHILIP: 'Okay, will do.'

06:20 (SA time) – Johannesburg

Cathy's mother, Patricia, had been listening to the radio on and off throughout the night. Then suddenly the news had come, and Jeremy Maggs was on the telephone.

JEREMY:	'How do you feel this morning, Patricia?'
PATRICIA:	'Afraid, excited and tremendously proud of what they have achieved.'
JEREMY:	'Last night, as you know, about midnight they were waking up in that small tent in camp 4, they had hundreds of metres to go to get to the top of Mount Everest, 8 848 metres to the top, how did you feel? Did you get much sleep last night? What was going through your mind as your daughter attempted one of the great physical feats that is known to mankind?'
PATRICIA:	'A feeling that one wants the younger generation to be thus far ahead of one. One wants them to realise one's own aspirations, one wants them to speak for the values of the country.'
JEREMY:	'Patricia, was she always keen? Was she always someone that you knew was going to do something special?'
PATRICIA:	'She was always keen, she was level-headed and has always had a wide view of the world. And she had the potential to do something different, something unique.'
JEREMY:	'So this doesn't really come as a surprise that she's actually done it?'
PATRICIA:	'Yes, it's in her character, it was there, it was a potential, but then so many of us have potentials that we don't necessarily realise.'

10:12 – Summit

Jeremy's voice came through faintly to the summit of the world.

JEREMY:	'Cathy O'Dowd, congratulations from all of us here at Radio 702. You're standing on top of the world at the moment. You've made it to the summit. Very simply, if my voice is coming through to you, how does it feel at the moment?'
CATHY:	'Hi, I guess that's my cue. I couldn't hear all of that, but, yes, I'm sitting, basically, gasping on top of the world and it's amazing. I can't believe that we've actually done it. And that after everything that we've been through we've actually made it up here.'

Then her mother's voice came through faintly from the black box.

PATRICIA:	'Hello, Cathy? Good morning, darling. You are the star for us.'
CATHY:	'Hi, Mom, it's great to hear your voice. It's amazing to be up here. We've been, we've been climbing since midnight and we've finally

made it. I can't believe we've done it. It's the most incredible feeling.'

PATRICIA: 'Cathy, darling, your team have done everything that South Africa wanted them to do. We are so proud.'

CATHY:
How strange it is to be so far away and yet so intimately connected, to stand on the summit of the world and speak to my mother in her living room in Johannesburg. It is a huge thrill to be able to share with her the very moment that I am on top. My parents have been so supportive through all the difficulty, never hinting to me what worries or fears they may have.

I try to sort my thoughts coherently, to be able to say something meaningful over the radio. But the emotions that are swelling through me toss my words into chaos.

06:30 (SA time) – Mpumalanga

Cathy's father, Michael, who was at a business *bosberaad* in Mpumalanga, was still in bed. Out of range of Radio 702 transmission, he had been phoning his wife each morning and each evening for news, and then relaying it to the directors of Anglo American and De Beers. The deputy chairman of Anglo American now came bursting into his bedroom, waving a radio. 'Michael, your daughter's on the radio. She's on the top.' They ran out on to the balcony, Michael still in his pyjamas. As they strained to get a decent reception on the radio, Cathy's voice came through faintly, gasping with the lack of air.

10:15 – Summit

Cathy was then asked to describe her surroundings.

CATHY: 'Well, Ian is busy holding the South African flag in my face. There are three of us, myself, Ian and Pemba, sort of crouched together in a huddle trying to keep warm, and we're just surrounded on every side by mountains and clouds. It's absolutely incredible. I've never seen anything like it. I haven't even really had a chance to look around me yet, but it's one of the most beautiful things I have ever seen. To be up here is a huge personal triumph. But for us it's much more than that, because we're here as South Africans, as the first South Africans. We're here with the flag on top of the world and it's really amazing to be up here, climbing as high as we can possibly get.'

Pemba, meanwhile, was packing up and Ian was beginning to become anxious to move as well.

IAN: 'Philip, Pemba wants to move down and I think that's a good idea. We just want one or two photographs and then we'll need to make a move.'
PHILIP: 'Okay, Ian, just stand by please.'

Brenda Woodall's voice came through faintly on the radio.

BRENDA: 'Hello, Ian, can you hear me? Ian, you're on top of the world, darling.'
IAN: 'Hello, mother. Yes, I can hear you loud and clear.'
BRENDA: 'Oh Ian, it's wonderful. Congratulations to you and to Cathy. I hope Bruce will be behind you soon. It's a wonderful achievement for you both.'
IAN: 'I couldn't really hear what you said, mother, but I'm sure you wished us all the best, and thank you and we will be safe. We're going to start leaving now.'
BRENDA: 'That's wonderful news, Ian. You're coming down soon. We wish you well. God speed. Take care.'

Philip then took over the radio again at base camp.

PHILIP: 'Thanks, Ian, that was great. We've done it the way we wanted. Almost.'
IAN: 'Okay, roger, Philip. We're going to sign off now.'
PHILIP: 'Okay, when will you call me again?'
IAN: 'We'll call you from camp 4.'
PHILIP: 'Okay, 10-4. We copy you now at 10:20.'
IAN: 'I roger that. This is the South African Everest Expedition on the summit of Everest signing off. Out.'

    IAN:
What must it take for parents to let go and support their children when they know they're taking such great risks? To sound so calm and in control when their emotions must be in such turmoil? The feeling of standing on

the summit of Everest is like no other, but the ability to share that feeling with one's team-mates, and most especially with one's family, even at such great distance, makes us all truly children of the universe.

CATHY:
Ian hands Pemba the camera and he and I clamber on to the summit itself, perched next to the tripod and flags, holding out Ian's ice axe with the Nepalese and South African flags hanging from it. The wind is so slight that we have to hold the flags out. After weeks of battling the most ferocious winds, the breeze is now not even strong enough to make the flags flutter.

I look down at the multi-coloured blaze of the South African flag with a shiver of excitement. I remember being a teenager, standing in my school hall in Johannesburg, mouthing the words of 'Die Stem' and wondering what it would be like to live in a country where one was actually proud to be a citizen, where the anthem and the flag really meant something.

And now I know.

I never expected to do something under the colours of my country, to make any kind of public contribution to the achievements of the nation. But now as I look down at what is for a brief moment the highest flag in the world, I am proud to be South African, and proud to have forged a small place in the history of my country.

As Ian moves down to begin packing his rucksack, I turn to look at what actually marks the summit of the world. The large metal tripod left by the Americans in 1992 as part of a re-surveying of Everest's height is almost covered in vividly coloured Buddhist prayer flags. Beneath them is a collection of tiny photographs in frames. They are presumably the family of some previous summiteer. Although I know we will not leave the South African flag on the summit but take it back with us, I am reluctant to leave no trace of South Africa's brief passage across the top of the world. I take off my gloves and fumble to remove the South African flag badge that is pinned to my fleece jacket. I place it in the snow and next to it put a tiny gold seal given to me by a friend and the film canister given to me by the trekker. When I promised him I'd leave it as high on the mountain as I could, neither of us ever expected that it would go this high, I thought with a private smile.

Part of me wants to relax, to sit down and soak in the sense of really being on top of the world. But that is overwhelmed by the nagging worry of the long, long way we have to descend. Every one of those steps so laboriously taken on the way still has to be taken before we are safe again at camp. The summit is not a finish in any sense, but only a halfway point. We have not yet succeeded at our given challenge. I know the risks of descent, the chances of making a mistake due to tiredness or simply lack of concentration. With the drive for the summit gone, all that remains to keep us moving is the survival instinct.

Ian and Pemba are packing up to leave and I join them reluctantly, with one last glance out across the hundreds of mountains below me. Whatever I climb in the future, I will never have to climb this high again. And thank God for that. To spend only 15 minutes on top after months of effort to get there seems less than logical, but now all that matters is the long descent. And in the end it has been about getting here, not about being here. I follow after Pemba with Ian bringing up the rear.

'Be very, very careful,' he calls.

I take a few photographs of Ian leaving the summit and of Pemba descending, before running out of film. Not wanting to dig around in my rucksack to find more, I turn to Ian.

'Ian, do you have any more film?'

'You shouldn't be taking pictures,' he explodes. 'You should be concentrating on getting down. It's very dangerous and this is no time for photography. We must just get on down.'

Yes, sure, Ian. We are going to go back to South Africa and we are not going to have a single damn photograph of the summit ridge. And you are going to wonder what happened. I'll take these pictures, and you'll love them. I decide to ignore him quietly.

IAN:
I want the sensation of being on top of the world to last forever. I want to stay here forever. Part of me wishes I could, but I know I'll have to go back down. Not out of fear, but out of responsibility. Maybe one day I'll be able to climb to the summit of a great mountain and make it my home forever, but not this one, and not now. I take one last quick look around and then begin to follow Cathy and Pemba back towards the Hillary Step.

10:35 – Summit Ridge

As they moved steadily down towards the Hillary Step, they encountered Jangmu and Ang Dorje moving determinedly upwards. A brief spurt of Nepali from Pemba informed them of the team's success. Wide, affectionate grins spread across their faces as they congratulated Ian and Cathy.

'Bara Sahib, Didi, *ramro*, very well done,' they said.

'You guys going on to the top?' asked Ian.

'Oh yes,' they confirmed.

The team-mates wished each other well and then split into those going up and those going back down.

IAN:
Our Nepalese team-mates are climbers and mountaineers, fathers and husbands, but most of all they are carefree spirits driven in search of the unknown. They aren't climbing Everest for the money or the prestige, they're climbing Everest to challenge themselves as individuals and as men. They are free to decide whether they continue on to the top or accompany us back down, and they have decided to go on. That's what being free really means.

10:55 – Summit

Ang Dorje and Jangmu slowly made their way up to the top of the snow slope, to the point where it went down on all sides. Jangmu had been here once before in his life, when he climbed Everest from the Tibetan side, but for Ang Dorje it was an unexpected culmination of his long career as a climbing sirdar. The two Sherpas solemnly shook hands and then Ang Dorje, his face split by a huge smile, pulled out his radio and called down to base camp to tell them all about it.

11:00 – Base Camp

At base camp the celebrations continued unabated, the mood one of joy and delight. People from other expeditions were coming across the glacier, shaking hands, hugging the team members, passing on their congratulations to the climbers.

'I'm so happy,' Deshun told Patrick. 'There were times on this trip when I just wanted to pack up and go home, but now I am so glad I stuck it out. My spirit was with them on the mountain all the time.'

'It was such a great moment when Ian radioed down and said he'd made it,' Patrick agreed.

'You know, a lot of teams who left thought us crazy for trying again,' Deshun continued. 'They said no one had ever climbed Everest that late in the season since Hillary and Tenzing did it. People just wanted to abandon the whole idea of climbing this season. They couldn't understand that after everything that had happened we were still pushing ahead. But I understood that we needed it for our country. All those other countries have long since had their first national ascent. So they don't understand the whole culture of "I'm doing this for my country" any more.'

'Don't tell me,' Patrick said. 'Tell South Africa. We've got a surprise for you back in 702land.' He handed her the telephone. She could hear Jeremy's voice bubbling with excitement on the other end.

JEREMY: 'So how does it feel, Deshun? Your team have made the top of the world.'

DESHUN: 'I'm obviously ecstatic because I'm part of the team, and I've been here, down at base camp, seeing everything through and really hoping that our team would make it. My jubilation is actually, I don't know, I can't put it in words ...'

Her mother was then patched through by telephone.

MRS DEYSEL: 'Congratulations for Cathy and Ian. I didn't sleep all night. I was climbing with them.'

DESHUN: 'Thanks for being with us in spirit, Mom.'

MRS DEYSEL: 'You must tell them I say congratulations and I was so glad I hoped I could shout at them through the radio, so that they could hear how excited I was.'

Radio 702 then spoke to Sir Edmund Hillary, the man who, with Tenzing Sherpa, first reached the summit of Everest on 29 May 1953.

SIR EDMUND: 'I would like to congratulate the South African team on their success. I think everybody in South Africa can be proud of their efforts. The descent of the mountain can be quite dangerous so I would imagine that they would be coming down very carefully indeed, and taking good care that they reach the bottom satisfactorily. I've always felt that it's one thing to get to the top, but the complete success is only when you get safely to the bottom again.'

11:00 – Summit Ridge

IAN:
I stand at the top of the Hillary Step and size up the options. Climb down or stay where you are. Yes, well, not exactly much of a choice. Normally climbing down is more difficult than climbing up, but in this case with such

heavy loads, the added bonus of gravity working in our favour really helps. The problem that troubles and concerns me most, however, is not the impending rock climb, but my glasses. Every time I look down to see where to place my feet the warm air from my oxygen mask condenses in a thick mist on the inside of the glasses and I'm immediately blinded, and 8 800 metres on Everest is not a good place to be blinded. I think of removing my glasses until I get safely to the South Summit but dismiss that instantly as one of the quicker ways of committing suicide, as within minutes of removing my glasses I'll be totally snow-blind from the intense glare of the snow and ice.

There's nothing for it, Ian, you'll just have to make do, climb down the step as best you can and then clean your glasses before edging out across the narrow ridge back to the South Summit. Settling on a compromise, I keep my glasses on but remove my oxygen mask, deciding that I can probably negotiate the climb down the step without bottled oxygen. So, frowning to myself and without much confidence, I gently lower myself down over the edge of the step.

I reach the small snow saddle between the bottom of the Hillary Step and the beginning of the narrow ridge, panting hard but without any major difficulties, although my glasses are completely misted up notwithstanding the removal of my oxygen mask. It's essential that I clear my glasses before moving on and, as it will take two hands, I look for a firm footing before starting the job. We're still unroped so any slip or stumble will certainly end in tears. Seeing the dark outline of a footprint in the snow through my misted glasses, I move my right foot and place it safely and firmly into the snow.

But there is no snow, only empty air. Empty air broken only by the bottom of the 2 000-metre drop down the South-West Face of Everest. Panic and fear chase each other up from my stomach, through my chest and battle to be first out of my throat, as I lose balance, and my heavy rucksack swings slowly but inexorably towards the drop and I begin to fall.

This is it then, Ian, the end of the road. Shame that it had to end this way. So I'm going to stay on Everest forever after all. The panic and fear have been replaced in fractions of seconds by logic and understanding. Damn, do I always have to be so logical?

I know that there's no way I can stop myself from falling, but my left arm swings my ice axe in a wide arc towards the narrow snow ridge, just for the hell of it really. Suddenly it grips and my left shoulder is wrenched as, after only a few metres, I stop falling and hang unceremoniously from my blessed ice axe, looking straight down the bottomless South-West Face. As I gaze down into the abyss I see a small South African flag floating gently towards the bottom. My beanie has come off in the fall and slowly, without any undue ceremony, offers to take my place on the sudden, downward journey.

CATHY:

I stop at Rob Hall's body for a few minutes, a tiny personal tribute to the life, the achievement and the tragic death of this talented climber. You must have been on such a different mountain from my Everest to have only got this far on the way back. It is so strange that we could both be climbing the same mountain and yet have such radically different experiences.

I cross over the South Summit and on to the steep ridge below. A small figure is visible below me, beyond Pemba, still moving determinedly upwards. Dear God, it's Bruce. I thought he'd given up. He is climbing up the steep ground above the rock step. I pause to take a photograph of him as Pemba passes him. He stops to wait for me and as I approach him he puts out his arms. He pulls me into a huge bear hug as we balance precariously on the ridge.

'Pemba gave me the news,' he says. 'Well done, woman. I'm so chuffed you guys have done it.'

We sit down together in the snow.

'Are you okay, Bruce? Are you having any problems?' I ask.

'I'm okay,' he replies. 'Just moving very slowly. It's mostly my own fault. I left camp some time after you. I was fussing around with my overboots and then trying to sort out Jangmu's oxygen. So what's the ridge like after the South Summit? How long did it take you to cross it? And how hard is the Hillary Step?'

As he quizzes me about the climbing above us, the nature of the difficulties, the length of time I had taken on each section, I realise he has no intention of turning back with us. I am not sure what to say to this. I wait for Ian to join us.

12:00 – Summit Ridge

Ian joined them and Bruce pumped his hand.

'Well done, mate. It's amazing you made it,' he beamed.

'Thanks, bro, I even surprised myself,' Ian joked in return, squeezing his best friend's hand.

'I guess there's life in us old timers after all.'

'It's not the age, it's the mileage. Listen, youth, are you going to come back with us?'

'I want to go on,' said Bruce firmly.

'Bruce, mate, I think you should come back down with us, you're not moving that fast,' Ian reasoned.

Bruce's ready smile in no way hid the steely determination in his voice.

'No, I've come this far. I'm going on.'

'Well, just go on for an hour, see how far you get and then turn round,' Ian said reluctantly.

Both Cathy and Ian assumed Bruce would simply go on to the South Summit, a major achievement in itself and then turn back from there.

'You must get a bottle of oxygen off Ang Dorje or Jangmu, and take Ang Dorje's radio,' said Cathy.

'Base camp is on permanent standby, and we'll be listening in as much as we can. If anything happens, just call. And call to tell us how you are getting on,' added Ian. 'And you know the route down? You remember where to turn off the ridge?'

'Yes,' said Bruce. 'I stashed a few things at the shoulder junction with the ridge in that Rymans bag I had. It's just straight down the ridge to there and then down the slopes.'

'Good luck then and be careful,' said Ian, shaking Bruce's hand again.

Ian and Cathy watched him move slowly on upward, before turning round to continue down the mountain.

> IAN:
> A man's a man who looks a man right between the eyes. Bruce is such a man. He is a better and more experienced climber than either Cathy or me. He has expressed his desire to climb a ridge that Cathy and I have just soloed ourselves. He has expressed his desire to fulfil a lifelong dream. Notwithstanding the insanity of trying to 'order' someone down or bodily restrain them in so precarious a position, Bruce is free to decide his future. Bruce is a man.

12:20 – South-East Ridge

A short while after leaving Cathy, Ian and Pemba, Bruce passed Jangmu and Ang Dorje, and took Ang Dorje's radio and another full bottle of oxygen. Ang Dorje also suggested that Bruce turn round, but he remained adamant. He opened up the radio to call down to Phil.

PHILIP: 'Bruce, there you are. Where've you been, my bro?'
BRUCE: 'I've been having a bit of a bad morning, Phil.'

PHILIP: 'How're you feeling, lad?'
BRUCE: 'At the moment I'm feeling great. Everybody has summitted ex-
             cept me. I'm about 30 minutes below the South Summit. What
             I'm going to do is press on on my own to the South Summit,
             keeping a very close eye on conditions and weather and myself. If
             everything's all right on the South Summit, I'm going to take the
             radio with me. I'll check in with you, and then I'll press on, just
             to see if I can top out.'
PHILIP: 'Great stuff, Bruce. Just watch it. If you feel bad, turn straight
             around. We'll be with you all the way, we're going to copy you on
             the radio. Sue's been on the phone a few times. I will phone her
             immediately and let her know where you are. Please call me as
             soon as you can.'
BRUCE: 'Yeah, okay. This is Bruce going clear for the time being.'
PHILIP: 'Go for it.'

12:30 – South-East Ridge

CATHY:
About halfway down the ridge I experience once more the slow sense of
suffocation that comes from wearing an oxygen mask when no oxygen is
coming through. My second bottle has run out.
    'I'm out of oxygen, Ian. I'm going to wait to see if one of the Sherpas has
a spare bottle. If not, I bet I'll find some half-used ones in the IMAX junk.'
    We sit down in the snow together and look down the ridge and out
across Tibet. Straddled across our line of view is the giant black pyramid of
Makalu, a classic mountain shape, emerging from a sea of low cloud. The
ridge normally climbed to reach the summit lies directly in front of us.
    'It's a magnificent mountain, Makalu,' I say casually.
    'Yes, and not an easy one,' Ian answers.
    'I'd love to give it a try,' I add even more casually.
    'Let's deal with one mountain at a time, shall we?' he replies.
    I know he plans to climb it sometime in the next few years, and I want to
be there. But let's get off this one first.

13:30 – South-East Ridge

Ang Dorje was climbing down very slowly, stopping to rest often, and looking very pale. He was constantly muttering incoherently to himself in Nepali

and seemed to be hallucinating. Ian found a discarded cylinder of IMAX oxygen, quickly replaced Ang Dorje's set and then sent him off in front to lead the team down. Realising he was in quite a bad way, Ian wanted to give Ang Dorje something to do, something to think about other than his exhaustion. He wanted to keep him concentrating.

Cathy eventually moved past Ang Dorje and continued down to the shoulder junction, where she sank down on her pack, deciding to wait, rather than tackle the steep slopes to camp 4 alone. She noticed Bruce's Rymans bag, held down by two oxygen bottles.

Ang Dorje led the others down to join Cathy and slumped beside her exhausted, his head in his hands. Ian arrived next and stood leaning on his axe waiting for the others to recover enough for the final stage back to camp. Jangmu, bringing up the rear, waited on the slope above.

14:00 – Base Camp

At base camp the waiting continued. In South Africa Radio 702 had been trying to contact President Mandela, and at two o'clock Nepalese time, they finally got him on the Jeremy Maggs show.

JEREMY: 'On the line from Cape Town we've now been joined by South African President Nelson Mandela. Mr President, thank you very much for joining us this morning, particularly at short notice.'

PRESIDENT: 'Well, thank you. Is that Patrick Conroy?'

JEREMY: 'It's Jeremy Maggs talking, Mr President. I'm going to put you through to Patrick Conroy in just a moment, but could I ask you how you feel at this particular point, the significance of what our climbers have done?'

PRESIDENT: 'Well, it is very important, not only for the purpose of inspiring the youth but for the whole country. We are all excited. All these achievements are putting South Africa on the map, and are inspiring everybody in government, in business, amongst the workers and throughout the various sectors of our community to emulate this example.'

The president was then patched through to Patrick at base camp.

PRESIDENT: 'Okay, I can't hear you very clearly but I just want to say that the news came to us as a real surprise, and also a cause for jubilation because of the fact that the conditions on top there were not

conducive to this achievement, but our children did very well indeed. And it shows the character of which all South Africans are
made of. I cannot wait long to welcome them back to the country.
I think that they deserve one of the highest recognitions that we
can give to people who have made this wonderful achievement. It
has created a tremendous ...'

PATRICK *(cutting in):* 'Mr President, I can confirm that they are a very determined bunch of climbers and they are very proud to be flying the
highest flag in the world right now on top of Everest. They're
making their way down and the last time we spoke to them, they
sounded safe and sound, and I'll be sure to pass that message of
yours on to them. I'm sure it will encourage them greatly to get
back, not only to base camp safely, but also back to South Africa,
sir.'

PRESIDENT: 'Thank you very much. If there is a possibility I would like to
speak to Cathy O'Dowd and Ian Woodall, but only when they
reach the area of civilisation when I can speak to them on the telephone. In the meantime give the children my heartiest congratulations.'

PATRICK: 'Mr President, we do have your numbers and I'm sure that as
soon as they are near a radio, the first thing they will do is they
will contact you. I'll make sure of that.'

PRESIDENT: 'Very good. Have you got our telephone? Let me give ...'

PATRICK: 'Yes, yes, we've got your number.'

Patrick interrupted, beginning to panic as he visualised President Mandela
giving out his personal telephone number live on air. He could imagine every
citizen in South Africa phoning Madiba up at home to complain about everything from the state of the nation to the neighbours' barking dog, and Patrick,
as a result, never working in media again.

14:00 – South-East Face

CATHY:
I dread climbing down the steep snow slope that I found so frightening on
the way up, but daylight and descent make it easier. We move across the
loose rocky ledges relatively quickly, passing Scott Fischer's body all
wrapped up in rope. Like Hall, his face and hands are covered. I am surprised by his location, because in the end he isn't that far from the South
Col. I move on to the fixed ropes, conscious only now of sore knees, deep

exhaustion and an overwhelming desire to reach the tents. By now the mist is swirling round us and light snow is falling.

I have moved ahead of the others, apart from Pemba, and am met at the bottom of the fixed ropes by Nawang, who moved up to camp 4 earlier today. He hands me a cup of tea from the flask he carries, and then a cup of soup. The hot tea burns a trail down my throat and I realise I have drunk virtually nothing since midnight and eaten nothing, not good planning.

'Didi, well done,' he says. 'I am sorry I wasn't with you. At camp 2 I had headaches and vomiting. I couldn't come that day.' He seems most anxious that I shouldn't think he has been neglecting his job.

I give him a tired smile. 'It really doesn't matter, Nawang. You were very sensible. It is just so nice to see you now.'

I walk slowly up to the tents, pull my pack off and simply stand there.

Thank God we're back. It's over. We made it.

I am too tired to feel anything much, but slowly go on with the chores of pulling on warm, dry clothing, while waiting for Ian.

IAN:

I'm beginning to get really tired now, nothing specific, just a general run-of-the-mill complete exhaustion. It's nothing to do with the time of day, and nothing to do with some ridiculous, arbitrary 'cut-off' time, but has everything to do with the fact that I've been climbing at over 8 000 metres continuously for the past 16 hours. I look with satisfaction at the figures of Pemba, Cathy and Ang Dorje safely in front of me and I know that Jangmu is only a few steps behind, so as long as Bruce can keep out of trouble, then we're doing well. I know I'm very tired but that's okay, I've been very tired before. I know I'm slow but I also know I'm in control. I reach the end of the short section of fixed ropes above camp 4 and sit down with Nawang for a welcome cuppa. A friendly smile from a team-mate and a warm drink, such are the simple pleasures of climbing big mountains. Well, best be moving on. The tank's definitely reading empty now, enough to get back to camp, but only just.

16:00 – Camp 4

Cathy waited for Ian, who arrived at last and stood exhausted by the tent door, huddled over, head down, hands jammed into his armpits. Cathy waited for a few minutes and then seeing that he seemed to be beyond moving, climbed out of her sleeping bag reluctantly. She pulled Ian's oxygen bottle out of his rucksack, fished out his down jacket and bullied him into the tent.

At twenty minutes to five Ian pulled out the radio and called Philip to report their safe return. His first concern was to make sure that base camp and the Nepalese government knew that the three Sherpas had reached the summit as well.

IAN: 'Thirty minutes after we topped out, Ang Dorje Sherpa and Jangmu Sherpa reached the summit of Everest as well.'

PHILIP: '10-4, Ian. We spoke to Ang Dorje on the summit. Shankar spoke to him as well.'

IAN: 'Oh, sorry I spoke. I didn't realise our Sherpas were that radio-oriented.'

PHILIP: 'That's a roger, Ian. We copied you on the summit at 09:52, we copied Cathy on the summit at 10:10, we copied you leaving the summit at 10:19 and we copied Jangmu and Ang Dorje on the summit at 10:55. Roger so far?'

IAN: 'Yes, I roger that. I can confirm that all the Sherpas are safely back in camp 4.'

PHILIP: 'Okay, that's great, but we're very worried about Bruce. We spoke to him at 12:22. He informed us he would be going for the summit alone and would call us, but he hasn't called since 12:22. We don't know where he is.'

IAN: 'I roger that. We met him on the ropes and we tried to convince him to turn round and come back with us. But you know, everyone's got to make up their own minds.'

PHILIP: '10-4, Ian. Do you know what the problem was? Why was he so far behind you?'

IAN: 'Basically, it's a hell of a long way. It really is steep, and he was just moving slower.'

PHILIP: 'Okay, 10-4. He said to us he had a problem but he didn't say what the problem was. I think you guys better settle down and get some hot drinks and some oxygen, and we've got a scheduled call at six o'clock, unless Bruce comes in earlier.'

IAN: 'Yeah, okay. I roger that. As long as he's sensible, which I'm sure he will be, he can keep to the trail we've broken and he shouldn't have a great deal of difficulty in getting back.'

PHILIP: 'Is it snowing up there, Ian?'

IAN: 'Yes, roger, it is snowing, the normal sort of rubbish we'd usually expect in the afternoons.'

PHILIP: 'Okay, 10-4. That's great. Well done, you guys. I don't know if you want me to read all the goodwill messages from South Africa now, or do you want to wait until six o'clock?'

IAN:	'Negative, Philip, we'll wait for Bruce to get here, because, whether he made the top or not, and I guess he didn't otherwise he would've phoned you by now, he's part of the team. So we'll wait for him to get in, and we'll go for the six o'clock call.'
PHILIP:	'Roger, Ian. We have a request from President Mandela. He'd like to speak to you directly. Do you want to do that at six o'clock?'
IAN:	'Negative, Philip. A little later if we can. It's a little fraught up here at the moment.'
PHILIP:	'10-4. We'll go by your timetable, whenever you're ready.'
IAN:	'Okay. I'll go with six o'clock. It's a rather knackered camp 4 signing off. Out.'

Both climbers crawled into their sleeping bags and lay there in the quiet of the early windless evening. Cathy reached across to hug Ian.

'I'm so glad you made it, and made it first,' she said. 'If any of us deserved that summit, it was you.'

And she meant it with all her heart. After all the effort he had put into organising and running the expedition, he had certainly earned that summit a hundredfold.

'No, if anyone deserved it, it was you. You were marvellous,' he smiled. 'I can't think of the right words for it now, but I guess I will later.'

They lay back in tired silence listening to the gentle, reassuring hiss of their oxygen regulators.

'I wonder where the hell Bruce has got to,' Cathy said.

'He should be back any minute now,' Ian replied. 'He must've turned back somewhere near the South Summit, though it would've been nice if he'd called us to say so. Anyway I told Phil to hold all the congratulations and the talking to the president until he's back.'

'For sure. It's a team achievement, whoever finally reached the summit,' Cathy agreed.

17:00 – Base Camp

Patrick and Philip stood back to look at the cardboard sign they had just constructed out of an old piece of computer packaging. It hung proudly, if somewhat askew, above the satellite telephone.

'Kind of sums it up, doesn't it?' said Patrick.

'Yep, that it does,' replied Philip.

The sign read: 'Our children did very well indeed.'

CHAPTER 12

Free to Decide

25 May
17:00 – Camp 4

Bruce's voice came crackling through on the radio that lay on standby between the two sleeping bags. Cathy and Ian, who had both been dozing, jerked up in confusion and Ian grabbed the radio, fumbling to find the call button.

IAN: 'Bruce, mate, where are you?'
BRUCE: 'I'm on the summit of the world.'

Bruce's voice came through strong and joyful. He sounded immensely proud of himself. Ian and Cathy stared at the radio and each other in horror.

IAN: 'You're not on top of the mountain at the moment, are you, you stupid tosser?'
BRUCE: 'Yes, I'm a stupid tosser.'
IAN: 'Firstly, congratulations, mate, and secondly, man, you've really got to get your arse down here.'
BRUCE: 'Yeah, thanks for the congratulations. They've been hard earned. Yes, I'm about to turn tail and head down.'
IAN: 'Bruce, be real careful, mate. What's the weather like where you are?'
BRUCE: 'Pretty benign, so I'm not too worried.'
IAN: 'Okay, well, it's really crappy down here. Are you happy to follow the ropes all the way down to where you left your Rymans bag, and then you've got to turn right off the ridge?'

BRUCE: 'Yep, I'm going to do my best. I've taken careful note on the way up. I'm just so chuffed that I've finally made it. It's been a long time coming, mate, and I'll be real careful on the way down.'

The point that concerned Ian most was that Bruce might miss the tents in the dark once he was off the ridge. The descent down the summit pyramid was relatively straightforward, but finding two black tents on the immense expanse of the black rock col could be hazardous.

IAN: 'Now, when you come down, you'll get to the bottom of the fixed ropes. If you need to, if it's a whiteout, stay and radio us from the fixed ropes and I'll send Nawang to come and fetch you.'

CATHY:
The summit! Bloody hell, what's he doing there? He's supposed to be making his way safely back down to us. And why did it take him so long?

But he's got guts, to keep going all that time, to get done what he wanted to do.

Shall I get on the radio and congratulate him? No, I'll wait. Let him concentrate on getting down and I'll give him an enormous hug when he gets back to camp.

Come on, Bruce. Get back down. We've all done it now and that's great. Now let's go home.

17:05 – Base Camp

Philip was hunched over the radio base station, attention fixed on every word. Bruce's girlfriend had phoned from London just as his call had come through. Ian signed off and Philip put her through.

PHILIP: 'Sue, go ahead.'
SUE: 'Hi there, how're you doing?'
BRUCE: 'Guess where I am.'
SUE: 'Please will you get down off there as fast as possible?'
BRUCE: 'Don't worry, I was on my own on Aconcagua and I'll be real careful coming down. I'm not going to rush everything. I've got too much to look forward to.'
SUE: 'I'm thinking of you all the way down. You need to be very careful. And make sure you find the oxygen dump. Be safe. Okay?'
BRUCE: 'Yeah, thanks ever so much for waiting. I love you dearly.'

SUE: 'I love you too. I'm with you all the way. Please come down
            safely. There's everything to look forward to. You'll be all right.'
BRUCE: 'Yeah, don't worry. It's just going to be one long plod on the way
            down.'
SUE: 'Okay, then please start off soon because I know there's not too
            much daylight left.'
BRUCE: 'Yeah, two hours should see me all right. I've left all the little bits
            and pieces up here that we spoke about. It's been a real pleasure.
            It's been a long, long road.'
SUE: 'You're damn right. It's been a very long road. So please, please,
            please concentrate from now on. Okay? I love you, all right. So
            please come down.'
BRUCE: 'Yeah, don't worry, there are one or two very sobering reminders
            on the way down, so don't worry on that score. I'll be down very
            safely. Don't you worry at all. This is the summit of the world
            signing off to Camden Grove and it's one hell of a pleasure.'

Patrick took over on the phone call to Sue. He reassured her that the weather
was good, and that Ian was giving Bruce very clear instructions about how to
get back and what to look out for. He promised to stay in touch and that, if
there was any news, she would be the first to know. Philip took over on the
radio.

PHILIP: 'Bruce, what the hell are you doing up there? How're you doing?'
BRUCE: 'Thanks very much for the patch to Sue, Phil, it meant a hell of a
            lot to both of us. Thanks a lot, mate.'
PHILIP: 'You're very welcome, mate. Don't linger around. Get your arse
            down. I think Ian's going to give you some pointers where the
            oxygen is.'
BRUCE: 'Okay, will do. Thanks a lot, mate.'
PHILIP: 'Okay, Bruce, well done. Keep in touch. This is base camp clear
            and standing by.'

17:15 – Camp 4

Ian was anxious to explain to Bruce the route back to camp 4 and where he
and Cathy had left extra oxygen if he needed it during his descent.

IAN: 'Bruce, how's your oxygen, mate?'
BRUCE: 'So far so good.'

IAN:	'Okay listen, youth, we've left two spare full bottles on top of your Rymans bag.'
BRUCE:	'Roger, Ian.'
IAN:	' So you must head straight down the ridge, and then turn right at the Rymans bag. From there it's straight down the snow slopes until you come to the fixed ropes. You can call us when you get to the bottom of the fixed ropes.'
BRUCE:	'Yeah, let's see how I go on that one. What sort of signal do you want?'
IAN:	'We'll have the radio on standby so you just have to buzz us.'
BRUCE:	'Yep, okay, I'll see how I feel by then.'
IAN:	'Is the weather holding up?'
BRUCE:	'Yeah, it's actually clearing up a bit up here. I think it'll drop into the valleys as I go down.'
IAN:	'Okay, Bruce, I won't keep you. Well done, but make sure you watch your arse on the way down.'
BRUCE:	'Yeah, thanks very much, mate. I'm so chuffed that I've made it. I'm not going to screw up now.'
IAN:	'Cheers then, youth, be safe.'
BRUCE:	'Yeah, I'll speak to you later, and thanks for all your support, mate.'

17:20 – Summit

Bruce pulled his camera out of his rucksack. He hadn't taken any photographs all day, but this was one scene that he was not going to miss. He pulled off his mitts, now wearing only his red inner gloves, so he could fiddle with the delicate camera controls. He fixed the camera to the top of his ice axe and looked through it carefully. He positioned it so that he could see the summit tripod, the blaze of prayer flags, the pyramid that made up the highest snow in the world, and the curve of the horizon so far beyond and below. Once he was sure it was in place, he moved round to position himself next to the summit tripod. As a last thought, he pulled round his green beanie so that the South African flag would be visible in the photograph. And with a big grin, he pushed the button on his remote control. He'd done it!

17:30 – Camp 4

Cathy and Ian looked at each other in consternation.

'I never expected him to go on for that long,' she said. 'I'd have thought he would have turned back hours ago.'

'So would I,' said Ian. 'But he sounded fine on the radio.'

'Yes, he sounded lucid and strong. Better than I must've sounded when I was puffing away on top, and he's just so thrilled, so excited to have done it.' She smiled at the memory.

'He's where he wanted to be, and in all conscience I don't think we could've denied him that, even if he'd listened to us, which he didn't,' Ian said thoughtfully.

'It meant so much to him to have got there. You could hear it in his voice,' Cathy added.

They sat in silence, the thoughts of all they had achieved, all they had been through to achieve it, and all that Bruce was still going through, circling inside their heads. Visions of the steep snow slopes, the broken, rocky ledges, the narrow, curving ridge, the small summit platform.

As darkness settled over the South Col, Cathy finally expressed her fears.

'Damn it, Ian. He's still out there. What if something goes wrong?'

'Nothing should go wrong,' Ian replied calmly. 'It's a clear, still night. He's had several hours of daylight to move down in before it got dark. He should be well below the South Summit by now. He's got a full down suit and plenty of oxygen. He can call us on the radio if anything goes wrong, and just like the rest of us he climbed up much of the mountain in the dark. There's no reason why he shouldn't climb down it as well.'

After a moment's reflection he continued.

'The history of Everest is full of people who've reached the summit late in the day. The first Brits to climb it stood on top at sunset, and on the American ascent of the West Ridge the climbers only reached the summit at nine o'clock at night. Remember the Yugoslavs a couple of weeks ago? They only got back to camp 4 near midnight. Bruce will either climb through the night or he'll bivi. He won't be the first climber to have bivied high on Everest either. Stephen Venables, Doug Scott and Dougal Haston all spent a night out above 8 000 metres on Everest, and Venables had climbed Everest without oxygen. Even this season Makalu Gau and Beck Weathers survived a night out in a storm, but tonight is clear, and much warmer for being so late in the season.'

'I guess so,' said Cathy. 'It's just having seen the bodies of Rob and Scott lying on the mountain and knowing that Bruce is out there on his own.' She hesitated. 'I guess this sounds silly to you after all your years in the army, but those are the first bodies I've ever seen.'

'Yes, but they're just bodies,' said Ian quietly.

'I know. It didn't particularly bother me when we were climbing, but it's the waiting now that's hard.'

IAN:
Well, youth, you decided to go on to the summit and you made it, but now you have to get yourself back down. You're not on your own, but the thread that holds us together is perilously thin.

18:00 – Camp 4

CATHY:
We don't have enough oxygen for the night, let alone to go back up the mountain for Bruce if that turns out to be necessary. I don't know if we have the strength to go back up the ridge if we have to, but I know that we have no chance at all without oxygen. Fresh we had little chance and now, after 18 hours of climbing, we have none.

I'm going to go on to the col in search of unfinished bottles. I fear we may need them, but it also provides a task to do, an escape from the waiting, a way to make time pass.

I move across the desolate col in the bitter cold of twilight, scrabbling through the piles of bottles left from teams in past decades, searching for the tell-tale orange of the Poisk bottles that fit our systems. In the confusion of their retreat after the great storm, the other teams didn't take down all their oxygen bottles. And once again there are a considerable number left by the IMAX team. Testing each bottle with my regulator, I finally find six with some oxygen left in them.

I sit for a moment in the chilly night air, looking up at the sombre pyramid of Everest, a darker shadow against a dark sky. I wonder where on its great slopes one man is moving. I look above it to the sky, clear and littered with brilliant stars. So beautiful but so unfeeling.

Amid the gloom of worry, a brief flicker of pride shines out. We did it!

While looking up at the mountain, I radio Phil to update him on conditions. He logs the call at ten minutes to seven. I can hear the worry in his voice. Unable to see the summit from base camp, he has no idea of what kind of weather Bruce is facing.

'Don't worry, Phil. It's completely clear and still. If there is any night for biviing on Everest, this is the night. And remember, Bruce might take all night, especially if he decides to bivi and climb on down in daylight.'

He agrees with me, and we discuss various possibilities with forced optimism. So we reassure each other, each hiding our own unease behind a brave facade.

I crawl back into the tent with my hoard of orange bottles. I settle down into my sleeping bag and pull on the oxygen mask, which has transformed

itself into a horrible alien object. Damp from the day of climbing and now
having been dragged round the col for use testing the bottles, the damp has
frozen, leaving a contraption of icy, hard leather, which irritates the skin on
my face, already chaffed by hours of wearing. But physical exhaustion soon
overcomes all such difficulties. I sleep like the dead, without waking or
dreaming.

19:15 – Base Camp

When Cathy signed off, Philip phoned Sue to tell her what little news he had.
Then they all returned to waiting. A while later he wandered out from the
comms tent to stare up at the white and black mass of the mountain. Somewhere in that vastness, out of his sight, seven very small people were pushing
the boundaries of survival. He looked up at the same stars Cathy had watched
earlier, that Bruce might be watching somewhere above both of them. Shankar
joined him and they walked across to the *chorten*, where they lit a fire of juniper sticks, the smell of which the Sherpas believed was pleasing to the
mountain god. Shankar walked round the *chorten*, sprinkling rice, muttering
his own prayers.

'You look exhausted,' said Patrick, when Philip returned to the comms tent.
No one had slept for over 24 hours and it seemed to Patrick that Philip had
aged visibly in the last few hours.

'Go to bed. I'll take the first watch on the radio. You can take over later if
you want,' volunteered Patrick.

While Philip snatched a few hours' sleep, Deshun tossed restlessly in her
sleeping bag on the floor of the comms tent. Her exhaustion was exacerbated
by nausea and Patrick joked with her that she was turning green.

Patrick sat by the radio base station, so keyed up from the adrenaline of the
radio filing that he felt no need to sleep. The radio was turned to full volume
so that any sound could be heard, but hour after hour was filled only by the
static hiss of the idle system.

26 May
02:00 – Camp 4

IAN:
My chest is burning, burning from the cold. I snuggle and creep further
into my sleeping bag and pull the hood firmly over my head. What's my
bloody chest's problem? I grumble to myself. Suddenly I realise. Oxygen,

oxygen, I can't taste the sweetness of bottled oxygen. With rising panic I clasp at the mask on my face. It's not there. It's no wonder my chest is complaining, as the intense cold of the raw night air grasps my lungs. Forgetting the hard-earned warmth of my comfortable position, I push myself up on to one elbow and begin rummaging around for my errant mask. In the darkness and without my contact lenses, I can only see the vague outline of our personal items strewn around the inside of the tent. The condensation from our bodies forms a gentle mist as it swirls around the tent before settling gently on every surface, forming a freezing layer of hoarfrost. My gloved hand stretches out in search of the mask and bumps into a body in a sleeping bag. Cathy mumbles and shifts in response to my prodding but fortunately doesn't wake. No mask on that side.

Cursing the inevitable loss of warm sleeping-bag air, I turn and shift on to my other elbow and begin feeling across the tent floor. Nothing. No mask on that side either. Nothing at all. Suddenly it flashes through my cold, oxygen-staved brain. Nothing, that means no body in a sleeping bag on this side of the tent. Christ, that means no Bruce! I grab at the radio inside my down jacket. Maybe it's switched off. Maybe the battery is dead. Maybe Bruce is okay but couldn't get through to us. Maybe he has been calling for help and we haven't heard him. I yank out the Motorola, but the tiny battery light shining out across the tent confirms that it's in perfect working order. No radio problem. I slump back down against my rucksack pillow, pull my lost mask from its hiding place behind my shoulder blades, stuff it over my nose and mouth, and bury my face in my hands.

Damn it, Bruce, where are you? Don't do this to me, I'm too old and too tired. I draw a deep breath from my mask and relax a little as the warm air flows into my lungs, soothing my burning chest. Think, Ian, think. Get a grip and think! Okay, right, Bruce isn't at camp 4 and he hasn't called us on the radio. So he's either fallen off the ridge or his radio isn't working, even though he used it to speak to us from the summit. Also, he definitely would've called us on the radio if he'd stopped to rest or to bivi for the night, that's assuming his radio is still working of course. So where does that leave us? Nowhere, mate, nowhere at all.

I look across at Cathy and wonder if she knows that Bruce is still out on the mountain. Should I wake her and tell her? We could discuss the possibilities together. I lean across and look at her still, peaceful face buried under waves of long hair and framed by the leather of her oxygen mask. I gently pull away some loose strands of hair stuck between her face and mask, which will be letting valuable oxygen escape. Let her sleep, Ian. Whatever needs to be done can only be done in the morning, and, up or down, she'll need all the sleep she can get. I settle back on my pillow, my mind churning.

Could we rescue Bruce if he calls us? Is it physically possible to rescue someone at this altitude? Do we have the bodily reserves to go back up? Do we have enough oxygen for such an attempt? And even if we reach him, if he's not mobile, we can't possibly carry him. Scott Fischer's team had to leave him tied to the mountain when they couldn't carry him any further. Would we fare any better? And what if he doesn't call, where would we look for him? Questions, a deep gasp of oxygen, but still questions, always more questions.

Okay, listen, Ian, if Bruce doesn't turn up and he doesn't use his radio to contact us, he must have had a sudden accident and in that case we are powerless to help him. The bottom line then, Ian, is will you go back up the mountain if Bruce calls for help? Christ, I don't know!

What will Cathy and the Sherpas do in response to a call for help? Will my decision affect theirs? If I decide to go, won't I be putting pressure on them to risk their lives? Although everyone has to make their own decision, how could Cathy go back and face South Africa if I went to help Bruce and she didn't? Will the Sherpas be fearful of not being invited on future expeditions if they decline to go back up the mountain? If he calls for help should any of us risk our lives knowing that there is very little chance of saving him? Is it worth going up just to be with him while he dies? What would Bruce want us to do? Maybe he hasn't called in order to spare us this fateful decision?

Excuses, Ian, aren't you just trying to find excuses?

I reach down to the frozen valve on my oxygen bottle and increase the flow rate to try to force myself to sleep and to push the avalanche of questions from my tired, confused mind. Sleep, Ian, there is nothing we can do until first light. Sleep … if only!

05:00 – Camp 4

CATHY:
I wake abruptly. It's morning, it's light. I look at my watch. Five o'clock.

No Bruce, no radio call.

He's dead.

No, maybe he isn't. Maybe he is still on his way down. Maybe he bivied and didn't call. Maybe he is nearly here.

But in the depths of my heart, after that long night with no communication, I know he's dead.

I lie very still, feeling the blood thumping through my pulses. I glance across at Ian, who seems asleep. I wonder if he has realised.

The radio crackles into life. Ian grabs it. He's not asleep.

But it's only Philip. He can bear the silence no longer. Ian has nothing to tell him. He says he will consult with the Sherpas and then call back. Soon after that a hand rattles the tent and a thermos flask of tea is thrust through the door.

'We go down today. We must leave this morning,' Ang Dorje announces firmly. Then he pauses.

'No Mr Bruce?' he asks.

'No, no Mr Bruce,' I reply.

He nods impassively and withdraws.

I watch him go with mixed feelings. I am aware of the prosaic attitude of the Sherpas towards death and have discussed it before with Bruce. He admired their calm stoicism in the face of the inevitability of human mortality. But I am still rather shaken actually to see their apparent disinterest.

06:00 – Camp 4

Once Cathy had drunk a few sips of the sickly sweet tea, she wriggled out of her down cocoon and awkwardly scrambled to look out of the tent door and up on to the high slopes of Everest. From their camp on the South Col they could see all the way up the slopes that had been so hard won the previous night, and then back up along the skyline ridge to the South Summit. The face was dotted with tiny black specks of rock, contrasting sharply with the brightness of the shining snow and ice, but there was no movement, none of the tiny black specks stood up and began to stumble back down towards the South African camp. There was nothing but the stillness of the altitude, and the heaviness of a missing comrade.

Cathy turned and shook her head.

'Bruce has probably bivied,' said Ian. 'He won't start moving down until the sun catches him and warms him up a bit.'

The two friends looked at one another. They both remembered standing on that high ridge in the light of the rising sun 24 hours earlier, and they both knew the sun caught that ridge very, very early.

'Listen, Caths,' Ian said quietly, 'we need to think about our options of helping Bruce if he calls.'

'Yes, I know,' she replied.

'There's nothing we can do if he doesn't call. But if he does, each one of us will have a decision to make.'

'Yes, I know,' Cathy answered slowly, before turning back to gaze up at the tiny black specks.

CATHY:

What do we do if he calls? If he is still moving, we could talk him down over the radio, we could go out and try to meet him on his way down. We'd all be pretty slow, but Nawang is fresh and both Jangmu and Pemba are strong climbers. But they want to go down.

What if he calls and says he can't go any further, like Rob Hall did? Do we listen to him die over the radio? Do we try to get to him when he'd probably be dead before we finally arrived? Or would we have to sit with him and watch him die, all the time wishing he'd hurry up while we still had some chance of getting ourselves down alive?

Do we have any hope of trying to drag six feet of massive male body back down the mountain? I doubt it.

Dear God, Bruce. Don't make us choose. But you won't. You won't call because you're no longer with us.

08:00 – Camp 4

PHILIP: 'Hello, camp 4, this is base camp. Come in, Ian.'
IAN: 'Hi, Philip, this is camp 4. Go ahead.'
PHILIP: 'Any news, bro?'
IAN: 'Sorry, nothing, nothing at all.'

There was silence for a few moments.

PHILIP: 'Hello, Ian, have you decided what you guys are going to do?'
IAN: 'Well, Philip, the Sherpas are adamant that they're going down this morning.'
PHILIP: 'What about you and Cathy?'
IAN: 'I've asked Cathy to go down with the Sherpas. We only have about a bottle and a half of oxygen left from the stock Cathy found yesterday, so there's not enough for everyone to stay here. Cathy's not very happy about going down, but she realises that it's the only sensible thing to do.'
PHILIP: 'What about you?'
IAN: 'I want to wait up here.'
PHILIP: 'For how long?'
IAN: 'I don't know. Maybe another 24 hours. As long as I can, really. I just want to give Bruce every chance to make it back.'
PHILIP: 'What does Ang Dorje think?'
IAN: 'He thinks I should go down.'

Seconds of silence tick away.

PHILIP: 'Just take care then, bro.'
IAN: 'No problem. If there's no sign of Bruce by noon, I'll release an official statement declaring him missing, presumed dead.'
PHILIP: 'Okay.'
IAN: 'Listen, Philip, can you check that the icefall can be held open for me? Probably for an extra three or four days or so. You may need to distribute some goodies to pave the way.'
PHILIP: 'Okay, understood. It shouldn't present a problem. We've got a lot of goodwill down here.'

Ian turned to Cathy.
   'Anything you'd like to add?' he asked.
Cathy shook her head.
'Just tell Philip I'll call him when I reach camp 2.'

CATHY:
Don't stay, Ian. Losing one of you is hard enough. I can't bear to lose both of you.
   But it makes sense. With so little oxygen left, it will last longer if only one person is using it. And for Bruce finally to crawl into camp, to find us all gone, would be appalling. Be careful. Come down.

IAN:
I sit with my knees hunched up under my chin, watching Cathy slowly and methodically pack up the last of her personal kit to take down the mountain. These things take time. She's keen to get away now that the decision has been made, but we're still at 8 000 metres and at this extreme altitude nothing can be rushed. Although her rucksack is bursting at the seams, she religiously finds space for her share of our rubbish, which needs to be taken down off the mountain. We don't talk. There's nothing to say. I start talking to myself again.
   I probably can't save Bruce, but I can't bear the thought that my friend might somehow stumble on his own back to the South Col, just as Beck Weathers had done a couple of weeks earlier, only to find his team-mates had left without him. I must give him every possible chance, no matter how small, no matter how unlikely.
   I probably can't save Bruce, but if he calls I'll have to make a decision. I want to be able to make that decision free of the obligations it may place on others. I want to be free to decide.

'Bara Sahib, come down soon.'

Ang Dorje's gruff voice brings me back to camp 4. It was definitely an order rather than a request. I smile at my co-leader and grab his hand.

'Thank you, Ang Dorje. Don't worry, I'll be careful.'

He raises his finger as though about to lecture me again, but then decides against it, smiles broadly and pumps my hand instead. With a nod he turns away.

'No go up, Bara Sahib,' pleads Pemba on the verge of tears.

I grab my team-mate by the shoulders and embrace him.

'*Ramro sa*, Pemba. *Ramro sa*. Everything will be okay.'

He smiles weakly in return and then turns quickly away before his tears overcome and embarrass him.

I reach across and gently brush Cathy on the nose, the icy morning air already making it cold to the touch. She flashes a smile in return. Our eyes are fixed together in the moment, passing lifetimes of information and feelings between us. No need to say goodbye.

'Be safe, youth.'

'You too, Ian.'

We exchange nods, then without looking back Cathy shoulders her rucksack and strides off towards the top of the fixed ropes.

10:30 – Geneva Spur

CATHY:

I stand alone on the slopes of the mountain, looking back up towards the summit. Our small unit of three friends is torn asunder, one member ripped away as from Siamese triplets, leaving a gaping hole from which blood pours out. I think of Ian, waiting alone on the col, nursing what we both know is the futile hope that Bruce is alive.

My last image as I left the tent was of Ian lying on his side, staring unmoving through the tent door at the slope above us. It tore my heart to see him sitting so still, so small. I know he is waiting for one of the black specks to stand up and begin a slow progress downhill. But they never do. They are only rocks, inanimate and immobile. There is nothing he can do but wait, and the longer he waits, the less chance there is of Bruce returning. It seems such a waste that everything he has put into the expedition should end like this, that his friend should be out there dead or dying and that we should be totally helpless.

'Damn you!' I shout suddenly, violently, not sure if I am addressing the mountain or Bruce.

'Damn you for killing him, damn you, Bruce, for not coming back. Don't do this to us. Don't be dead. Come back, for God's sake, come back!'

The mountain looms over me in impassive silence, its vast bulk beyond all understanding of small human miseries.

I walk on, waves of anger and despair rolling over me. My worry for Bruce is mingled now with worry for Ian, waiting alone. Forgive me, Bruce, if my concern is increasingly for him rather than you. I believe you are safe, enjoying the adventure of whatever comes next in the universe. But we are still so vulnerable, ants on the side of this mountain.

By the time I reach the top of the Geneva Spur I am calmer. I turn for what will be my final view of the summit pyramid.

Goodbye, Bruce. If you have to be dead, there can be no finer tombstone.

I turn away, drop over the edge and begin to move down towards the Lhotse Face.

As I climb alone down the mountain, I am glad of these hours of solitude in which to try to absorb the enormity of what has happened, before returning to the agonised concern of those who wait at the mountain's foot. As I move, I replay through my mind all that happened. I analyse our decisions again and again, and I can't find it in myself to think that, knowing what we did when we did, we would have decided differently. I discover that it is difficult to climb downwards when your eyes are full of tears, that blurred vision interferes with placing your feet. Already the pragmatism of living is taking over from the seemingly insurmountable trauma of Bruce's death.

10:30 – Base Camp

Philip wandered aimlessly across the glacier, smoking continuously, kicking idly at the many small stones that had been released from the glacier's icy grip by the rising temperatures. He had decided that Bruce was dead around midnight the previous night. He had worked out for himself how long it should take Bruce to return to camp, and when that line was crossed, he came to his own conclusions. Thereafter he spent little time in the South African camp but took to taking long walks, as if movement would keep him from being flooded by his feelings.

Deshun sat in quiet bewilderment. She didn't know whether she should be happy or sad. She didn't know whether being pleased about the achievement was belittling what was happening on the mountain with Bruce. She felt a deep sense of disorientation.

A profound silence hung over base camp. No one said anything because no one knew what to say. Deep down inside they were waiting for the radio to crackle and Bruce to say, 'I'm just a few hundred metres away from camp 4.'

Morning – South Africa

Back in South Africa, people who had never met Bruce, who were of a different nationality from him, who had never even seen a snow-covered mountain, joined together in churches throughout the country on that Sunday morning to offer up prayers for his safety. Radio 702 listeners all over Gauteng remained close to their radios in hope of further news.

10:30 – Camp 4

> IAN:
> I sit alone with the minutes ticking by. I glance at the radio. Silence. I look up at the South Summit of Everest. Nothing moves. No sign of Bruce, but a wave of relief sweeps over me and I burst out laughing. Relief at being on my own. Relief at not being responsible for anyone else's decisions. Free to decide my own course of action. Free to decide. And if Bruce calls for help I'll go, even if I can't save him, I'll go. Even if it's just to be with my friend while he goes to sleep, I'll go. It's worth taking the risk to be with him, that's what team-mates are for, that's what friends are for, and if I don't come back, then so be it. We'll both be our own heroes, just for one day. If he calls, I'll go. If he calls.

10:40 – Camp 4

As Ian sat quietly, a signal came through on the radio.

PHILIP: 'Hello, Ian, this is base camp.'
IAN: 'Hi, Philip, go ahead.'
PHILIP: 'Are you on your own?'
IAN: 'Yes, everyone's on their way down to camp 2 by now.'
PHILIP: 'Okay, I roger that. I have some news on the icefall.'
IAN: 'Right, go ahead.'
PHILIP: 'The icefall Sherpas say they will start clearing the route on the twenty-ninth. That doesn't give you much time, bro.'

IAN:	'It'll have to do. Any news on the weather?'
PHILIP:	'Not good, I'm afraid. All the reports indicate that the monsoon is expected to hit Everest any time now.'
IAN:	'You're right, that's not good news.'
PHILIP:	'Ian, you can't risk being caught on the mountain when the monsoon breaks.'
IAN:	'Yes, I know. Don't worry, I'll keep my eyes open. I should be able to see it coming. That'll give me a couple of hours' notice at least.'
PHILIP:	'Okay, bro, be safe.'
IAN:	'Yeah, cheers. Speak to you soon.'

IAN:

I run my hand along the cold metal of the two oxygen bottles at my feet. One full, the other half full. The relationship between us is a close one: without the bottled oxygen I would be dead by now, but with careful use I should be able to stay up here for another 24 hours. After that, who knows?

I find my eyes constantly drawn back to the radio. Please ring. Please don't ring. Please don't ring? Christ, Ian, what are you saying? I don't believe I just said that. Furious with myself for even thinking such a thing, I grab my oxygen regulator to make sure that it's still working and that I'm not going delirious with hypoxia. Get a serious grip now, Ian! I reach across for the radio and shake it up towards the mountain. Ring, damn you!

11:30 – Camp 4

The radio buzzed by Ian's hand. He jerked out of his reverie to grab it. It was Cathy, calling from camp 3.

IAN:	'You've made very good time. You aren't moving too fast, are you?'
CATHY:	'Not at all. I feel as if I am crawling. My knees are killing me. Is there … any sign of anything on the mountain?'
IAN:	'No, love, there's nothing.'

Cathy waited at camp 3 for the official announcement, as it was then nearly noon. Putting her radio on standby, she sat on her rucksack, staring down the Western Cwm and out to the distant peaks of Pumori and beyond that to Cho Oyu. A little after noon Ian's voice came over the radio, reading out the announcement:

'The First South African Everest Expedition regretfully announces that team member Bruce Herrod has been missing on Mount Everest between the summit and the South Col for a period of 19 hours, from 17:00 on 25/05/96 to 12:00 on 26/05/96.

'Ian Woodall will remain on the South Col for 24 hours pending Bruce Herrod's possible return. No further communication will be given.'

IAN:
Thank heavens for radio, I think as I slowly switch off the Motorola and place it near the open tent door. The voice is heard, but the tears are hidden. The official announcement, missing, presumed dead. Is there still hope for Bruce, or is this the beginning of us all adjusting to Bruce being gone forever?

I wipe away my tears and look desperately at the radio again.

12:15 – Base Camp

The base camp team were left with the grim duty of getting the news out to the rest of the world. The British and Nepalese authorities were notified. Philip had spoken to Sue intermittently throughout the course of the morning. Now he held back tears as he telephoned her once more. Deshun and Patrick just hugged each other. Patrick then had to file to Radio 702.

PATRICK: 'Bruce Herrod last spoke to us from the summit ...'

As he read the line, Patrick knew that Bruce was dead. There was nothing to tell him definitely, he just knew it inside. His voice broke and then he started to cry.

PATRICK: 'Call me back in a few minutes.'

He put the phone down and walked outside. He found Philip sitting on a rock outside the tent, also crying. He sat down next to him, putting an arm round his shoulders and for a while they sat together in silence.

'It's so damn difficult to report on the death of somebody you knew,' Patrick said eventually. 'I can understand now why friends and relatives sometimes feel so hostile towards the media.'

He walked back into the tent and phoned the radio station again. This time he managed to get through the report, but he could hear the sorrow in his own voice. Radio 702 news editor Debora Patta came on the line.

DEBORA: 'Are you okay? If you want to talk, just call.'
PATRICK: 'I'd rather not.'

It was all he could get out. He walked outside again, found a big rock far away from base camp, all on his own, and there he let his grief run wild.

12:00 – Camp 3

CATHY:

I turn the radio off and sit alone on the vast expanse of mountain and cry. My feelings swing between a certain amount of acceptance of Bruce's choices, of the risks of mountaineering, and overwhelming pain and sorrow that he isn't coming back. I run through it all over again. It is, I realise, a catch-22 situation.

I really felt that in Bruce I had found a friend for life. And I admired his confidence and determination. And yet I knew it was that determination that had kept him going late in the day, and slowly. To wish him to have turned round was to wish him to have been another person. Yet it was the person he was that I liked so much.

I have no answers.

But now descending safely has to claim all my attention.

I clip my safety sling to the fixed rope, just below an ice screw anchor point, and ease my weight on to it. The screw wobbles alarmingly. I turn to inspect it and realise that, with the ever-rising temperatures, the surface layer of ice is melting and the anchors securing the fixed ropes are coming loose.

My heart sinks. Just when I want nothing more than to put my mind in neutral and slide on down to rest and safety, I will have to check each point, to remain totally alert, never trusting the ropes fully. The descent becomes slow and painstaking, but at last the bergschrund is in sight. I reach the lip to find the anchor at the top of the abseil has vanished. I will have to trust my full weight to a dubious snow stake far above me that I cannot even remember checking.

As I move over the edge, I find that both the ice screws that secured the diagonal abseil have pulled out. To go straight down means to go straight into the gaping chasm below. I inch diagonally downwards and then swing out right, feet landing on solid snow. And sinking immediately through it into the hole below. I wallow in the snow, kicking my feet out in search of solid ground.

If it was bad for me, it will be worse for Ian. Be careful, Ian, be careful.

14:00 – Camp 4

IAN:
I try not to doze off, but I've had so little sleep lately that I can't fight it any longer. I place the radio inside my jacket shoulder, ready to wake me in an instant, and let myself relax. Relax and doze. Doze and gently sleep …

I sit bolt upright gasping for air. I check my regulator and see that it shows an empty oxygen bottle. I look outside before unscrewing the bottle and reaching across for a full one. Without giving it much thought I start to screw in the new bottle, but it won't fit. Concentrating properly this time, I try again. It definitely won't fit. With a tinge of panic I grab for another, but with the same result. I try bottle after bottle, but although they may have fitted Cathy's regulator, they don't fit mine. I'm at 8 000 metres on the afternoon of 26 May and I'm out of oxygen. I'm in desperate trouble!

I'm sorry, Bruce, but I can't wait any longer. If I try to stay up here without oxygen, I'll die for sure, and I don't think you would want that. It's already very late in the day to be going down, but down is where I must dash, before the lack of oxygen holds me up here forever.

14:30 – Camp 4

Having decided that the South Col was really not the place to be, Ian radioed down to Philip to say that he was going to start down. Cathy was by then at camp 2 and picked up the call on her radio. She butted in to warn Ian of how bad conditions were on the Lhotse Face and to urge him to be very careful.

IAN:
I stand on the ridge of the Geneva Spur looking up at the summit slopes of Everest for the last time. My closest friend is up there, but it's time for us to part. I stand there for a few moments, tears welling up in my eyes, contemplating calling his name, but I know that isn't fair. Bruce has made his choice, and as much as it hurts, I must respect that decision. Standing to salute my friend in our parting, I take a last look back before starting the long, lonely journey home on my own, my throat taut with emotion.

21:00 – Camp 2

Ian had arrived in camp 2 to find only two tents left standing in the whole of the area that had once housed eleven expeditions. Cathy's tent had been taken down, and she had moved into his, in Bruce's place. As they lay together in the dark they talked softly. Although both physically very tired, neither was ready for sleep, their minds full with the events of the past 48 hours.

'This probably sounds chauvinistic, although it isn't meant to be,' said Ian. 'But in the end a man has to be allowed to make a man's decision, because if he isn't, then he isn't a man. And Bruce made his decision.'

Cathy smiled to herself. She knew what he meant, although she wasn't sure about the way he chose to phrase it.

'What do you think happened to him?' she asked.

'I think he fell off the mountain,' Ian answered firmly. 'And that, unfortunately, is the number one risk when you choose to try to climb up them. Think about it. If anything else had gone wrong, if he'd felt sick, had been running low on oxygen, or whatever, all he had to do was to open up the radio and call us. We might not have had the strength to get back up to him, but you and I both know that we would've tried our damnedest.'

'At the very least we could've tried to talk him through it,' Cathy said.

'Exactly. And those things are so unlikely anyway. He had plenty of oxygen and he had the gear for a night bivi.' He thought about it for a minute and then continued. 'So either something went wrong very quickly, he had a heart attack or a stroke, or he fell. He would've called us when he reached the South Summit. It's a major landmark and the end of the difficulties. But nothing. I think he fell from the ridge. Probably where it's at its most narrow, near the Hillary Step. I took a short fall there myself and I know how easy it is to do.'

'I can believe that,' said Cathy. 'I found that each time I looked down to try to place my feet in the path, the hot air would rush out of the top of my oxygen mask and mist up my glasses instantly. And then I'd be balanced precariously while I tried to de-mist my glasses with icy gloves. I felt like throwing them away sometimes.'

They sat in silence for a while.

'Thinking about the summit, my one miscalculation was to assume we would all reach the summit together, or that I'd be the back marker,' said Ian.

'Yes, but it doesn't work like that, does it?' Cathy replied. 'Once people start moving unroped at their own pace, they string out. The only surprise was that you were in front, rather than in your usual position at the back.'

CATHY:
I lie wide awake in the darkness. We are only 36 hours away from the summit that all six of us reached, one by one. And only a day away from the base where we will have to rejoin a world filled with other people.

Last night exhaustion and bottled oxygen brought sleep. But tonight I cannot sleep, feeling sick, restless and battling to breathe. I toss and turn, jerking upright periodically with the fearful feeling of suffocation. Initially Ian tries to comfort me, but I can feel his restlessness and then irritation at my continued movement.

'Get angry,' he tells me. 'Channel your pain into anger.'

'No,' I reply, horrified at the thought. I see anger as destructive.

'Well, for God's sake, don't get all girlie on me,' he says. 'Not yet. We're not off the mountain yet.'

'Sod off, Ian.'

I immediately get angry, with him. Who is he to assume that 'girlie' emotions are weak? That if I don't suppress them I might not be able to get myself off the mountain safely? Is his bottled-up anger and hurt and fear a better, stronger way of coping?

How can he be both so compassionate and so chauvinistic? As we lie together in the tent I feel so far away from him and his understanding of this mountain, as if we really did originate from different planets.

But it works. In my anger with him, my distress eases and sleep eventually comes.

27 May
05:00 – Camp 2

Cathy shook Ian by the shoulder. She had woken up at five, as agreed. They needed to get moving. Both the Sherpas and Philip had warned them that the icefall was in a very bad condition, and they needed to get through it quickly, before the midday heat melted what little stability was left. Ian snuggled down into his bag, pulling it firmly shut over his head.

'This is the last morning I ever have to wait for you, mate,' she muttered under her breath, and began to pack. After she had packed and drunk two cups of coffee, he was barely beginning to wake.

'I'm leaving,' she announced, and crawled out of the tent.

The Western Cwm had changed dramatically with the rising temperatures and had many more crevasses. Now there was no stopping to gaze at the beautiful scenery. She moved on as quickly as possible. This time it was really over, and it was time to get home.

06:00 – Camp 2

Ian had purposely stayed in bed, hoping that Cathy would leave without him because the unenviable job of packing up Bruce's personal belongings at camp

2 had fallen to him, and it was going to be difficult enough without having to do it in front of Cathy.

Spared an audience, Ian could weep unashamedly as he took Bruce's effects and packed them away for carrying down to base camp. The two men had shared a tent for weeks on the mountain and as Ian held each item he could vividly remember a time when Bruce was either wearing it or using it.

Having packed up Bruce's equipment, Ian shouldered his own large load including his share of expedition rubbish and made his way down the Western Cwm. He was amazed at how many crevasses had materialised, and with his tiredness and grief he had to use all his mountaineering experience and judgement to weave a safe path through the maze of danger.

As he climbed through the icefall he passed under the wave, the giant roof of ice that Mal Duff had so confidently predicted would collapse within a week. Many things had collapsed around it, but this edifice still stood. In the end the mountain was beyond the prediction of the humans that trod upon it.

10:00 – Base Camp

Philip lowered the South African flag that flew above base camp to half-mast. He had done it two weeks ago for other teams' members. He had never thought then that he would be doing it again for one of his own.

Then he settled himself on a large rock just outside base camp and began the long wait for his brother and his friend. He was still exhausted, less now from lack of sleep than from the emotional toll of the extreme swing of emotions experienced over the past few days.

12:00 – Khumbu Icefall

Ian arrived at the foot of the icefall to find Cathy dozing on her pack, scarf over her eyes, Walkman in her ears, escaped briefly into another world.

'What are you doing here?' he asked.

'Waiting for you,' replied Cathy. 'We left base camp as a team. I thought we should arrive back as one, such as we are.'

They walked on together, over the endless glacier. They passed through the IMAX camp and one of their members came over and shook their hands. He asked them if they would like to stay for some tea.

'Thank you, but no,' said Ian. 'If we sit down now, we're likely never to stand up again.'

David Breashears watched in silence as they walked on past.

13:00 – Base Camp

Philip watched the two little figures stumbling towards him. Ian looked even worse than when he had come back from the storm, with a deeply sunburnt face and chapped lips. Cathy had again lost weight and the bones of her face stood out starkly against sunken cheeks.

He hugged Cathy and shook Ian's hand.

'Welcome back, love. Welcome home, bro.'

They walked on together in silence. All the staff came out to greet them. The climbers dumped their packs for the last time and reached out for a welcome cup of juice. The base camp team stood around them awkwardly, not sure whether to offer congratulations or commiserations. But mostly they were just grateful to have the two climbers safely back and off the mountain.

* * * * *

'More fried eggs, anyone?' asked Philip.

'Sure,' replied Cathy and Ian simultaneously through full mouths, both reaching for their third helpings of fried bread and egg.

'How was the climb down?' asked Philip at last. He desperately wanted to know all that had transpired in the last 72 hours but wasn't sure how the climbers felt about talking about it.

'Bloody dangerous,' Ian replied. 'We really pushed it to the last possible minute.'

How could the climbers explain all that had happened to them, to people who had never been there? Words became inadequate.

The silence was broken by a cannon-like crack followed by the swelling roar of an avalanche. An enormous piece of serac had broken off from the Lo Lha and was crashing down towards the glacier. Cathy grabbed her camera and finally managed to photograph an avalanche in action. She thought with a smile of Bruce, who had tried so often to capture the avalanches around base camp but, because he'd always had to dive into his tent to find his Canon, had never succeeded. Now she had it, and she would never be able to show him.

'Well, I guess that's the mountain declaring that Everest is now officially closed,' she said.

'Yes,' Ian replied. 'The last man is off the mountain and it's time to go home.'

CATHY:
I disappear into my tent for a total wash, or the best that can be done with a bowl of lukewarm water and a flannel. I peel off layer after layer of clothing

that have not been removed in weeks, to discover the strange phenomenon of a body beneath. My hands are the colour of ochre, my forearms little lighter, while the rest of my body is so white it resembles a grub reluctantly dragged to the surface. And everything is so thin. My skin is stretched as tight as a drum top across my ribs. My forearms are stick bundles of sinew and muscle. I am so tired. I feel as if every bone is filled with lead, every muscle reduced to cotton wool. But at last it's over.

IAN:
I laugh out loud as I look at myself in my small mirror balanced precariously on a barrel in my tent. At least I'm consistent, I say to myself, I look as bad as I feel!

19:00 – Base Camp

The soup tureen and peppery poppadoms had been taken away and Cathy, Ian, Patrick and Deshun waited for the next course, which Philip had disappeared to find. He came back with a huge variety of pots.

'I got Ang Mu to cook up some hill food,' he explained. 'Cathy, the last of the chicken casserole for you, and Ian, chilli con carne.'

'I don't know if my system is ready for this,' Ian joked while eyeing it hungrily.

'And then lots of veggies, for a change from all that packaged food you've been eating,' Philip added.

'Veggies? You mean cabbage, again,' Cathy said sarcastically.

'Well yes, cabbage. But also cauliflower and some funny local stuff all chopped up into bits in the pasta. You'll have to wait a few more days for real variety,' Philip explained with the air of a master chef.

'Fresh fruit and fresh bread. That's all I want. A decent salad sandwich. Oh, and some roast chicken,' said Cathy thoughtfully.

'Well, eat up. Ang Mu has put together something special for pudding.'

The team munched steadily through the offerings. At last every plate was scraped clean, and they were ready to wash it all down with coffee and hot chocolate. Ang Mu arrived, carrying the final course. The rest of the cook staff were clustered behind him, eager to see the reaction to their surprise.

He held a cake, covered in white icing and pink, blazing candles. A message in pink writing was scrawled between the candles: 'Everest Hippy Nice Samit'.

Everyone began to laugh. Philip pulled a hidden bottle of Nederburg from under the table and put it with the cake. He then brought out his camera.

'Come on, you two, pose nicely. This really is a once-in-a-lifetime picture.'

Cathy and Ian posed with the cake. Their blue down jackets framed faces lobster-red from sunburn, with their eyes staring out from rings of white skin left by the protection of their sunglasses.

The cake had broken the mood of tension and exhaustion that had dominated the camp all day.

Patrick opened the Nederburg and filled each of the metal cups with the red wine.

'A toast,' he said. 'To our team's success! South Africa did it, despite everything.'

They all drank. Ian refilled the mugs.

'A toast. To absent friends!' he said.

They all drank once more.

'Come on then. Tell us all about it,' Patrick demanded.

The evening was spent in a mixture of laughter and tears, as the celebration of the team's triumph mingled with the acknowledgement of the tragedy. Cathy and Ian took the rest of the team through their summit day, the others listening intently, trying to understand what had really happened, out of sight, so far above them.

24:00 – Base Camp

CATHY:
No, that's wrong, that's not it at all. That's not how it happened. I can't quite explain why, but that's just not quite right. I slide awake to find myself wrapped up in a knot in my sleeping bag, sweating from the unaccustomed heat of base camp.

Tangled wisps from some incredibly complicated dream about what had happened on the mountain still hover in my mind. All I know is I was dreaming about what happened on the mountain, and that the dream had it all wrong. Just subtle things, all wrong. Even as I was dreaming I knew it was wrong but found myself powerless to stop the dream, unable to pinpoint the problem, powerless to explain ...

28 May
09:00 – Base Camp

Base camp had changed dramatically. The glacier surface was melting and the tents now stood on ice pedestals, like strange mushroom houses. Avalanche and rockfall became ever more common. Giant boulders left teetering on narrow stems of ice crashed down one by one. Even the tents began to become lopsided as the ice beneath them melted. It felt like still living in a house when the demolition squad had already started work.

'It's quite depressing in some ways,' Cathy commented to Patrick as they walked together to breakfast. 'It's like being the last people at a party, surrounded by empty beer cans and dirty plates, with nothing left to do but start clearing up the mess.'

The climbers sat on stools in the sun, eating fried eggs and toast, and watching yaks head off down the glacier with the loads of the IMAX team. Patrick stood restlessly near them, watching Ian.

'Ian, South Africa is desperate for news,' he said at last. 'Since your official announcement two and a half days ago there has been nothing. Everybody wants to know what happened, and if you won't tell them, they'll just make it up. Everybody is speculating.'

'Patrick, I appreciate that as a journalist you want news, but we were the ones who were up there, and we'll talk about it when we are good and ready, and not one minute before. I don't know about Cathy, but I'm not ready yet.'

'I don't mind,' said Cathy. 'I've had a lot of time to think it through in the last few days and I'm happy to talk. I think Patrick is right. Let South Africa hear it first hand, rather than as rumours.'

'Will you go on the John and Dan Show this morning?' asked Patrick. 'That will be 12 o'clock our time.'

'Sure. And if they ask an honest question, they'll get an honest answer. If they don't, I'll put the phone down,' Cathy stated.

11:50 – Base Camp

Cathy sat in the comms tent, waiting on hold to go on to Radio 702. She could hear the programme playing as she waited. The radio station had interviewed English mountaineer Chris Bonnington, leader of five Everest expeditions, and who had reached the summit of the mountain once. He said the South African team should not accept any feelings of guilt, that Bruce was determined to climb to the summit.

'It was a risk he took. I mean, he obviously pushed it to the limit. I suspect he pushed a lot, lot further than was wise, and he paid the price,' he concluded.

Sue had also been contacted. She described Bruce as 'an extremely sensible person. Which, I can understand, may make many people wonder why he went for the summit so late in the day. As I say, I have no answer to that, apart

from the fact that he clearly thought he could do it, and when I spoke to him
on the summit he believed he could get back down again.'

When pressed by the presenter she continued, 'When I asked him, "Will
you feel absolutely confident when you're on the mountain, both with Ian
Woodall and the other members of the team, that if the chips are down, you
will be okay?" he had no hesitation in saying yes.'

12:00 – Base Camp

At twenty minutes past eight South African time Cathy joined the John and
Dan Show.

JOHN: 'How does it feel to have successfully climbed the highest moun-
             tain in the world?'
CATHY: 'I'm not sure. It really hasn't sunk in yet. But every so often I
             think, "Dear God, I've done it! I don't believe it." It seems in-
             credible.'

They began to talk about the loss of Bruce, Cathy trying to explain her
enormously mixed emotions of sorrow at losing Bruce and pride at his
achievement. She told John how they'd met Bruce on the ridge, how he had
decided to go on, and how each climber moved solo, accepting total responsibility for their own safety.

JOHN: 'So, Cathy, when you crossed there was nothing but encourage-
             ment and congratulations? There was no attempt either by you or
             by Ian to try to talk Bruce out of his summit attempt?'
CATHY: 'No. We simply discussed with Bruce what he wanted to do.'

    CATHY:
    I speak with complete conviction, although I am aware I'm not telling the
    whole story. As far as I'm concerned, my and Ian's misgivings about Bruce's
    decision, and Ian's attempt to get Bruce to turn round, are our affair. Bruce
    is gone and it is left to us, the survivors, to defend his decisions.

JOHN: 'So it was just an unfortunate tragedy?'
CATHY: 'That's what we feel. It's a risky sport, and those are risks we have
             all thought through and accepted before we take on the challenge.
             We believe that it was an unfortunate accident, one of the risks in-
             herent in the challenge he undertook.'

JOHN: 'Cathy, there is no doubt that you've made history by becoming the first woman on Everest from South Africa, and Africa. Will you do it again?'

CATHY: 'No, never! There's no way. I'm never coming back. I'm terribly proud of what I did and I've enjoyed much of the expedition. It has been some of the best days of my life up on the mountain with Ian and Bruce, but I won't be coming back to this mountain again.'

14:00 – Base Camp

Cathy was sitting in the comms tent, struggling to write a letter to Sue when Philip walked in.

'Christ, this is hard,' she said. 'How do I even begin to put into the blandness of words on paper all that Bruce meant to me, to all of us?'

'I know, love. None of it is easy. I brought you a cup of tea and a biscuit. I thought that might help.' He smiled sadly.

She went back to staring at her piece of paper. She wrote:

> *Dear Sue*
> *All the members of the First South African Everest Expedition*
> *would like to express our profound sorrow at the loss of Bruce.*
> *Although not South African, he was completely dedicated to the*
> *aims of the expedition and we could never have achieved all we did*
> *without his participation and enthusiasm. More than that, he was a*
> *good friend to all of us and we feel his absence keenly. We are very*
> *proud of what he achieved on Everest, both for the expedition as a*
> *whole and for himself. He played an important role in our lives*
> *and we will never forget him.*

It seemed so inadequate to sum up a life of such joy, happiness and vitality.

Cathy passed the note around and each member added their own message.

'Eight months is not long enough to have a friend like Bruce. I miss him. All my love and support,' wrote Philip.

'At the going down of the sun … With love,' wrote Ian.

CATHY:
The letter comes back to me. I stare at it and then scrawl along the bottom: 'The days with Bruce and Ian on the mountain were some of the best of my life. I will always treasure the short time I was able to spend with Bruce.'

And it's true, I think. They *were* some of the best days of my life. Far better to be here sharing the experience to the full than to be stuck at home, waiting. Our pain is not for the person we have lost but for ourselves, left to live our lives without them.

IAN:

'At the going down of the sun, and in the morning, we will remember.' Those immortal words haunt and dominate my thoughts, control my actions. Yes, we will remember you, Bruce, and we will come back. We'll come back to base camp again soon and remember you. We'll build you a memorial overlooking the mountain, so everyone passing this way will remember you. Wherever you are now, and whatever mountain you're planning on climbing next, we will remember you.

18:30 – Base Camp

The group sat silently round the dinner table, the only sound the clink of cutlery against plates. It had been like that all day, animated talk interspersed with long silences, as each person sank into their own thoughts.

Cathy, seated nearest to the tent door, heard the clatter of the fax machine. She walked across to the comms tent to investigate and came back, fax in hand.

'It's from Sue,' she said. 'In response to our letter.'

Cathy read it aloud:

> I am heartbroken, devastated and at the same time pretty pissed off with Bruce for walking out of my life big time. But whatever the controversy back in SA, I would like you all to know that I hold no one responsible. I need to talk to Cathy/Ian about the earlier part of the summit day and what happened, but there is no doubt in my mind that Bruce's decision was his alone. It just happened to be a monumental cock-up!

The group sat in silence. It was very difficult to know what to say.

'Next time you or Philip speak to her,' said Ian, 'ask if she would like to fly out to Kathmandu and spend some time with us when we get back there. Then we can go through everything step by step.'

'When will we get back?' asked Philip.

'We'll be able to leave the day after tomorrow,' Ian replied. 'We've sent word down the trail for the yak herders to come up and move the majority of the loads, but it will take them several days to get here. However, we need to get out as fast as possible. Apart from the fact that I guess we're all more than ready to go home, you can see the monsoon clouds building up. If we don't hurry, we won't be able to get a helicopter out of the Khumbu area. The weather will just be too bad for them to fly, and that means instead of having a three-day walk to get out, we'll have a ten-day walk.'

'God no!' Patrick exclaimed. 'Can't we leave tomorrow?'

'If we go, what happens to all the kit?' Cathy asked.

'We need to finish packing everything up into yak loads, which we'll have to do tomorrow,' Ian explained. 'Then Shankar will stay here to ensure it all gets packed on to yaks and taken down. If it gets caught in the monsoon, it may take weeks to move it all to Kathmandu, possibly even months, but Shankar has got enough porters up from the local villages to carry our personal stuff down with us.'

29 May
10:00 – Base Camp

The contents of the camp were slowly packed into barrels until only the basics remained. The appearance of the camp wasn't the only thing to be changing. As each climber got a chance to shrug off their climbing clothing and clean up a little, new people emerged. Cathy and Philip sat outside the mess tent, watching the Sherpas appear from their tents.

A wash had altered Ang Dorje's matted mass of black hair to a chaos of curls, which, combined with some clean clothing, transformed him from the hardman sirdar to the urban playboy. His teenage son had walked up to base camp to meet his father. The son was the mirror image of his handsome father, and clearly soon to be something of a heartbreaker in the villages. Now he was enjoying the reflected glory and fame of his dad, telling everyone he met that his father had just reached the summit of Everest.

'At camp 2 after the storm Ang Dorje told me that he wasn't too taken with extreme high-altitude mountaineering,' Cathy said to Philip. 'He wanted to stick to leading expeditions on 7 000-metre mountains. Now suddenly he is all talk of joining an expedition to Tibet in the autumn season and climbing Everest from both sides in one year.'

'Yes, he's done very nicely out of it,' said Philip. 'And all the Sherpanis eyeing him seem to think so too.' Various local women had arrived at the camp to help carry loads down the trail and to bargain for expedition leftovers.

Pemba emerged next, sparkling clean and shirtless, enjoying the sun on his skin. The months on the mountain had left him with a lean, muscled torso.

'There is some serious Sherpani-pulling-power there,' Cathy laughed.

'Of all the Sherpas, the change in him is the greatest,' Philip said.

She could only agree. A shy young man on his arrival at base camp, cautious in the company of westerners, his confidence had grown in leaps and bounds as he progressed up the mountain. Returning now with the summit tucked under his belt, he had the air of a seasoned mountaineer.

12:00 – Base Camp

Cathy and Philip watched Ian tread a path through the confusion of half-packed barrels on his way to the comms tent. He had agreed to be interviewed on the John and Dan Show. They listened as he began to talk to Dan.

DAN: 'So how was the experience for you? You on Radio 702 and talking to your mother, and the president sending messages to you?'

IAN: 'What you have to do is narrow your vision down considerably because while you're talking on the radio you can't wear your oxygen mask, so you're getting very little oxygen, and you are very tired. So it does take a long while for anything to sink in. I don't think the impact of what has happened has really sunk into any of us as yet.'

JOHN: 'We absolutely congratulate you on achieving your mission, and you won't believe the impact of your mission and success. The reaction has been fabulous! But there are questions to be asked because of the tragedy. When you were up on the summit, did you think about Bruce at all? Did you discuss him at all? Were you worried about him?'

Ian explained how he had asked Cathy for news, and then about how they had met Bruce on the way down.

JOHN: 'Now he was two hours behind you. Were you surprised when he indicated a desire to push on by himself?'

IAN: 'No, no, not at all. People think of mountaineering as perhaps two or three people tied together, and you belay yourself at each stage. Everest isn't like that. It's too big. You have to move too quickly.'

He explained that each climber moved as an individual, climbing without ropes, except for the very limited fixed ropes in place, and some climbed faster than others.

JOHN: 'But surely the time factor is vital. If you're too late up on the summit, it means you're going to have to spend a night up on Everest with no tent, no sleeping bag. You're virtually going to kill yourself!'

IAN: 'Not necessarily, no. Bruce had a good three hours of light left and a torch, and if for any reason he wanted to stay out, he had a full down suit, which is warmer even than a sleeping bag, and he could have sat on a ledge all night if he wanted to. The weather was quite superb.'

JOHN: 'Did Bruce ask your opinion when you met when he was going up and you were coming down?'

IAN: 'Yes, he did indeed. The three of us sat there together. First of all he quizzed Cathy about the climbing, in other words, about how long from where he was to the South Summit and then to the main summit, and so on. Then he did the same to me.'

DAN: 'Tell us, Ian. Would you attempt to summit Mount Everest again?'

IAN: 'I'm not sure I would go back to Everest again. It has obviously got considerable memories, both good ones and not so good ones. Cathy and I have talked about other mountains, but not about Everest again. In actual fact, what we've talked about most is a good crayfish thermidor.'

30 May
09:00 – Base Camp

Patrick and Deshun set off down the trail together.

'And?' he asked. 'What did all that mean to you in the end?'

'It's hard to say. There are so many things that I experienced on this expedition that I never, ever bargained for, that just don't cross your mind when you are in the average humdrum of suburban life.' She paused in thought.

'I would like to climb it, but I would leave it to the mountain to decide whether I would get up it or not. That respect for the mountain is the one big thing that overshadowed everything else that I learnt, because I've seen big people going up there and not coming back.'

09:30 – Base Camp

Ian and Cathy walked over to where Philip was standing staring up at the icefall. 'So, are you ready to leave?' she asked.

He turned to her and smiled.

'I have mixed feelings about leaving. It's been home for me for so long. I had my daily routine. It feels wrong to abandon it. During the last two days of packing I've spent a lot of time just looking at the icefall. Every 10 or 15 minutes I would glance at it, expecting to see a little black dot sitting up at the top. But now I realise I'm ready to go.'

CATHY:

Yes, I want to go too. I want to be able to move down the valleys, walking fast and light, without the weight of mountaineering boots and crampons, without the constricting bulk of heavy clothing, without soft snow and a heavy rucksack.

I want to go down the trail and see running water and green trees and people living on the land. I've had enough of these barren wastes.

Enough for a while, anyway.

IAN:

We came to climb the highest mountain in the world, and after a considerable struggle we stood proudly on its summit. I'm glad we did that, but the mountain has taken our closest friend and it won't be giving him back to us. I once considered staying on Everest forever but decided against it. So no, I'm not keen to leave, but this time I will.

09:35 – Base Camp

Ian, Cathy and Philip stood together, taking one last look at the area of rock and ice that had been their home for the last nine weeks.

'Time to say goodbye,' said Cathy quietly.

'But we'll come back soon,' said Philip.

'Aye, that we will,' confirmed Ian.

Epilogue

17 April 1997
12:00 – Base Camp

'Well, we're back,' said Ian, staring dubiously at the pile of rubble where, a year previously, the South African base camp had stood. No one was camped there in the 1997 spring season and the only way the climbers had found the site was by placing it against landmarks on the horizon. They had walked slowly up the glacier, watching the surrounding mountains, until suddenly the panorama slid into the old, so familiar formation that they had seen each day from their base camp mess tent.

'Yes, in a way,' Cathy replied, kicking at the stones that had once surrounded their flagpole. 'It's odd, really. At a distance it's just like last year, all the little tents huddled together in their various camps, all the climbers trying to reach the top. I've even seen a few people who were here with us last year but didn't make the summit and are trying again. And both Mal Duff and Henry Todd are back with expeditions. Yet it's not like last year at all.'

She knelt down to pick up one of the fragments of grey-silver rock, turning it over and over in her hand.

'This is the site but it's not base camp, or not ours anyway. It's another year, another group of climbers, another challenge. Our year has been and gone, and all that is left are photographs and memories.'

The South African team had returned to close the circle, to build a memorial to Bruce Herrod in the shadow of the mountain, as a way of saying a last formal farewell to him and to give themselves the freedom to move on, to move away into their own futures. Futures that Bruce would have no part of, although memories of him would always accompany them. But futures that had been profoundly affected by him, by all that they went through together on Everest.

18 April
12:30 – Bruce Herrod Memorial, Gorak Shep, near Everest Base Camp

The mysterious Buddhist chant rose from the small, grassy hilltop, swelling outwards to fill the giant horseshoe of mountains, dominated by Nuptse and Everest, and broken only by the Khumbu Glacier as it swept down and away from the Khumbu Icefall. The lama sat cross-legged on the icy grass, his port-red robes arranged decorously over his grey and red padded mountaineering jacket. From beneath the robes, thick, woolly socks and leather boots protruded.

Spread out in front of the lama were the implements of his craft, the metal bell, the incense sticks, the bowls of rice and oil. He was looking at the front of the stone memorial. For two days two stone masons had sat on that hilltop, with chisels and hammers, cutting the nearby rocks into smooth squares that could be stacked one on top of another. The structure stood square and proud, chest-high, without the help of any cement.

Set into the side that looked out on to Everest were photographs of Bruce and a stone carved in his memory. The stone, which had been engraved at Namche Bazaar, had been carried for four days up the trail.

The lama read from complex papers covered in Sanskrit script, the words running into each other as his voice rose and sank in an endless plainsong chant. Hidden in the words were an understanding of life, death and the Himalaya that was beyond the ken of the western climbers who sat huddled round the memorial. It was an understanding that Bruce had sort to comprehend during his many trips to Nepal.

The South Africans sat bundled up in their giant, blue down jackets and black, fleecy salopettes, in woolly hats and gloves. Sherpas who had known Bruce, and who had made the pilgrimage to join this memorial, stood silently around them. A bitter wind swept up the valley, swirling round the stone memorial, penetrating every chink of their clothing. A weak sun shone down, illuminating the scene but providing no warmth.

Slowly wispy clouds crept up the valley and the peaks around them gradually vanished behind misty veils. Even the lama began to feel the chill and hurried through the remainder of the ceremony so that he could retreat to the warmth of the smoky lodge in Gorak Shep. The westerners quickly returned to the shelter of their mess tent, now erected on a patch of yak dung-covered grazing ground. As they walked, they passed other *chortens*, erected over the years in memory of those who had given up their lives on the slopes of Everest, Lhotse, Pumori and Ama Dablam.

'You know, I think that would have appealed to Bruce's sense of humour,' said Cathy, teeth chattering as she piled into the tent. 'All of us standing around, freezing our butts off, listening to a whole lot of chanting we didn't understand. Hell, he would have laughed.'

Philip pulled out a bottle of Remy Martin from the depths of his jacket. He looked at it solemnly for a moment and then grinned.

'This brings back such memories. All those times sitting in the mess tent with Bruce, late at night, when the rest of you had gone to bed. All that rubbish we talked. Bruce always said Remy was terrible stuff, but that didn't stop him drinking it when nothing else was available.'

Philip poured out a measure into each of their metal mugs.

'To absent friends!' said Philip. They drank.

Cathy refilled the mugs and they raised them again.

'To the highest mountain in the world, and the fact that we've been there, done that. And we need never go back.'

They drank again.

19 April
08:00 – Bruce Herrod Memorial

The wind had died, the clouds gone. The sun shone down on the small hilltop with a welcome warmth. The great sweeps of Nuptse gleamed as if made of burnished silver, while their knife-like edges glinted gold in the sunlight. Lesser mountains ran round them in a huge circle, sparkling in the crystalline air. The sky rose over the mountains in a monumental blue arc.

The South Africans stood silently next to the stone memorial. They had returned to perform their own ceremony, spoken in the language they understood. From the little Walkman speakers propped up on top of the memorial Eric Clapton's voice rose plaintively.

> *Would you know my name*
> *If I saw you in heaven?*
> *Would it be the same*
> *If I saw you in heaven?*
> *I must be strong and carry on*
> *'Cause I know I don't belong here in heaven.*

Philip stepped forward to talk quietly, personally, to the stone memorial.

'I have come here today, Bruce, to lay a stone in honour of a mountaineer, photographer, but above all a very good friend. During the short time that we knew each other, I would like to think that I was as good a friend to you as you were to me.'

He stopped momentarily, tears streaking his grey beard. 'Goodnight, Bruce. God bless you.'

CATHY:

I watch Philip turn away. Suffering and success seem so inextricably interlinked in all we have done. Still watching him, I begin to recite from memory a poem written by one climber for another climber, somewhere else in the world. But the sentiments remain the same.

I would give all my world to have you back,
Remember you not in a photograph,
But in your smiling eyes and wild ideal.
And yet I would not pay a price too high:
I would not dream of asking you to change.

I first saw the poem stuck to the wall of a London flat, a flat I was sharing with three other mountaineers. Two years later one of them found the bodies of the other two lying, still, at the foot of a great ice-face in Peru. I turned to the poem then to give voice to the complexity of my feelings about death in the mountains, just as I do now ...

If you were with me now, I would still help,
Encourage you to reach for mountain tops,
Would watch you strive for where you should not go.

And you would go again and die again,
And I would cry – but cry how much more
If you should ever cease to be yourself.

Ian's voice fills the ensuing silence. For a man so self-contained, he expresses his pain with a raw honesty that, for the first time today, reduces me to tears.

Ian looked down at the words he had written on the scruffy piece of exam-pad paper. They were inadequate to the experience, but then all words were, he felt.

For taking in the rain when I'm feeling so dry,
For giving me the answers when I'm asking you why,
And my-oh-my, for that I thank you.

For taking in the sun when I'm feeling so cold,
For giving me a chance when my body is old,
And don't you know, for that I need you ...

Oh! but most of all, for crying out loud, for that I miss you.
Oh! but most of all, for crying out loud, for that I love you.

With a deep breath, he looked up from his piece of paper and began to speak.

'Many have questioned Bruce's right to live his life in the manner he chose, but to those of us left behind he was a true free spirit. He was a man who took it upon himself to live his life to the full. He was free to decide his future, and he exercised that right.'

He reached across to the Walkman and put in another tape. The song 'Free to Decide'. Cranberries singer Delores O'Riordan's voice emerged strongly, travelling through the thin, clear air, reaching out to the surrounding mountains. It was a song that had become something of a theme tune for the expedition members, expressing what they felt they took away from the experience. As the last words of the song faded into silence, Ian reached out for Cathy to hug her. Then Philip joined them in their embrace, and the three friends, the three team-mates, stood in heavy silence, emotionally exhausted.

'Bruce would have liked that,' Cathy said softly. The tribute of the great open spaces, the proud beauty of the icy mountains, the love and pain of those who had walked so far to see the tribute made, he would have appreciated it. 'If it ever comes to it, I'd like something similar for myself.'

'No, I never want to have to do this for you,' replied Ian abruptly. 'I've done this too often in my life already.'

IAN:
We said we would come back, Bruce, and we did. If any South Africans should pass this way, keep an eye on them for us. Goodbye for now, mate. See you soon.

5 May
11:00 – Kathmandu

Cathy and Ian walked in tense silence through the crowded Kathmandu streets. The hubbub of Nepal's capital rose all around them, as they dodged rickshaws, cars, cows and people. The streets were filled with the dense smells of food, dust and animals. The heat of approaching summer beat down on the urban chaos. The two South Africans saw none of it. They were in search of answers to the question first posed five days before, when they heard the rumour that Bruce's body had been found high on the slopes of Everest.

The Indonesian team that was supposed to have found it had reached the summit in late April. They were the first team to summit Everest from the south side since the South Africans 11 months previously.

'I can't believe it,' Ian said suddenly. 'Even if he did die on the ridge, I just don't see how the body could have managed to stay there. The winds of the monsoon or of the winter would have blown it off. Maybe they are confusing him with Rob Hall.'

'Well, we'll soon find out. We've had nothing but confused, contradictory reports ever since we first heard the rumour,' Cathy replied.

The Indonesian climbers had been out of contact with Kathmandu since they'd reached the summit, as they had to walk back down through the Khumbu valley to catch a helicopter to the city. They had arrived back the previous day and Ian had arranged for Cathy and himself to speak to Appa Sherpa, the Indonesians' sirdar. A highly experienced mountaineer, he had just reached the summit of Everest for the eighth time.

They found him in the lobby of the team's hotel, surrounded by piles of equipment just ferried back from the mountain. Seated together on the lobby's shabby lounge suite, Ian asked him to take them through his summit day, from the South Col to where he thought Bruce's body might be. Appa Sherpa described the long haul up the South-East Ridge, and then the steady plod up the ridge to the South Summit.

'I come over South Summit and I expect to see Rob Hall's body, but it is covered over with snow. I start to climb along the ridge towards Hillary Step. It is very narrow, very dangerous. At the foot of the step I see a man sitting. He wears a blue down suit and a red rucksack.'

Ian and Cathy glanced at each other briefly. They had their answer. It had to be Bruce.

Appa Sherpa continued. 'I stop to look who it is. He is clipped on to one of the fixed ropes on the Hillary Step with a jumar.'

'So that's why the body didn't blow away,' Ian muttered. 'Sorry, go on.'

'His face is mostly covered by the oxygen mask.' Appa shrugged. 'There are no other signs of what went wrong. We didn't touch him. We climb on to the summit.'

14:00 – Harati Hotel, Kathmandu

'So we still have no answers,' said Cathy thoughtfully, staring out across the lush garden of their hotel. 'Just a whole lot more unanswered questions. Like why didn't he call us on the radio? Why did he stop there? But I guess we've just got to learn to live with that.'

'At least we know where he is now. We're not going to have to deal with unconfirmed sightings every few years, as happens with some mountaineers who go missing,' Ian replied, staring down into his glass of Coke. 'I tell you what, though, he's got a hell of a view from up there.' He seemed unusually pensive, sunk deep in his own thoughts.

He looked up slowly.

'You know, I have to ask whether it's worth it, given the price we pay.'

'Whether what's worth it?' Cathy asked, although she was fairly sure she knew what he meant.

'High-altitude mountaineering, of course,' Ian replied with a smile. 'It's no good trying to fool ourselves. It's a high-risk sport. Think about it. When Bruce and I stumbled on to the South Col in the middle of that mini-storm on 9 May last year, I took shelter with Scott Fischer and his sirdar, Lobsang Sherpa. Bruce took shelter with Rob Hall and one of his guides, Andy Harris. A year later, of those six climbers, I'm the only one left alive.'

Rob Hall, Andy Harris and Scott Fischer had died in the great storm. Lobsang Sherpa had been killed in an avalanche while climbing on the Lhotse Face above camp 3 on Everest in the autumn season of 1996.

Cathy watched Ian silently. There were no easy answers to these questions.

'In a year,' he said quietly, 'I've lost my two closest mountaineering friends, and both have died on Everest.' He shook his head in bewilderment. 'I still can't believe Mal Duff's dead.'

'No, it seems so unreal,' said Cathy. 'To have sat there with him in base camp a few weeks ago, having a cup of tea, and then to hear last week that he'd just passed away in his sleep in his base camp tent.'

'I guess it's real enough,' Ian replied grimly. 'Too real by half. But there has to come a time when you have to take stock, to ask yourself if continuing to do this is the right choice.'

It was a choice they had to face up to rapidly. They had been spending time in Kathmandu chasing permits for other mountains, for future projects. There were so many potential challenges. Mountains South Africans had never climbed, mountains that nobody had ever climbed. But no challenge came without risk.

'Well, it's a choice we each have to make on our own,' Cathy said slowly as she tried to find words to express her feelings. 'And I guess everybody hits their own limit eventually. I've never been able to come up with a pat answer when I get asked "Why do you do it?" Lots of people know the famous Mallory answer, "Because it's there", but I think he had it wrong. I reckon we do it "because we're here". It's part of a drive, in whatever form, to challenge our limits, to try to express the infinite potential we carry within us. That drive is part of what it means to be human, and everyone is free to decide whether the risks are worth it for them.'

Ian stared at her with raised eyebrows.

'What's this? Zen and the art of mountain climbing? You'll be applying for an American passport soon if you carry on like that.'

She smiled back.

'Hey, at least I'm trying to find some answers for you. Let's have a little gratitude here.'

'Sod it,' said Ian, 'forget answers. Let's just go climbing.'

14 June
23:00 – Rivonia, Johannesburg

Cathy and Ian sat together, staring down at a photograph. Their hands were cupped round china coffee mugs, rather than metal ones. They were wearing jeans and jerseys, rather than down jackets and salopettes. But the face that stared up at them out of the photograph was unchanged.

'It's been a long year,' said Cathy. 'We've come a long way.'

'It's not the age, it's the bloody mileage,' said Ian dryly.

Most of the first six months since their return to South Africa from Everest had been spent honouring commitments to sponsors. The rest of the first year had been spent telling their story to South Africans all over the country. They had seen over 25 000 schoolchildren since their return, and many adults, as part of their charity audio-visual presentations. They had raised R250 000 for the Nelson Mandela Children's Fund. They had published some of the 10 000 photographs they had brought back from Everest. They had returned to Nepal to build the memorial for Bruce. They had started to plan the next expedition.

They both looked back down at the photograph.

'Maybe it was worth it after all,' said Ian.

Bruce's face grinned back at them, still in his green South African beanie and his blue down jacket. His face was split in a smile, his eyes screwed up as they always were when he was happy. The joy of his spirit shone through as brightly as ever. Next to him was a metal tripod and a blaze of Buddhist prayer flags. Behind and far below him was a curving horizon.

'So chuffed,' murmured Cathy. 'That's how he put it when he was on the radio to us. And that's just how he looks there.' She touched the photograph gently. 'Of it all, the only thing I regret is that I didn't tell him over the radio how proud I am of him.'

One of the other teams that had reached the summit of Everest in the spring season of 1997 had moved Bruce's body off the trail and retrieved his camera. Cathy and Ian were now staring at the last photograph Bruce had ever taken, the photograph he took of himself as he sat on the top of the world.

'"It's been a long time coming, mate." That's the other thing he said to me,' Ian recalled. 'Well, it's been a long road for all of us, but now we know how he looked when he got there. And he looks fit and happy and proud. You know, looking back on it now, if we had to do it all over again, God forbid, knowing only what we knew then, I think we'd make all the same decisions. Now we really can close the book on this one and move on.'

He took one last, long look at the photograph and then put it carefully away.

'So are you coming, youth?' he asked.

'Coming where?' she replied.

'On the next great South African adventure.'

She grinned at him.

'Don't even think of going without me.'

Expedition Daily Movement Log

6 April
Arrive at base camp (5 340 metres)

7–9 April
Base camp – preparation and acclimatisation

10 April
Base camp – *Puja* ceremony

11 April
Base camp – preparation and acclimatisation

12 April
Ascend to camp 1 (6 100 metres) and return to base camp

13–16 April
Establish and equip camp 1

17–18 April
Establish and equip camp 2 (6 500 metres)

19 April
Ascend to camp 2 and sleep

20 April
Camp 2 – acclimatisation

21 April
Camp 2 – acclimatisation
Philip arrives at base camp

22–23 April
Camp 2 – acclimatisation

24 April
Return to base camp

25–28 April
Base camp – rest days

29 April
Ascend to camp 2 and sleep

30 April
Camp 2 – rest day

1–4 May
Camp 2 – establish and equip camp 3 (7 400 metres) and camp 4 (7 980 metres)

5–6 May
Camp 2 – weather-watching

7 May
Ascend to camp 3 and sleep

8 May
Camp 3 – weather-watching
Patrick arrives at base camp

9 May
Ascend to camp 4 and sleep

10–11 May
Camp 4 – storm-bound

12 May
Descend to camp 2

13 May
Descend to base camp

14–17 May
Base camp – rest days

18 May
Ascend to camp 2 and sleep

19 May
Camp 2 – rest day

20 May
Ascend to camp 3 and sleep

21 May
Descend to camp 2

22 May
Camp 2 – rest day

23 May
Ascend to camp 3 and sleep

24 May
Ascend to camp 4 and sleep

25 May
Ascend to summit and return to camp 4

26 May
Descend to camp 2

27 May
Descend to base camp

28–29 May
Base camp – packing up

30 May
Depart base camp

1st South African Everest Expedition Sponsorship Listing

Expedition sponsors are listed in alphabetical order.

702 Talk Radio
Atomic Energy Commission
Apple Computer (SA)
Backpacker Products
Bollé
Cadac
Cadbury Schweppes
Cape Union Mart
Citylab
DAKA Technologys
DHL
Duracell
Europ Assistance
Flagcraft
Fortibix
GEC Marconi

Gentek Systems
Glaxo Wellcome
Kodak (SA)
Megapak
Motorola
Nestlé
Pharma Natura
Reebok (SA)
Samsung (SA)
Singapore Airlines
Standard Bank (Rivonia & Sandton)
Stantek Electronics
The Internet Solution
Thin Air Expeditions
Tongaat Foods
Uniross Batteries

About the Authors

Cathy O'Dowd grew up and finished her schooling in Johannesburg. She was completing her master's degree in journalism at Rhodes University in November 1995 when she saw an advertisement for a woman team member on the First South African Everest Expedition. Having successfully been selected, six months later she became the first woman in Africa to reach the top of the world. Previous climbing expeditions have taken her to South America, Europe and elsewhere in Africa. She now lives in Johannesburg, where she speaks and writes professionally.

Ian Woodall grew up and completed his schooling in Cape Town. After working in the catering industry and as a high-school teacher, Ian left South Africa to serve as an officer in the British Army. On completion of his military service, he returned to South Africa in July 1995 to plan and organise the expedition. He has taken part in many other Himalayan climbing expeditions. He now lives in Johannesburg, where he is planning his next mountain adventure.

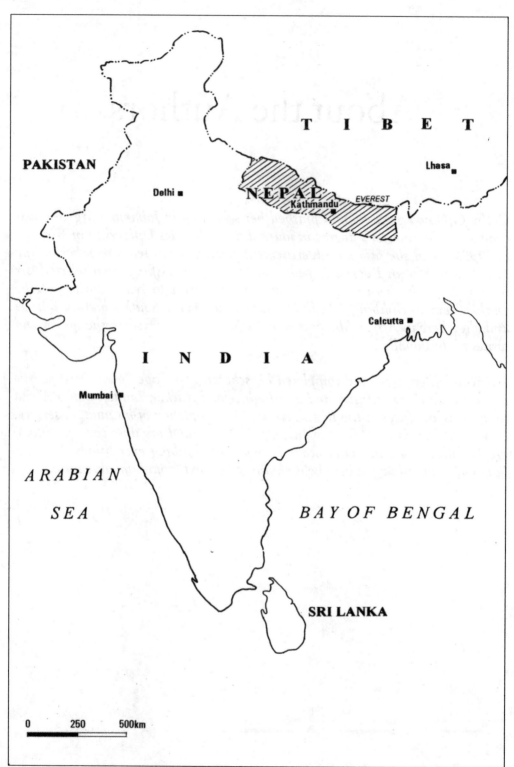

The Indian subcontinent

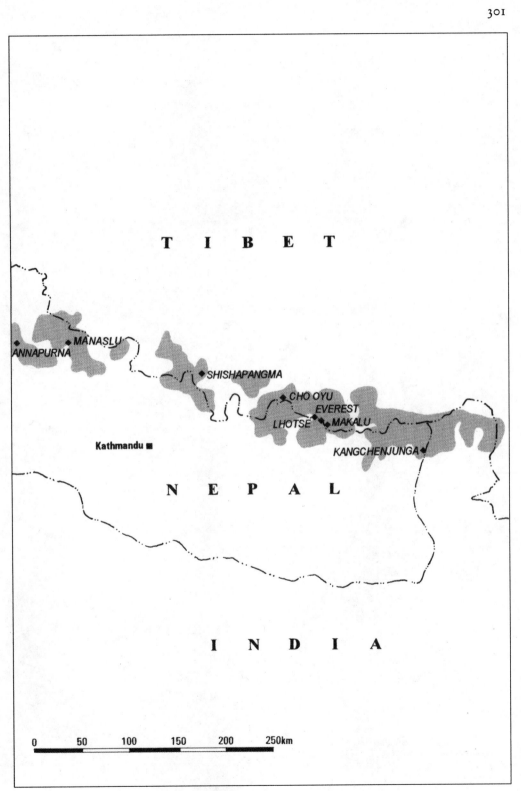

The Himalayan range

Himalayan Academy 98
(in association with the 1st South African K2 Expedition)

Candidate Application Form

In 1996 the 1st South African Everest Expedition chose a woman climbing member from a selection process called Himalayan Academy 96: Woman on Everest. That successful candidate subsequently became the first woman in Africa to climb Everest.

In 1998 the 1st South African K2 Expedition will attempt the classic North Ridge of Everest as part of their K2 training programme. In conjunction with the Himalayan Academy 98 project, two climbing places and six support places are available on this expedition, all expenses paid.

Selection of Everest Climbing Places

From these applications three men and three women candidates will be invited to take part in a selection expedition to Aconcagua in South America. From this selection expedition, one man and one woman will be invited to continue on to Everest.

Selection of Support Staff

Two places are available for base camp co-ordinators (technical experience an advantage), and four for first-time radio presenters (two English speakers, two Afrikaans speakers). This selection will be made in Johannesburg.

Conditions of Entry

Candidates must be at least 18 years of age and South African citizens. They must be available for the period 1 February to 31 May 1998. No previous climbing experience is necessary. Woman on Everest candidates are welcome to re-apply. Applications must be submitted by 31 December 1997 on this original form (*no photocopies*) and returned to: Himalayan Academy 98, PO Box 1621, Gallo Manor 2052.

Applications should include a recent passport photograph and a written motivation as to why you should be selected for your chosen category, and any other relevant information. Potential radio presenters should include a demonstration cassette tape.

Surname:. . . . .   First name:. . . . .

Postal address:. . . . .

Contact telephone number (with code):. . . . .

Category of application (select *one* only): Male Everest climber ❏

Female Everest climber ❏

Base camp co-ordinator ❏

Radio presenter English ❏

Radio presenter Afrikaans ❏

Home language:. . . . .